Stephen Walder was born in Bromley, Kent, on the 25th of January 1981. He lived in Bromley for the first quarter of a century of his life, where he slowly lost his way. He moved to Swansea in 2006 and has spent all but two years of his life there since. He has recently begun a career helping others with their substance misuse issues, a cause very close to his heart.

To everyone fighting a battle with themselves. Please keep fighting. You can beat this.

Stephen Walder

THE DAY I CHOSE TO LIVE

A Normal Boy's Descent into Drink,
Drugs and Despondency

AUSTIN MACAULEY PUBLISHERS™

LONDON ∗ CAMBRIDGE ∗ NEW YORK ∗ SHARJAH

A CIP catalogue record for this title is available from the British Library.

ISBN 9781528999984 (Paperback)
ISBN 9781528999991 (ePub e-book)

www.austinmacauley.com

First Published (2021)
Austin Macauley Publishers Ltd
25 Canada Square
Canary Wharf
London
E14 5LQ

Huge thanks to my fantastic family for putting up with all of the hurt and disappointment I have caused them and for continually supporting and believing in me. Thanks to everybody who has shown me a little kindness over the years. Thank you, my friends, old and new. Thank you to the staff, volunteers and service users at Barod in Swansea, UK SMART Recovery in Swansea and Swansea Mind. You have helped set me on the most wonderful path. Thanks to everyone at Austin Macauley for allowing me to believe in my words and helping to make this book a reality. Finally, thanks to my beloved Cath. We're going to be all right. We are! x

Chapter 1

Origins of an Outsider

I was born on Sunday, 25 January 1981 at 12:05 p.m. to two loving and caring Christian parents. I was the youngest of three, a pain in the arse to an older sister and brother. My father at the time was a minister and had to miss preaching that day in order to be at my birth. Maybe I was doing the devil's work from the start. I preferred to think of it as arriving just in time for pub opening hours!

I have been told that I was a well-mannered, obedient and serious child. I didn't smile a lot. I always had a thirst for knowledge; my siblings would say that I had swallowed an encyclopaedia. Once I was able to operate the TV, I would come downstairs in the morning at the weekends and sit in front of the TV and watch 'The Open University' programmes. I wouldn't speak until I was nearly four years old. Apparently, I was intelligent enough to manipulate my siblings without the use of words. What a thing to tell the parents of a young child!

At school, I was a studious boy but not in the slightest bit artistic. Every time that I was asked to draw something, I would just scribble with reds, oranges and yellows and say that it was an explosion. I actually had some success with the girls. On only my second day of primary school, I asked a girl if she would like to be my girlfriend. Astonishingly, she said yes and we remained 'boyfriend and girlfriend' in some capacity until we were fifteen

I never had a rebellious streak in those days. If a parent, teacher or any authority figure told me to do, or not to do, something, I would obey. One of my earliest memories is of a school play we put on. I was in the choir and we were all told to sit up, nice and straight on the benches. I was the only child who did and I can clearly remember a couple of the mothers pointing and laughing at me. In spite of this, I maintained a straight back. It was most probably around this time that I started to have recurring nightmares involving two crocodiles that walked around on their hind legs, one black and one white. I think that we'll leave the symbolism of that to the professionals!

I was academically gifted but lacked the confidence to exhibit it in any way other than in my exercise books. In group work, even if I knew better than my peers, I never felt as though I could exert my point of view on people. This led to me turning down a good educational opportunity.

On my eleventh birthday, I was due to sit an entrance examination for a selective school in the area. This would have led to a much higher level of education than I eventually received. I used the fact that it was my birthday to avoid this, for reasons only known to me at the time. Looking back, I realise that this is the first instance of the fear of failure outweighing my desire to succeed. This is something that has blighted me all through my adolescence and adulthood.

As I said, I was a quiet, reticent child. As I left primary school and went on to secondary school, I became more withdrawn. Although I made friends at my new school, I always felt on the periphery, like I didn't belong, a feeling that has always accompanied me.

That sense of isolation was one of many themes that first showed themselves around this time. The first manifestation of addictive behaviour surfaced in my obsession with collecting football stickers. I would also steal to fund my addiction for the first time, taking ten pounds from my mother's purse, being rumbled as soon as I walked back through the door. My first suicidal thoughts occurred too. On bad days, I would cycle to a railway bridge somewhere and stand there, watching the trains coming and going underneath, thinking to myself, *It'll only take a second; you won't feel a thing. It could all be over soon.*

Chapter 2

Sowing the Seeds of Waste

Although supposedly a gifted student, secondary school never engaged me. I found the academic subjects easy. We were tested every half term for banding reasons, always under the pressure that we might be moved into a different class, but I found that I would always be in the top one or two with minimal effort. Soon I stopped doing homework altogether and developed a cynical streak and a smart mouth. Having had no detentions in year seven, they become a very regular occurrence thereafter.

By the time year nine had finished, I had become a habitual truant. Being a bit of a rebel, I didn't conform to the usual stereotype and would take a change of clothes and sit in the public library every day. I would read about many subjects, from sport to history and politics. I had made myself believe that I was in some way different from the other kids and tried to find some answers in psychology and psychiatry books. I convinced myself that I had some obsessive, compulsive traits, and very nearly came to the conclusion that my inner dialogue was schizophrenia. These 'findings' were extremely detrimental to my mental health and accelerated what I can see now as the total erosion of my self-esteem.

When I was fourteen, I started doing a paper round. This was the only little thing that gave me a sense of worth. I made sure that I was the first boy in and that I did the job to the absolute best of my ability. I have tried to be this way throughout all subsequent employment, or so I thought. Sadly, diligence isn't always rewarded!

It was around this time that I started drinking. I discovered drink much the same as every other teenager. I found that it gave me confidence and it was some common ground with the more popular kids. I found that I could always find access to alcohol, and although it wasn't a conscious decision, I set out to be the best at it.

Before long, I was drinking somewhere most weekends and, on one occasion, led an expedition of my mates to the pub closest to my school. I have always felt comfortable in small, local pubs; even when I was clearly underage, I would act like I belonged. So, it was that five of us, all aged fifteen and sixteen, wearing matching short-sleeved sky-blue shirts, ended up at the pub during our lunch break from school. I approached the bar and ordered five pints of Stella.

"You kids aren't from the school, are you?" Without thinking, I came back.

"No, British Gas, mate." That was all that was needed to 'prove' our age! Times have changed, thankfully.

I breezed through my GCSE's and attained good grades across the board with the minimum of effort. I could have had my pick of sixth forms and colleges but decided to stay put. Better the devil you know.

Chapter 3
Studies in Failure

I carried on with my A-levels and actually started with a little new resolve. Realising the step-up in standard, I would throw myself into my coursework assignments. However, I would hand work in only to never see it again and receive no feedback whatsoever. I soon lost faith and motivation. It would turn out that the headteacher of the school, an ex-nun of all people, had been embezzling money. Eventually, she was convicted and served two-and-a-half years for taking anywhere between £100,000 and £1,000,000. The affair would later be made into a docudrama called 'The Thieving Headmistress', where she was played by Pauline Quirke.

Looking back, it is easy to see that something was wrong. The school only had a library while I was in year seven. Every winter, we would be sitting in our thick coats in class, being told that there was another problem with the boilers. There wasn't; there was no money to fund heating. A proposed swimming pool never materialised, even though funding was apparently secured. We had to share textbooks, and in the last two terms of my A-levels, teachers were taken out of our year thirteen classes in order to cover GCSE revision classes because there was a shortage of teachers as word had got around, and nobody wanted to teach at the school.

My GCSE results and previous academic record were enough to land me an interview at Girton College, Cambridge to study mathematics. Woefully underprepared by myself and my school, I never stood a chance and had only covered the material for one of three separate interviews. The turnover of staff at my school meant that I had seven different teachers for my two-year maths A-level course. Once the inevitable rejection letter came from Cambridge, that was it for me and education. I couldn't give a shit anymore.

By this time, I had started doing some shifts in my local newsagents, as well as helping my father a bit in his accountancy firm. I was earning the money to drink four, five, six or even seven nights a week. I played on this at school and started to identify myself as such. I was a drinker, and a fucking good one! In the end, I scraped two Ds and an E.

On the day of my A-level results, I went to collect them in a homemade spray paint T-shirt with the legend 'Pimped by the National Curriculum' on it, whatever that meant. As soon as I got home with my disappointing grades, I retired to my bedroom with a bottle of vodka to prepare for one hell of a night out.

My most tangible achievement was at the leaving do when joke awards were handed out. I received a certificate proclaiming me 'Most Likely to Die of Liver Failure'. I wore this as a badge of honour. It was still on my bedroom wall earlier this year.

Throughout my A-level course, outwardly, it would seem that I was enjoying a thriving social life. I was out at the pub most nights of the week, going regularly to the football and my earliest and best friend and I had formed a band. I was the drummer.

However, I was starting to struggle when in solitude. I was into my music, Manic Street Preachers especially, and reading a huge amount. I became very self-analytical and was only too aware of my own failures and underachievement. It was shortly before my eighteenth birthday that I took my first tentative steps into self-harm. It seemed fairly innocuous at the time, just dragging a razor blade across my forearm, barely scratching, just enough to draw a little blood. I thought that I was in total control. I have had the word 'FAILURE' indelibly marked on my left forearm since I was eighteen.

Chapter 4

A Degree of Incapability

I resolved to find myself a full-time job after my results came out, but early the next week, I received a call from the Physics Department at Swansea University inviting me to join their Physics Foundation course. I chose to defer for a year and they kept the place open for me.

I looked to find some work experience in Accountancy for my gap year but couldn't find any, so I carried on working in the newsagents and doing some part-time work for my father. I earned decent money over the year which allowed me to carry on with my 'socialising' and also save some money towards my education.

September 1999, and I found myself on my way to Swansea University. Swansea was a city that I knew fairly well, having had many holidays there. Both of my grandmothers were originally from the area. I settled into my room in the halls of residence and kept myself to myself for the first couple of nights. *I can do this*, I thought to myself. I had no real worries about the study. Entering at foundation level, I knew that it was material that I could handle.

On the third night, I joined some of the other new intakes from my floor in the common room. The bottle of Jack Daniels that my boss at the newsagents had given me as a leaving present was opened and emptied. What followed next were a great couple of riotous nights out as we all got to know each other and enjoyed our freedom.

When it came time to start my studies, I pledged to myself that I would throw myself into the course. However, entering at the foundation level, I was not at all engaged. On one of the maths courses, we spent two hours on number lines.

"Next week, it will get harder," said the lecturer. I thought that it would be worth sticking with. Until he immediately followed it up with "We are going to tackle negative numbers". I only attended one more of his lectures, towards the end of the term after two hours in the Union and twelve pints of Snakebite and Black. I must have been an absolute arsehole to everybody else in that lecture who wanted to learn.

Slowly but surely, all of my studies went by the wayside as drinking became the priority. My days were spent in the Union bar, and if there was ever a night out to be had, I was there, even with people that I had only got talking to that day.

Having deferred a year, my Local Education Authority screwed up my student loan. By the time that this was sorted, the cheque cleared in my account on the day that my father and brother came to pick me up for Christmas. I already knew that I wasn't going back in January. It was fucking party time!

The next ten days were spent out on the piss with my mates, acting like Billy Big Bollocks and showing off the amount that I could drink. To become 'Wenglish' at university, I had downed half a pint of top-shelf. My party trick on Christmas Eve was to do a pint! Christmas passed off uneventfully and fairly pleasantly from what I can remember. Next up: New Year's Eve!

Yet another mammoth night out. When I got home, I thought that it was the perfect time to let my parents know that I was quitting university. The best way to do this, I concluded, was to pack a bag, leave a note and walk out in the early hours. That night, I slept rough in a corridor at the block of flats where my sister lived. The next evening, I returned home at about 6 o'clock. A quick shower, a couple of cursory words to my parents and back out on the piss.

Within the next couple of weeks, I did a circuit of the employment agencies in Bromley. I was immediately placed in an admin job with the local authority in their Special Educational Needs Department. This was a job that I could do easily, but I struggled when it came to having to take initiative. I was asked to contact local minicab companies in order to ask quotes for the school run. I found myself unable to make a single call.

Working full time gave me the perfect excuse to carry on drinking. I was earning well and, even though I had written to cancel it, I was sent the second instalment of my student loan. Ding! Ding! Round two, boys! Rather than catch a bus that would drop me off at the end of my road, where I could be seen from my house, I would catch one that would leave me a walk past my local. Without fail, I would pop in and be there at closing time, often ordering two or three pints at the final bell!

Looking back now, I can see that it was around this time that a drink stopped being a reward for a day's work. A day's work became the justification for a drink or a session. I have been deluding myself for years, and it is only writing this now that I realise that my main reason for getting out of bed in the morning, since I was 20, has been to have a drink. Shit!

One morning, I woke up unable to stand up straight due to the pain in my kidneys. I went to the doctor's, ridiculously expecting some sympathy. He said that the first thing that I needed to do was to change my T-shirt when I got home. I looked down and I had a white T-shirt on emblazoned with the slogan 'Hug Me! I'm Drinking Labatt Ice!'. I didn't even realise.

Chapter 5

No Way Out

One day, I was asked to do some photocopying. I noticed that those were the CVs and applications for the job that I had applied for. Mine was missing. Why hadn't somebody told me beforehand? This seemed such a bad way to learn that you haven't got a chance. In my head, it was personal, cruel and spiteful. This was all the excuse I needed to go out for lunch, straight into a pub, never to return. Cue another week of constant drinking.

After a little while, I started working back in the newsagent's six days a week. I loved this job, but it did nothing to curtail my drinking. At the start of May, I went full time with my father's accountancy firm, continuing to work at the newsagent's on Saturdays. It was just my parents and myself, and I would be based at home most of the time. 30 April. My last night of freedom as I saw it. Time for a piss-up! I only had to get downstairs by 9:00 the following morning to be on time for work. That proved too much.

I did start becoming more reliable while still making drinking basically my full-time hobby. Within three weeks, on a no-mark Thursday, I broke my elbow in my local pub. Mucking about with mates, I fell on it. I was sitting there flexing it; you could feel bits moving inside. I thought that this was so funny. I stayed until closing, with my arm now seized in a straight position, three hours, and most probably the best part of ten pints later, and caught the bus to A & E. This was about midnight on Thursday. They couldn't operate until Saturday afternoon, having me on a saline drip the whole time.

I returned to work with my father and things settled down a bit with the only sticking point being when I would come down for work, stinking of booze from the night before when we were due to visit a client. This was beyond the pale for my father. How unreasonable, eh?

I had blown all of my student loan money plus everything that I had earned. I was at my overdraft limit and had maxed out my credit card, so I went along to the bank to see what they could do. They said that they could consolidate the overdraft and credit card bill into a personal loan. Perfect. "Would you like a bit of money to keep you going too?"

"That'll be nice. What can you do?"

"We can make the loan amount up to £5,000."

"Thank you very much."

By the time that I was outside, there was three and a half grand in my bank! The show must go on!

I continued working and drinking, and soon a couple of mates and I had transformed the garage at the end of my garden into a smoking den. Just a couple of spliffs after an evening on the beer. Where's the harm? Nights when I went home alone, I started to self-harm again. Slowly, I started to increase the severity with which I would cut myself, and I started occasionally putting cigarettes out on myself. When was this supposed to start hurting?

I was playing with my band and we were doing a few gigs around London. I was also going to watch Charlton Athletic, my football club, on a very regular basis. The club was doing well and the ground was a great place to be around. Both of these pursuits allowed me an excuse to drink in large quantities. After all, it was the done thing. I was funding the whole band thing. Paying for practice time, transport for the equipment to gigs and even paying for the initial studio session to record our demo. Nobody else ever seemed to have any money, so I would buy all of the drinks on a night out, thinking nothing of spending a three-figure sum, even when they had invited me out. Why couldn't I see that I was being taken for an absolute fucking mug?

I was convinced that I was winning at life. I was earning decent money, both my band and my football team were on the up and were great releases. I was popular, I thought, surrounded by friends. So why did I feel nothing? Why did I constantly want to alter my reality? Why did I want to spend every solitary moment hurting and tormenting myself?

Later on that year, I received a letter calling me up for Jury Service. Early in the new year, I was to report to the Centre Court in Elephant & Castle. I was told that this was a very prominent court, second in seniority only to The Old Bailey. I started to worry, initially, that I would drink too much one night and not get there on time. The more this consumed my thoughts, the more I started to analyse other aspects of this. I was being asked to make a decision that could majorly affect somebody's life after listening to potentially weeks of evidence, most of which I wouldn't understand. What a responsibility for a 20-year-old who sometimes was so racked by anxiety that he couldn't make the simplest of decisions that carried no consequences!

I continued to drink heavily outside of work, now ingrained in a routine that just undermined any feeling of self-worth that I had left, but I was coping, I thought.

On Christmas Eve, we had a cracking night down the local. Loads of friends, loads of drink and an amazing atmosphere. When I went home, I went upstairs to my room. The thoughts came again. I hadn't bought any Christmas presents for anyone. Why was I such a fuck up? I convinced myself that I was going to ruin some poor stranger's life through Jury Service. Why could I never do anything right? Why did I always hurt people?

Around 2 o'clock on Christmas morning, I sent a group text to every contact on my phone basically saying goodbye, got under my duvet, slit my wrists and lay back, waiting to die.

Chapter 6

A Lost Little Boy Finds a Home

Waking up that Christmas morning, I was hit with conflicting emotions. Initial relief that I hadn't succeeded, followed by almost instant guilt and shame for the number of Christmases I had ruined and the worry and turmoil that I had caused people close to me. However, the strongest feeling was one of despondency at my failure. I couldn't even fucking get this right!

I got up and showered. After drying myself, I looked down at my wrists. It looked like Jabba the Hut's eyes were staring back at me. I dressed my wounds, then headed downstairs. My parents were out at church and my brother hadn't surfaced yet. I sat outside chain-smoking and making myself cups of tea. My brother came downstairs just before midday. "Are you alright, Bruv?"

"Yeah, sweet as, Bruv. Just a bit pissed up last night."

"OK, pub when it opens?"

"Fuck, aye!"

Our local was open from 12 until 3 on Christmas Day and, even though I knew I would have to explain things to some people, I knew I could laugh it all off. Never had the phrase 'What makes you bad, makes you better' been so relevant. A couple of pints would push any emotion down and I would be back, right?

After a couple of hours, it was time to go home for dinner. I refused to go, and this led to a row with my brother. When the pub closed, I took a bag of carry-outs home, went straight up to my room, lay face down on my bed and cried for the best part of an hour.

After another visit to the doctor's, I was prescribed with Diazepam to help with the withdrawal from alcohol and was basically sent on my way with a note to excuse me from Jury Service. I stayed off the booze for a couple of weeks, after New Year's, of course, returning to work for my father on reduced hours, to begin with, but I gave up my Saturdays at the newsagent's.

Now, my 21st birthday was coming up, and it happened to fall on a Friday. I was never going to miss out on this opportunity, so I went about restoring my tolerance levels in the run-up to the big day. What other choice did I have? I didn't want to make a fool of myself.

Friday 25 January 2002, I took my seat at the bar at midday, ordering my first pint so that I could toast the minute that I turned 21 years old at 12:05. Bang, we were on our way. All afternoon in the pub. Home for an hour for dinner and a quick change and back out to my adoring public. Getting absolutely smashed, barely having to put my hand in my own pocket. My only memory of the evening is of being sick into the urinals after a couple of cocktails. Marvelling, almost proudly, about the bright pink colour of my vomit.

As I returned to a more settled routine, my drinking became more settled and routine. A dozen or so pints after work? No harm done. Now with my Saturdays free, I could start regularly going to the football. I had met a couple of Charlton fans a couple of years younger than me, and we started travelling to away games. This was a different experience from going to football with my Dad or my sister. These weren't away days; these were fucking sessions! Good times, and I do look back on the next few years going to watch The Mighty Addicks as the happiest time of my life.

I've alluded to the feeling of never being a part of everything. With Charlton, the biggest group of people that I have ever knocked about with, numbering several thousands, I was part of something. The club was punching well above its weight and the relationship from the boardroom, through the management and playing staff, to the fans in the stands was exceptional. Everybody was pulling in the same direction, and in going to the ground to shout and sing for two hours, I was in no doubt that I was doing my bit.

This brings me to a weekend in October 2003. I had a trip down to Fratton Park, Portsmouth planned on the Saturday with a couple of mates. Friday night was spent down the local, and then a few of us headed back to mine. This included my oldest friend and a friend of his whose influence had led to me leaving the band that I had formed and bankrolled for years.

Now, this boy was a Billy Bullshit Cunt of the highest order and would boast about all of the drugs he had taken. We thought that we would teach him a lesson. Other than my oldest friend, who didn't touch ecstasy, we all triple-dropped.

This was par for the course for my three friends and me. For Billy, as I shall call him, this was like nothing he had experienced before.

Within five minutes, he had come up and he was flailing about wildly on my brother's bed, kicking and punching in all directions. I jumped on him and tried to hold him down as we all tried to subdue him, as my parents were trying to sleep in the next room. This wasn't working, so, as I held him down, my brother punched him and knocked him out. He came straight back around. My brother and a friend then took it in turns to punch his jaw. Every time his eyes rolled back, and straight away, he was conscious again.

This must have happened at least half a dozen times after which we picked him up, one on each limb, and carried him, still writhing about, out to the back garden.

We dumped him on the lawn and watched him, calling him every name under the sun. We had a green size-1 football in the garden, and I threw it at his head. "Eat the apple!" I said.

"It's not an apple; it's a potato!" he replied.

"Well, eat the fucking potato then!" I snapped back at him. He then proceeded to try and take a bite out of a leather football.

After a while, he had calmed down a bit and we sent him on his way, still in no condition to make his way home. Although he was an arsehole and he rubbed a lot of people up the wrong way, he didn't deserve what we did to him, anything could have happened to him. It was incredibly callous. We saw him the next day at the pub, fat lip and bruised jaw. He kept apologising to us! After what we had done? At that point, I had nearly as little respect for him as I had for myself.

I got up the next morning, right as rain, not giving the previous night's events a second thought. A day out in Portsmouth with the boys! I picked up some beers and jumped on the train to meet my mates, who had got on a stop earlier. There was only three of us making the journey, but we knew that we had sold out our 2,000 allocation. The team was playing well, and we were riding high in the Premiership. It was going to be fucking noisy!

Wherever we travelled, we always did what we called 'The Station Walk'. Without looking who was around as soon as our feet hit the platform, we would start singing. Today, the whole train seemed to spill out Charlton fans, and within seconds, hundreds of us were singing *Valley Floyd Road*, the Charlton anthem. What a buzz! I never took drugs at football. I never needed to; this shit was better than anything chemically induced.

After a few pints, we went to the match. When we got in the ground, there was a boy of no more than ten, and my mate saw him turn to his dad and say, "Oh good, they're here. We're going to be loud today." I felt ten feet tall! Don't get me wrong; we were no great faces or anything, but we were doing a lot of away games and we always sang throughout. When you know that you have mates who will back you up and join in, you have no worries about starting a song.

We were sat in the front row and we were singing with a few other pockets of Charlton from the moment we got there. Charlton fans were always noisy from the get-go at this time. At half-time, we were one down. Us and a couple of other small groups kept the noise up in the second half and, even though as time ticked by, the chance of victory was ebbing away, more and more joined in, and soon we had all 2,000 travelling Addicks on their feet belting out their support. I'm probably romanticising a bit, but at the time you could see the lift that the Charlton players got and they came storming at Portsmouth, attacking the goal in front of us. We scored two in the last 15 minutes to win the game. The equaliser came from John Fortune who ran straight in front of us, and stood, arms stretched out, looking at me and my mates, one by one, nodding as if to give us recognition. What a result! The perfect smash and grab raid! It may sound self-congratulatory, but I know that the three of us contributed in a way that day. We travelled home, drinking and singing all the way, and entered our local that night as conquering heroes! What a feeling!

Anyway, back to 2002. My sister was getting married in July that year, and my drinking, along with my brother's, was a very real concern for them, and they seriously considered holding their reception in a church hall and making it a dry occasion. In the end, they did book a hotel with beautiful grounds, and I behaved well, my brother too.

The day before, however, we had gone to get our hair cut and pick up our suits. After we had everything, we decided to have a couple of pints in the town centre before going home. My brother received a text from the landlady of our local, saying that her ice machine had broken down. We supped up went straight to Waitrose and filled a cab with bags of ice and took it down the pub. We were sorted out a couple of pints for our troubles. In the meantime, I received a text from Mum asking where we were, as she and Dad were worried. Well, that was it. They were obviously going to be a nightmare, so best to stay out of the way.

We had started drinking about 11 in the morning and carried on until being kicked out at midnight. Luckily, we had a henry of Charlie to sort us out! I got my head down about 4 o'clock on the morning of the day that I was due to be an usher at my sister's wedding. I was up at eight, bright and breezy. The day went off without a hitch. I was charming, polite and did everything asked of me. So, no harm done then.

Before my sister's happy day, there was the small matter of the World Cup. England had a decent team at a time when there was no standout team in the world. We had a very real chance. Best of all, though, it was being hosted by Japan and South Korea. Early morning kick-offs! In the pub at silly o'clock, and then win or lose, we're on the booze!

England's first game was on Sunday, the 2nd of June, 2002 against Sweden. A 1–1 draw was incidental as we were getting pissed. Early evening, some of my mates went off to a barbecue, but I decided to stay in the pub. I was only just around the corner from home, after all. After closing, I was drinking a couple of take-outs at home, watching a Queen Concert on the TV. My phone rang and a mate was calling me from the hospital. There had been an accident, a mate's car had hit a tree, and one of my boys was gone! Dumbstruck, I sat back down to finish my beers and soon realised that *The Show Must Go On* was playing. This is one of the most poignant moments of my life. I resolved there and then to sort myself out. After I finished the beers that I had brought home, of course.

Chapter 7
Life Becoming a Pharmacy

We all agreed to meet up at the tree where the accident had happened to lay flowers and leave mementoes. Nobody knew exactly what to do, so we all found our way back to the pub to raise a glass. I couldn't quit drinking on that day. That would have been disrespectful. The one thing that I prided myself on was that I was always respectful. Wasn't I? After a good time in the pub, it was time to go home.

The next few days followed a similar pattern. Most of the afternoons and all of the evenings were spent in the pub and then usually back to someone's afterwards to continue drinking. I was doing alright, I thought. *This grief thing is a piece of piss!*

My sister came to the funeral with me as some moral support. It was a huge turnout. We could only get into the foyer, and there were many people actually outside. As U2's *With or Without You* played over the crematorium PA system, we knew that the coffin was going down. I looked at my sister; tears were streaming down her face. We just held each other as I too cried, and cried. I wouldn't be able to cry for the next fifteen and a half years. Death wouldn't affect me during that time either. I was completely dead inside!

The upshot of the accident was that there was a big group of us which became really tight, united in our grief. All of a sudden, there was always somebody to get off your box with. Pills became the order of the day, especially at the weekends. They weren't always suitable for a school night, so sometimes, the Charlie would have to do. Besides, a couple of grams of Charlie after a bellyful of lager staved off a hangover and left you feeling fresh the following morning. You only needed a couple of hours' sleep each night anyway, didn't you? Football provided me with all of the surrogate emotions that I needed. I had found a way to deal with life, and I felt fucking great!

At some point, my band played a gig in our local. It was packed. We played the gig of our life and it was a great evening. Needless to say that I never played sober. As we lapped up the atmosphere, I had no idea that this was the last gig I would play with the band that I had founded and funded.

My oldest friend had met a boy at work who was a decent guitarist while they were doing their part-time jobs there. He became our new lead guitarist. In their free time, they would spend the time together working on new material and deciding a new direction and name for the band. All of our back catalogue was out the window. We couldn't even play any in practice. As the drummer, I loved warming up for a session with a couple of the faster ones, but hey-ho.

The new fella was going to a university in London in September. He had access to free practice space, all be it during the day. It made sense; after all, it would save the band money. Save the band money? What the fuck did they know? I was the cunt that had worked full time, sometimes longer hours, for years to finance everything, including the social side. What did they mean the band's money? We never made any money. It was my fucking money! Oh yeah, and I was still trying to work full-time, so I couldn't commit to midweek practices. But this was my issue to fucking resolve. I jumped before I was pushed and walked away from something that I loved, and had put my absolute all into, with barely a whimper or crossword. Why the fuck would I go to their gigs and continue to pay for their drugs?

I realised, at this time, that quite a few of my social group started going out to Bromley town centre at weekends, never inviting me. Was I becoming a problem? Was I just unlikeable? No, it can't be that. Someone would always be in touch after kicking out time to carry on the party. That had nothing to do with the fact that I had money, a cracking supply of disco biscuits and nosebag and I was always fucking up for it! That couldn't be it. They must like me after all. Besides, I had my local. I could sit with absolutely any one of the regulars. Any time of the week, I could walk in there and find someone to share a drink with. If not, there was always the bar staff. I was known in my local. I was liked and respected, wasn't I?

The boy who had been driving when the crash had occurred remained a good friend of ours. He was a good lad, had only just been going over the speed limit and it was only a couple of days since he had passed his test. He pleaded guilty to death by dangerous driving. This carried a minimum sentence of a year and a half. Many people wrote character references for him. Even though I was by far the most eloquent of my mates, nobody asked me.

The day of his sentencing arrived. We all expected this to be the last time that we saw him for a long time; he ended up with a suspended sentence and some Community Service. Loads went to the court to show support. I was sat at my desk at home, working. Nobody had bothered to tell me. I clearly wasn't invited. I was just a liability.

At least, I had my football. Charlton players were going really well at the time, and it was a great thing to be involved in. I had a good group of friends, and we had a good supply of top-notch drugs. I had no reason to feel sad or doubt myself. I was happy; life was fun.

Chapter 8

Anti-Depressants and Anaesthesia

The next couple of years carried on in much the same vein. Drinking, sniffing, popping pills. Generally, loving life. I and three others started to bulk-buy ecstasy. £700 for a thousand. Top-drawer narcotics they were too! We would sell them to friends and people we knew and just have ours for free. We weren't into making a profit. We weren't dealing. That's clear, isn't it? Whatever was left after the weekend, we would just finish on Monday night to ease us into the working week.

On a long weekend evening in the summer, a few of us were at mine, my parents being away. A few cold beers and a few Jack & Jills. This was living. I needed a slash, so I went to the toilet, sat down and relaxed. On the pills, it isn't always the easiest to piss, so I settled in to take my time.

Ah! Here we go. Why am I getting wet? I was so mashed that I had totally forgotten to take my jeans and pants down. Oh well, I was at home, quick shower and change and back on it. Actually, fuck the shower. Just dry yourself, change your clothes and a quick splash of Lynx Africa and back to the business of getting cunted. Class act, eh?

Occasionally, I had moments of lucidity. I had one sometime around a couple of years later. We ended up with quite a surplus one week. It was about three o'clock on a Thursday morning, and the four of us were sitting in a bedroom, chewing our faces off, trying to play Monopoly. Even in that state, I knew that this was ridiculous and it had to stop. We carried on until we had done them all, missing work on Thursday and Friday, but I would only do the gurners on a couple of other isolated occasions. Anyway, I still had booze and Charlie. The fucking power couple!

Now, I had a good, reliable source for the old Peruvian Marching Powder. The word was starting to get around, and I became the middleman for a lot of people. I didn't need money for drugs anymore. I just passed on enough and made mine for free. A little commission, if you will. I never held any stock, so obviously, I wasn't dealing, right?

When nobody wanted any, I had money of my own, and I could always get a line of credit! When you get your first tick, it feels like you have made it. This purveyor of the fine extra-curricular trusted me. No greater sign of respect. The opposite is true. This is when they've got you. Pay them back promptly a couple of times, and the sky's the limit. Now, I was looking to get higher than the sky! The best bit? Never having to go without a buzz. At least cocaine is an everyday drug!

November 2003. My grandfather died of Bronchial Pneumonia a week after having his flu jab. Coincidence? Who knows, who cares! A great man who I looked up to. He was a reservist before the Second World War and signed up immediately after war was declared. Part of the British Expeditionary Force, he would end up spending three days and three nights in Dunkirk. Once evacuated, he would fight in North Africa and then up through Italy, Hitler's soft underbelly. In my eyes, an absolute hero, but never a killer. He just did his duty, and he never wanted to be thanked. I felt a little sadness but no great loss. He was old; he'd been in poor health for a while. He'd had good innings! The show must go on! I could kill a line!

With no end of credit and quality Class As around me, I never wanted for company. I could play Charlie Big Potato. Literally. One time, I called in a shopping list, and while we were waiting, the three of us decided to go to a different pub. My man came and we jumped in, and he dropped us at the other pub ten minutes down the road. I slipped him some cash and out we jumped. One of the boys I was with offered to pay for the cab.

"How much?"

"£120. That was my geezer!" I could tell he was well impressed. I was a fucking top boy, wasn't I!

One of the boys who I used to go to football with turned 21 in May of the following year. He remains my best friend to this day. He had been a very close friend of our mate who died, and it was that mate who introduced us. He had a garden party, and all of the boys were around. A good drink over a sunny Sunday afternoon and a good group of us headed to the pub. Always one to feel a stranger in a crowd, I was well aware that everybody else had known him much longer.

We had a good drink and a cracking Charlton sing-song in the pub. We were the ringleaders. The two of us, arms around each other, belting out the favourites.

Why did I go home feeling like an outsider?

Obviously, a skinful was never enough, so I took a bag full of bottles home and carried on drinking, just me and my thoughts. *I am never going to fit in anywhere. What was the point of living life on the outside, or worse, on my own?* I checked the cupboards, and there was a good stock of various painkillers. I got a plate, popped them all out and counted them. 93 pills: Paracetamol, Solpadeine and Co-codamol. That should do it. One last cigarette, and then to bed.

I took my remaining beers to bed and took a sip, then took a tablet. Then a sip, then a tablet. I got into a good rhythm, and soon all the tablets were gone with one bottle of lager left. I thought that I would savour this last taste of heaven before I slipped into eternal peace. I wasn't savouring anything at this point in my life, and it slipped straight down. I closed my eyes to die.

My stomach had other ideas, and I was violently sick throughout the night. To my parents, I put it down to having had too much to drink. Until this day, nobody knew that I tried to end my life that night.

After a couple of days recuperating, I returned to work and my regular routine. I had always wanted to be in a relationship and wasn't necessarily that bothered in casual sex. If I had been a bit more successful in finding it, I probably would have taken to it. If I liked a girl, I would say something, but always to no avail.

In the summer of 2004, there was a girl working in the local, and living above. We got on well, and I would often stay behind for a drink after the pub closed. I asked her if she wanted to start seeing me a couple of times, but she declined. She started to get some attention from a bloke I knew. Now, he was a cunt and only interested in one thing, but he was a good-looking, confident cunt. I warned her that he would do the dirty on her, but they started seeing each other anyway.

Soon after, he got together with another girl in our local while the girl I liked was working. After work, I was comforting her and she came out with the cracking line, "Why can't I find someone like you?" Now to most people, this might seem like a compliment. In my mind, it finally proved to me that there was something intrinsically wrong and unlovable about me. That was it. I would never allow myself to develop feelings for another girl. I was destined to spend my life alone. Oh well, I still had my favourite two girls, Stella and Charlie.

My parents had been thinking about moving to Swansea to take my mother's mother and aunt home for their final years. The plan was that I would stay up in Bromley and run the accountancy firm for them, with my father coming back up for two or three days a week.

I had been made partner, somehow, by this time. I think most probably to try and motivate me. In all fairness, I was doing the hours required, but not on a 9–5 basis. By now, I had built up a lot more debt, and my finances had been consolidated into another, larger loan, that my father paid directly and deducted from my salary. Often, to make the hours up, I would be in the office until 11 or 12 on a Thursday night.

Anyway, the move to Swansea was gathering pace. My nan's and great aunt's houses had sold and a property in Swansea was purchased. My great aunt had a fall, broke her hip and went into a home that she was never to leave. My father had been struggling health-wise for a while, and he was eventually diagnosed with Non-Hodgkin's Lymphoma. A non-aggressive form of cancer. It was my time to step up, as he was to undergo chemo. In all fairness, I did, for a while.

In the spring of 2005, my nan was found dead in her bed. Neither was to make it home to Swansea. This was possibly a blessing in disguise, as my mother would be able to concentrate on my father's recuperation as he was now in remission. I had started to increase my drinking and cocaine consumption again. This led to me becoming unreliable, and I let my parents down badly.

With Dad not well enough to travel regularly between Swansea and Bromley, and me struggling to cope, the decision was made to sell the company. I cherry-picked some of the regular jobs to give myself an income, but the inescapable truth was that I had destroyed my father's legacy to me. A successful company that was as old as I was, and I had fucked it up in little over six months.

My brother and I had always had a fractious relationship growing up. We were born only 17 months apart and shared a bedroom until I was 12, and we seemed to be around each other in a lot of what we did, which caused friction. Although both having similar interests, we failed to find much common ground. This was finally rectified by drink and drugs. We had something that we could do together. For a long time, it worked well and we grew close. Some people knew us as the chemical brothers. Charlie, pills, ketamine. Fucking love it. Looking back, there were a lot of flashpoints all along. These definitely escalated throughout the years leading up to our parents' departure, with several violent encounters.

I can look back now and see that we both were in a terrible place mentally, and we both chose to deal with it the same way. However, the difference was in our mindsets and the way we coped with our frustrations. I would blame myself for absolutely everything that was wrong in my life, as well as much more. I internalised my anger, and I would cut myself or put cigarettes out on myself. My brother always had to blame somebody else, usually me, and would lash out at someone, usually me. Obviously, with a shitload of lager in me, I wouldn't take it.

We had many tear-ups, but it would be over and we would be drinking together the next day. It must have been hell for my parents, especially when my father got ill. My father would always choose to have a go at me, as I was never going to attack him. Everything seemed like my fault, even the night that my brother came into my room with a knife or the time when they were away and I had to barricade myself in my room all night because he was chasing me around the house with a baseball bat. It all reminded me of the numerous times that I was told that I was the cause of all the aggro in the house while I was growing up.

In October, that year, my parents finally made the move to Swansea. My brother and I stayed in the house together, barely speaking to each other except when we filled the house with people, beer and drugs. We definitely weren't getting on but had found a way to co-exist. If we weren't getting off our tits, we just avoided each other.

Shortly after Mum and Dad's departure, the boss of a building firm that I did the accounts for went on a month's holiday, leaving me in charge of everything, including getting payments. I knew that he didn't have any faith in me.

This was a client of over twenty years standing of my father's, and, although I had basically been doing everything there for over a year, I had found out that he had been getting someone in to check some of what I was doing. This bloke couldn't have been much cop, as, although my work was good, there were a couple of occasions when, doing the payroll, I had paid myself a bit extra to pay off a tab, and nothing ever came of it. I really was dragging my father's good name through the mud.

Anyway, by the beginning of the third week, I was sinking fast. On Tuesdays, I would do the payroll. Timesheets and invoices had to be in by midday. I had

had a blowout over the weekend, to escape, I suppose. Anyway, I didn't get up to do the payroll, and by lunchtime, there were a couple of his staff members knocking on my front door.

What the fuck do I do now?

After I had slit my wrists that Christmas Eve, someone got wind that I had cut across. I think that they were trying to expose me as a fraud and had said in front of a lot of people, "Across for attention, down for death!"

Thanks for the tip, I now thought. I also realised that the blood had clotted that first time. Armed with all of this knowledge, I ran a bath, opened up a new razor and got in. I slit my wrist, the proper way, and lay with my head under the water.

Almost immediately there was a knock on the bathroom door. I tried to ignore it. They kept knocking, and it turned out that it was our neighbours from across the road, very good friends of my parents. I knew the game was up, and I felt terrible that they were going to find me, so I got out of the bath and opened the door. They took me to the hospital and called my sister. Once I was bandaged up, I went back to my sister's flat to stay the night, feeling like the worst person to ever have lived. I obviously couldn't kill myself by cutting, so I wouldn't do it anymore.

My brother and I now totally avoided each other. I spent all of my time in my room. In fairness, I must have been an absolute nightmare to live with. Imagine returning home every day, almost expecting to find your brother dead. Over the summer, he had been working on my parent's house in Swansea and had met a girl. That Christmas, he moved to Swansea to live with her. I was now free to do as I pleased.

All of my regular work had gone by the wayside now. I would do a little bit here and there, earn a bit, and then lock myself away with a load of beer, fags and Charlie. I became an absolute recluse. I never opened the curtains, and the house was an absolute state. I only spoke to people to buy something or other and still had some decent tabs that I could run up. I always made my best for football. It was the one time that I functioned, that I felt alive.

Eventually, it was agreed that I should move back with my parents in Swansea. A date was set and tickets purchased. I was to travel after Charlton's FA Cup Quarter Final against Middlesbrough. A 0–0 draw meant a reply. I didn't get on that train, I had a day out first. We took over five and a half thousand up to the Riverside that night for the replay.

As the club laid on the transport as a 'thank you' to the fans for their support, everybody was deposited in the ground two hours before the kick-off. The beer was flowing; everybody was up for it, and the songs were being belted out. The game started, and it sounded like Charlton were the home side; we were that loud.

We came straight out of the blocks and should have been ahead a couple of times early on. As it happened, we were to lose 4–2, but we absolutely embarrassed their support, outsinging them from the first to the last whistle. Even though I was pissed off that we had lost, I was fucking buzzing. As I had known all along, this was my drug. This was where I was supposed to be. This was what I was supposed to do. This was where I belonged, where I fitted in, where I was somebody, somebody alive. I reflected on this and the fact that I had to leave this all behind me for the duration of the long coach journey back south. How had it come to this? Why had I fucked this up for myself?

Chapter 9

The First in a Series of False Dawns

So, I moved to Swansea. A fresh start, a new beginning and a chance to create a new me. I had some renewed optimism, and I set about the task of finding work. I did a circuit of the employment agencies and sent out several CVs. After a couple of months, I got a temporary placement in the Finance Department of a Housing Association. The work was nothing that I couldn't handle, and my colleagues all seemed pleasant and easy-going.

A couple of weeks after moving down, the FA Cup final between West Ham United and Liverpool was played in Cardiff. My brother received a call that morning from a friend of ours saying that he was on his way to Cardiff with his girlfriend. She was a West Ham fan and she and some friends had tickets to the match. He didn't, so did we fancy meeting him for a drink. Rude not to! My brother's partner had gone away for the weekend, so we had had a good drink the night before, leaving his local pub well after two. I left with my glasses taped up after losing a screw.

So it was that we got straight up, quick showers and into town to get my glasses fixed and jump on the train to Cardiff. A few cans for the journey, and then we were amongst it. We found a pub that was majority West Ham, found a plot and waited for our mate. He arrived shortly and we were on our way.

There was a cracking atmosphere in the pub, and West Ham is a club that I have always had a soft spot for, so I was far from neutral. There were a couple of scuffles elsewhere in the pub, but this just added to the atmosphere. I have never been a purveyor of violence, but being around violence didn't particularly bother me, I was prepared to do much worse to myself than anybody else would do to me!

A couple more hours of drinking after the game, which had gone the distance, and time for the journey home. By this stage, we had probably been drinking for the best part of ten hours on an empty stomach after one hell of a session the night before. My brother made a call on the train home to book in some extra-curricular, and we were on our way. This was getting better and better.

We got back to Swansea and back to my brother's house. My brother went to call his mate to say that we were home. He had lost his phone. Soon he would pass out. If there was no Charlie, what was the point in staying there?

I got a kebab, called a cab and headed for home. Why go home when the pub is still open? I popped to the pub closest to my parents' house and stayed until it closed. There must have been one hell of a state on me.

My first day at work happened to be the day before my brother's wedding, so straight from work, I went to meet him and his future father-in-law for a couple of drinks. The wedding was arranged at short notice to fit around a pre-booked holiday. This was his stag do, and we took full advantage. Somewhere along the way, I lost my signed timesheet for the one day that I had worked and had to sheepishly ask for another one on Monday. Good fucking start!

The wedding was a low-key affair. Just immediate family in the registry office, and then to a pub in town for a meal. After that, we went to the pub where the two of them had met. They had only told those who were to attend the wedding about their upcoming nuptials, so it was a surprise to everyone down the pub. Word soon got around, and soon the place was heaving. This pub was starting to become my local, and I was meeting all of the regulars and characters. Well, that was it; this was where I was going to spend my spare time.

Work continued, fairly mundanely, and I would be in the pub every evening after work, either in town with a friend or alone in my local. My local was exceedingly quiet during the week, often just being me and the staff. This suited me; it gave me someone to talk to. They were duty-bound after all.

My brother and I would have the odd Friday or Saturday night out that would end up getting way over the top including masses of cocaine. This was almost always on me. His wife took a strict line with their money and certainly didn't encourage us to drink together. I took his mates' number and I was all set now! I managed to keep the drugs to the weekend to start with, but it started creeping into school nights when I had a good drink.

I started to get disillusioned at work. I had applied for and been selected for the permanent position of the role that I had been filling, but things seemed like they were changing. I was moved to a different part of the department to do monkey work. I was also not being selected for certain training.

Although I wasn't properly qualified, I was told that I was qualified by experience by several very credible sources. There were people in higher positions, as well as people on my pay grade, who might have had qualifications but didn't have the experience or understanding of accountancy that I did. My father was old school, and I had learnt using pen and paper, the proper way. I had a real understanding of the theory. So why was I being excluded? I was convinced that I and seven clones could have run that department more efficiently and effectively, but I was moving backwards.

My new role was processing invoices for payment. Part of this was to get invoices approved by the various department heads. I kept getting told to sit on invoices, hold payment on this and that, that one's in dispute. My head of department kept telling me to get these old invoices sorted. The heads of departments were older than me; they had been there longer than me and were a lot more senior. I didn't think that I had the authority to chase them, and I certainly didn't have the confidence, so things kept piling up.

On a Monday night, I went for a couple of pints with my mate from work and stayed on after he had gone home, drinking alone. I had become accustomed to this by now and proceeded to stumble from pub to pub. Once my money was gone, I started to walk home, with just my thoughts for company.

How have I allowed myself to get to this point again? I noticed that the tide wasn't too far out, so I cut through to the beach. I walked along a bit where I thought that I wouldn't be seen and started to walk out into Swansea Bay. I am not a good swimmer, and once you get out far enough, the seabed is basically like heavy, sticky mud. I knew I wouldn't have to go far until my feet would stick and I could just let nature take its course.

The water was nearly up to my waist when I heard someone calling from the shore. I ignored and kept moving forward. I would have continued, but then he shouted, "Don't make me come and get you!" I realised at that moment that I could end up putting him in trouble, and he was completely innocent. He was prepared to put himself in danger for me—a stranger. After a little thought, I turned and made for the shore. He walked me all the way to home in Mumbles. I was genuinely humbled by the kindness of this stranger. *I can't let this happen again*, I thought.

I had totally forgotten about this chapter of my life before I started this process of documenting my struggles. What the fuck is wrong with me? Has the decision to end my life become such a regular thought that it ceased to be exceptional? Has a suicide attempt stopped being a major event in my story?

I had kept my season ticket at Charlton going and would travel back for all the weekend fixtures, travelling back sometime on the Friday and coming home on Sunday, having used my sister's place as little more than a bed & breakfast from which to stage a 36-hour bender with my mates. Fridays were the only holidays I booked, and I would sometimes travel after work so as not to take the piss.

Charlton's season was not going well, and we were mired in a relegation battle that we were doomed to lose. Towards the end of March, we had a fixture to play against Wigan. A bona fide relegation six-pointer! I just had to be there. I needed to be there. My team needed me to be there.

I had booked the Friday off as usual, and travel was arranged. The week before, I was told that if I didn't rectify my backlog, I wouldn't be able to have the following Friday off. Were they taking the piss? I had volunteered for everything. I had been part of the skeleton staff between Christmas and New Year. I had over a week in flexi-time.

That weekend, I did my usual session after work on Friday with a nice bit of chop for afters, followed by an all-dayer, pretty much alone, on Saturday. On Sunday, I arranged to meet my brother, knowing that it would turn out to be a big 'un. I went out that Sunday, knowing that I wasn't going back to work. The session was going to be my excuse, and I was going to let what came after be my catalyst back into my depressive cocoon. Most of all, I would make the football!

I made the Wigan match and we won 1–0, with a late penalty. The place was buzzing; we had a real chance now. I had made the right choice. A great weekend with the boys. Good company, good beer, good class As! Oh, and a little time with my sister, my kind host.

Chapter 10

Safety in Solitude

I never did return to my job. Charlton eventually got relegated and the last time that I saw them, I travelled with my father to Blackburn. We were among over 6,000 Charlton fans. We lost 4–1, and that basically secured relegation. The fans were magnificent singing until the end.

Just before the final whistle, everybody was on their feet, singing *Valley Floyd Road*. What a noise, in adversity. What a place and time to be in. This was what I needed in my life. Out of pride, I felt a lump in my throat and the tears form. This was the closest that I would come to crying during this soulless, emotionless, despondent period of my sorry existence. I was aware that I had fucked it all up again, and I had no way to facilitate my favourite experience. If I ever picked myself up this time, would I ever be able to watch my team play again?

Over the next couple of months, I slipped into a nocturnal existence. My parents didn't know how to encourage me and didn't know how to handle me. I was a shell. My personal hygiene went by the wayside, and I realised that, by staying up all night and hiding away in my room during daylight hours, I would hardly have to speak to anybody. On one of my clandestine expeditions to the shop for cigarettes, I clearly saw the man behind the counter wrinkle his nose at my smell. What had I become?

The problem with this was that it was too comfortable. I never really considered suicide because I was safe and sound within my dark cave. Depression has always seemed very self-protecting to me. If left to your own devices, you will continue to wallow. You will do what you have to do to get back to your hovel and look inside yourself at everything that disgusts you. We put on a mask in public, over-compensating, being the joker, just to avoid the awkward questions. I found that if I could totally withdraw from life, then my mental health wouldn't become terminal again. Allowing no outside influences meant that I wouldn't be exposed to the added stresses that might tip me over the edge. I wasn't living, so much as existing. But existing was better than dying, right?

In trying to help, my parents arranged some counselling for me. This was through a church-based charity and was something that I was never going to be receptive to, being led back to the faith. Don't get me wrong; I have the highest respect for peoples' faiths and belief systems. I know what it is like trying to find a purpose and a way through the day. I will never become an aggressive atheist, but religion hasn't worked for me.

Anyway, the man I had the sessions with soon established some common ground in the fact that we had both been in The Boys' Brigade. I never felt like he listened to me and would regularly talk over me. Eventually, he came to the conclusion that I was comfortable doing what I was doing and didn't really want to get better. *Well, fuck you then, Cunty!* He was right.

After about nine months of existential limbo, neither wanting to live nor die, my brother came up with an idea. He had worked in the building trade straight from school, and he needed an extra pair of hands for a couple of weeks. I was to cycle into Swansea each morning, basically just to pass him tools and materials.

After months of inactivity, any strength that I may have once possessed, which would only ever have been negligible, had completely atrophied. I had once been quite a fit boy, now I couldn't cycle a mile without my legs aching and gasping for breath. I let down one of my tyres and proceeded to push my bike for the duration of the journey. I turned up well late and claimed to have had a puncture. What was meant to be a short-term thing would shape my next decade. I would be next to no help, and I would be paid £25 per day for the privilege! How had it come to this? From being an Oxbridge candidate to being a charity case, grateful for earning a pittance in an industry that I was never going to succeed in?

Chapter 11

Growing Stronger yet Fading Away

I settled down to work with my brother, struggling to lift a 25kg bag of cement, such was my lack of physicality. My brother made sure that I was alright, always working closely with me, but I knew that I was much more a hindrance than a help. At least this gave me some money to resume drinking at the weekends.

Sometimes, my wages would go on a Friday night, out on the piss, pretty much on my own. This would usually end up in my 'local' sat on my own, pouring pint after pint of Stella down my throat. At least, there were other people in the pub, so I wasn't technically drinking alone, right?

After finishing the flats that they were building when I joined, we started doing total renovations of houses, totally gutting them first. This was work that I could do. Knowing that I would never let myself believe that I could ever do anything constructive or technical, I put all of my effort into the rip-outs.

I felt my strength slowly increasing, and I was sure that if I put my heart and soul into the work, that would be noticed and I would be offered more money. I want to iterate that my brother wasn't in charge of my pay, but it would be 9 months before I would be on £30 a day and a further 18 before I would receive £40, barely a decent wage. My brother had to push for this, as I had absolutely no faith that my work had any value.

Early one year, my brother had a short separation from his wife. He found himself in one of the flats that he had built. Well, working together and now living near the City Centre, we were on the piss every night and then back to his flat for a big, fat toot. I would sleep curled up on the small living-room carpet using a pile of clothes as a pillow for the first week or so. After that, it was the comparative luxury of a small sofa bed.

That month, things started to get very fractious between us. He was probably pissed off with the amount of money that he was spending on me. I never asked him for anything. I spent what little money I had, and then the financial burden was on him, but he wanted me around to support him through this difficult time, so I wasn't taking advantage. Bollocks! I knew exactly what I was doing. Besides, he was practically insisting that I stay with him as much as I would have liked to have had a night at home. We were both getting what we wanted, and it didn't matter that we would have mammoth fucking rows at work. We could argue while working, the job would get done, and then we would be off to the pub where we were best of friends.

After about a month, my brother reconciled with his wife and moved back home. We were working six or seven days a week now, so even my meagre wage would give me a little bit of wedge to have a drink after work every night and still enough for a big beer and Charlie binge over the weekend evenings.

Work has always been essential to my self-esteem, and gratitude has always been as good as a day's wage to me. I was getting very little money and absolutely no fucking gratitude. My confidence a year after starting was exactly where it was when I started: six foot under. I knew that there was never any future in this sort of work for me, and the job was sucking what little life I had left out of me, but it was a means to an end. It facilitated my using.

I was on the scrapheap and I fucking knew it. This was my life from now on, and I didn't deserve any better. I had done this to myself by my own decisions, and I deserved to feel like a worthless cunt for another half a century, or however long my pitiful existence would last. I was just counting down the days until I died, hoping that it would be sooner rather than later.

One Friday, I spent the day alone, picking rubbish out of a huge pile of dirt, getting it ready to be taken away. Apparently, this needed to be done so that it could go through the processing plant. I don't fucking know whether there is any truth in this or whether it was just a fucking joke at my expense. I didn't fucking care.

Anyway, my boss turned up to pay me for the week. He handed me the money and said, "I've only got 20s; can I owe you the fiver?"

"No worries," I replied. I counted it, and there was £140; he had overpaid me. I was straight over to him to give him £20 back, and he turned to his mate and laughed.

"He's giving me money back! Steve, I'll have that fiver on Monday." Then he was gone. This was the level of respect that I commanded at that time. I carried on working for another two and a half hours, waiting for a call to tell me to pack it in and go home. That call never came. When it got too dark, I walked into town for a pint. This was the level of respect that I had for myself at that time.

As I said, I was a good hard worker. Now, usually, this would be rewarded you would think, but not here. People would come to do some labouring, do fuck all of the dirty work, bitch and moan about it and soon be moved onto more constructive work, learning new skills.

Me, because I could be left alone in a house on my own to just crack on, saw no advancement opportunities whatsoever. I was always bottom rung. Everybody else came in on the second rung. New kids that hadn't done any work in the building trade came straight in on better money from the start and were soon moved onto more involved work, just to give our boss a quiet life. Still, I couldn't speak up.

Driving was a bone of contention. Because I didn't drive, my boss would have to drop the tools off to me at each new job. It wasn't really that big a deal, Swansea is a small city, and besides, the lazy cunt never did anything. He was so lazy that he had his father tiling a splashback in a kitchen during a course of radiotherapy, while he swanned about, as if he was Billy Big Bollocks. One day, he asked, "Are you interested in driving?" I replied,

"I'm not operating a vehicle on these wages." This was the full extent of the conversation. That was it. The word was out very quickly that, even though he had offered to pay for my lessons, tests and a van with insurance, I had flatly refused him. This is so far from the cunting truth! It was not a flat-out refusal; all I wanted was some more money if I was going to be driving. This was the only time that I ever tried to further my earnings here.

My brother started to get quite a bit of private work in, and we started working the majority of weekends. This was a totally different experience. My brother was much happier working for himself. He knew he wasn't being taken advantage of, which, to be fair, he was with the amount and quality of work he got through between Monday and Friday. I could tell that he knew I would give him a good day's work in both effort and quality. In exchange, he would pay me a decent whack and a couple of pints after work. I had gained a little respect from him, but very little from myself. When we worked together during the week, things weren't always so harmonious.

This was the pattern that life followed. We started to knock about with a couple of boys from a different part of town, and there were drugs available when I wanted. I was earning the money as well. A few pints after work in the week, and then a session of drink and drugs over the weekend, still OK to work seven days a week. This was my lot for the rest of my days, remember, but I could exist like this. There was something in it for me now. Escape!

Our first job one year was to renovate a house that had been left to one of our bosses. The two of us did most of the work together with nobody else. This was quite a pleasant period and we were getting on pretty well. By the time that we had finished the house, my brother and his wife split up. He would be moving into the house when it was done. Working together, it would make sense if I stayed with him most of the time. The Chemical Brothers were back, and we were going to put a major dent in the trade deficit of South America!

Chapter 12

Perfect Purgatory

A couple of weeks before my brother moved into his new gaff, I had an accident at work. On a different job, I was pushing wheelbarrows up scaffold boards to empty into a skip. The shit work again! There were a couple of skip rats going through the crap, looking for some flagstones that we had taken up. I was pushing a full barrow up when the scaffold boards slipped and I fell to the ground, with the full weight of everything coming down on my left elbow.

I got up, gathered myself and tried to carry on. I could still lift a barrow, but when it came to pushing forward, the pain was too much and I couldn't exert any force on the left-hand side. I was convinced that the skip rats had moved the boards, as I was quite particular about resituating them after every couple of loads. However, I still saw fit to apologise to my boss before I made my way home. He said that it was alright, but I could tell by his manner that he felt as though I had let him down.

Anyway, a visit to the hospital that afternoon, followed by a visit to the Fracture Clinic the following day, confirmed that I had chipped my left humerus. I had the full set now!

The upshot of this was that I would have time off work. Illness and injury was the only time that I had off work. Now when I had broken my right humerus, I had an operation to put a wire in and correct the break. This fracture apparently wasn't serious enough, so it was just left. The fragment of bone would just dissolve over time and there might be some muscle damage. My right arm recovered full mobility; my left I can never fully extend or flex. The lesson here is that, if you are going to break a bone, do it fucking properly. Entirely up to you if you want to involve alcohol or not.

I had three weeks off work altogether; I was in no rush to get back, and during this time, my brother moved into his new home. As I wasn't working, he asked me to sit in one Friday to wait for his Sky to be installed. When he came home that night, he had four cases of lager. Housewarming here we come!

A couple of his mates came around; he was living a lot closer to them now, and we proceeded to have one hell of a lost weekend. There were times where my brother was clearly upset about his marriage, but he was dealing with it in exactly the same way as I would have. Get fucked and push any feelings so far down that they will never resurface. We both knew that this worked and allowed you to get on with your life. Provided that you didn't stop.

I think that it was this weekend that our mate's brother, a heroin addict, refused to share a note with us. We thought who does this junkie think that he is? He's the dirty one; he's the one who might have diseases. He told us how Hepatitis can be passed by sharing notes to sniff. He was much more aware of the health risks than us, and our behaviour or habit certainly wasn't any better than his, but because we never touched heroin, and of course never would, we thought that we were somehow superior.

On Sunday, it was just the two of us by then, and he suggested that it would be easier if I slept over for work on Monday. I said that I wasn't ready for work yet; I couldn't fully turn off a tap with my left hand; how could I do my job? I could have easily gone back to work then, but I didn't particularly have any desire to return to work earlier than I absolutely had to. Besides, we had had an absolute fucking monster of a weekend, and I could do with a couple of days in bed. This, understandably, led to a row and I headed off home. I went back to work that Thursday.

It was in the spring of this year that we tried Meow. This shit was cracking value for money. You could be going all weekend for what you would spend in an evening or quicker, on cocaine. It had a stinking comedown though, so we only ever really tried it on a few occasions and preferred to stick with the Charlie, no matter how shit it was. After all, Charlie was a drug you could do on a school night.

One weekend, when we were on a Meow binge, my brother, I and a friend were watching football at my brother's house. It was Saturday afternoon, and we were having a laugh, nicely anaesthetised from the real world. My brother threw a flip flop at me, for a joke, and it hit my glasses, breaking one of the lenses. We all thought that it was quite funny, and I managed to tape part of it back in place, and so I just carried on.

Most of the weekend was spent looking through one eye on the old Meow anyway. I stayed until the Sunday night, made my way home half-blind and completely off my box and went straight to my room. I got up the next morning and took myself into town to Vision Express. I had an eye test, and the woman said that I had very healthy eyes. Not from my fucking viewpoint, they weren't! A couple of ton later, and I was back to work the following day.

We carried on working six or seven days a week. Whenever there was private work to do, we would take it on. Evenings and weekends. Regardless of what time we finished in the evening, there was always time for a couple of drinks, and that usually meant some barley as well.

The only time that was sacrosanct from work was Wednesday evenings. On Wednesday evenings, we would be back home by six, usually after a speedy few pints in the pub, with a couple of crates of lager. A quick call to someone, we had plenty of contacts now, and if we owed somebody, we could always get our chang somewhere else. With a henry on the way, it would be quick showers and then our mate would turn up, usually with a quarter of green, and we were all set. A night of FIFA on the Xbox! I loved those evenings.

Really chilled, the three of us got on really well. Good drugs, good beer, good company, good times. Our club nights gave me some structure to my week. Whereas, going to Charlton had been what got me through the weeks back home; now it was football on the computer. It gave me something to aim for.

The funny thing to look back on, though, is that we would do something like this most evenings. Not always FIFA, usually just the two of us, but for some reason, Wednesday was different; a special occasion. As I write this, I actually look back on this time with some fondness. I didn't enjoy what I did for work, and it seemed at the time to be an interminable slog, but I genuinely enjoyed the downtime. Yes, there was the odd row. There always is going to be where oceans of beer and mountains of class As are concerned, but my brother and I were, for the main, comfortable in each other's company and genuinely got on well.

We were the only ones at work that we could rely on to put in a proper graft. It was us against the world and all of those gym bunny cunts that we worked with could fuck off with their health kicks. We would put our bodies through the absolute fucking ringer and we would still show them up for the fucking pussyhole little pricks that they were. They had bigger muscles than us, but ours weren't made for the mantelpiece. Ours were functional, not for show. I definitely had a sense of pride about what I was doing then, even if I have only realised that now.

Chapter 13
Mixed Signals

The times that I spent at home at my parents' house were characterised by drunken nights, alone in a roomful of people. My local was my refuge, and I could drink in a darkened corner. I knew plenty of people, but everybody knew somebody else better. Some nights, you would get into a conversation and that was nice. Other nights, I was left alone to deal with my personal issues the only way that I knew how, and that was nice.

One day, I was the only person in the pub and three boys came in. They immediately struck up a conversation with me, and it turned out that they had just moved into the flat next door, above the shop. They had all just finished at Swansea University and were staying in the area. They were great lads and I felt at ease with them straight away.

After a few pints, they invited me back to theirs and we shared a couple of spliffs. I have never been a big one for weed, but they were such easy company and the conversation could get quite deep at times and was always stimulating. In most of my experiences of the building trade, any sign of intelligence or knowledge is taken as a weakness or shameful, and I had learnt to just keep my mouth shut.

"You're not paid to think!"

Now I had an outlet, a place where I honestly felt that I could be myself. I should have hitched myself to them closer. These were good boys.

Most of my life was still spent with my brother, and when I was back at my parents', I would drink in the pub alone and quite often go on a mission to find some coke to sniff alone at home. I had several contacts, but none that were 100% reliable. This was something that I definitely missed from London.

I never contacted the lads next door to see if they wanted to meet up. I couldn't understand that anyone would want to volunteer their free time to listen to me. I was always excited to receive a text or phone call from one of them to see if I fancied a drink. I knew that I would have a good time, and that I would end up getting stoned. One day, one of them made the mistake of telling me to knock anytime that I fancied.

On a Friday or Saturday night, they would often have a group of friends around. All good company, but again, another group for me to be welcomed into to feel excluded from. They didn't exclude me and made every effort to involve me, but again, I had trouble accepting friendship, and it was another situation where everybody else had a lot more history with each other. Always made to feel welcome, but never even close to feeling comfortable.

In my head, I think that I believed that I could have my cake and eat it. When I had a weekend back 'home', I would have a good drink on Friday night and go on my usual magical mystery tour for cocaine. If that didn't happen, I would look up at their window on my way home after the pub had closed, and if the light was on, I would knock. Someone would throw down the keys to me and I would let myself up.

Most of the time, it was only one or two of them, and I would feel a little at ease.

Walking into a bigger group really brought out the anxiety.

Anybody who has enjoyed their cannabis knows that the last thing that the atmosphere needs is a pisshead to enter. Occasionally, they would ignore the knock and the keys weren't forthcoming, even though I heard them chatting, and they knew that it was me. I don't blame them one bit. I was starting to take the piss and ruin their nights. In fairness, I would always get an invitation around or out for a drink soon after. Occasionally, I would take some marching powder around and we would sniff that together, and they would seem satisfied that this was ample recompense for the countless joints that they gave me. The cocaine-cannabis exchange rate has always been in favour of the cannabis user. Not in this case.

The trouble with being a drinker hanging out with experienced smokers is that they like the good quality dope, and you have little or no tolerance. Add to that a bellyful of lager and it is a bad combination. It was a three-bedroom flat and they were all en suite. I think over my time there, I was sick in three toilets, three basins, two shower cubicles, one bath and the kitchen sink. I did once wake up at home to a text asking me to come around to clear up the sick that I had left in one of the basins. The boy whose room it was hadn't even been home that night. Still, they refused to cut me loose.

From time to time, one of them would move out and someone else would move in. Every time, the new tenant would make me feel at home and welcome me straight into the fold. One of the lads was there throughout the entirety of their stay. The two of us would strike up a friendship that even I could see as being true. We could talk forever about any subject for any length of time.

One morning, I woke up on the sofa with his hand in my pants and mine in his. How did that happen? Oh, well. Home for some kip. This happened a couple of times and I said nothing. I still needed to change my reality one way or another.

One day, the two of us went out and had a good drink on a Friday night. We went back to his, and I expected to have a couple of spliffs as usual. A friend of his was around with a load of MDMA. Now I love Mandy and he was happy to share. When he was leaving, my mate asked if he had any more. He did and now we had a nice bit for the two of us. I'd been expecting it for a while, but I was still quite surprised when he asked me if I wanted to go up to his bedroom. I wasn't really up for it, but then his flatmate's girlfriend said, "You're both single; why not?" Now I'd never thought of it like that, yeah, why not?

So over the next 36 hours, I experienced my only homosexual encounter.

No bum fun and nothing done to completion. Nothing is ever done to completion on Mandy! It wasn't something that I enjoyed or hated, but it was nice to feel some affection and intimacy for once.

I knew after that weekend that I was definitely not gay and I can say that with more certainty than most. It's a shame really because if I was, I would have had a lot more sex. It turns out that there are plenty of men sitting deeply in the closet around my area. I think that I must give off a vibe that Welsh gay men misread. Probably a translation issue!

Chapter 14
Friendships Revisited

In the spring of 2008, there was a new addition to the family. Mum and Dad had registered to puppy walk a guide dog. This basically entailed homing a puppy for a year, teaching him the basic commands and generally preparing him for selection and subsequent training as a guide dog for the blind.

So it came to pass that a tiny seven-weeks-old black Labrador retriever called Klint was delivered to us on a Tuesday. When Guide Dogs have a new litter, all of the puppies are given the same initial. Klint suited him. He definitely wasn't a Kevin or Keith! *Here is a little playmate for me*, I thought.

He was a little bundle of energy who would play until all of his energy resources were expended. He was always ready to greet me from work with a little jump and plenty of kisses. I was left in no doubt that he loved me, and I had absolutely no hesitation in accepting his friendship. Nobody had known him longer than I had, after all. He became my best friend; most of the time, I was convinced that he was my only friend.

It was a joy to see him grow and mature. Watching him learn how to use his paws to manipulate things was brilliant. There was no doubt that he was an intelligent dog and so affectionate with it. Guide Dogs wanted him to be handled mainly by one person, so my father was in charge of his walks. He would join us on family days out, and seeing him off-lead, exploring every new environment was brilliant.

He had his health issues during this first year. He somehow contracted conjunctivitis and this developed into kennel cough, which is, apparently, closely linked. He would become a regular at the vet's for a while, as this then became a chest infection and he would have to be kept inside for over a month. This would have a bit of an effect on his development. I became convinced that he had been talking to some older dogs who had told him what they were going to do with his bollocks. He did manage to hold on to them for a month or two longer, but ultimately they had to go! The Puppy Walking co-ordinator said that the operation was pretty non-invasive. My father and I caught each other out of the corner of our eyes. Yeah, like fuck!

The literal black dog was never far from my side when I was around. The figurative black dog was always close, no matter where I was. There were a couple of times when I had Klint for the day or afternoon. I thought nothing of leaving him alone for an hour or so to pop out for a pint. Quite often, this became an expedition for drugs and he would end up being left for around three hours. The guidelines that we were given was that he shouldn't be left for more than four hours, and I was always comfortably within this time. It still wasn't the right thing to do. I loved my time with Klint, but I prioritised my drink and drugs.

Due to his illness, Klint was kept with us for an extra couple of months to allow him to develop once more. I went out to work one morning, and when I came home, he was gone. I was alone again. Alone but surrounded by people.

We got word that he had qualified as a guide dog. Mum and Dad got to see him one more time and we received a graduation photo, and that was that. He was gone.

We learnt that Klint had gone to Buckfast in Devon to work.

We all agreed that it was far too much of a wrench to do that again. It is impossible not to get attached. A dog would never let you spend a year in their company without becoming absolutely besotted. Luckily, there was a guide dog trainer who lived locally and needed somebody to board his dogs during their training.

The first dog that came into our home was a big, black Labrador retriever called Taylor. He was a beautiful dog. Very reticent and lacking in confidence but had real substance to him, and oh, so obedient. We were told that we didn't have to be strict with him as he actually needed bringing out of his shell. Game on.

Plenty of playtime and attention, and Taylor soon became a big, gentlemanly hooligan! That was incredibly rewarding, and he ended up being the only puppy from his litter to make the grade. His parents wouldn't be mated together again. He went out to a smallholding in Carmarthenshire to live.

Next up was Frances. She was a small, black Labrador bitch and was very intelligent and affectionate when she wanted to be. She seemed totally content to lie down on her blanket under the TV and watch us. You could almost think that she was following the conversation. She went off to Carmarthenshire to assist a partially sighted showjumper.

Last up was another small, black Labrador bitch called Nan. Now, Nan was a lovely-looking dog but an absolute pain in the arse. No food was safe, and she was always on the lookout for mischief. Although not as affectionate as the others, and there were many discipline issues, we all grew very fond of her. She would be placed with a blind man in Swansea Marina. I kept an eye on the local news, waiting to hear reports of a blind man who had starved to death due to his guide dog stealing all of his food. I have not heard anything yet.

About a year after Klint went, I returned home from work to find out that we had had a phone call. The relationship between Klint and his handler had broken down and Klint was being withdrawn from service and, as we had puppy walked him, we were to have first refusal. It was a no-brainer.

It turns out that Klint had taken his blind man to the shops one day and just sat down, refusing to take him home. He was the third dog to lose his discipline with this handler. It had all turned into a bit of a power struggle and Klint had actually become quite ill. He had regular ear infections, that they put down to stress. He was actually on medication when he returned home, but he was never to have a recurrence with us.

Our home was complete again, and I had a healthy outlet. Although I was around less and less, spending more and more time with my brother as we worked for longer hours to finance getting on or off it incessantly, when I did come back, I could go out for hours with Klint. When the two of us were out, I didn't have a care in the world. OK, I wasn't dealing with my problems, just temporarily forgetting them like I did with drink and drugs, but my time with Klint didn't exacerbate them.

Unlike my parents, Klint didn't give a shit what state I came home in. If I was pissed, I was more likely to give him some of my dinner. If Mum and Dad were out and I came home with some nosebag, he would get the fucking lot. He would sit up with me while I had a toot some nights, so I wasn't always doing it alone in my room. Fuck me! Did I really equate sniffing Charlie in the company of a dog as some kind of a social event? The lies you tell yourself to justify what you do!

Occasionally, we would pop to the pub for a pint. Only a couple at this time, very reserved. This would change after my couple of years back up in London. He was my little ray of sunshine in those dark days, and when we were together, it was the closest thing that I felt to happiness. He helped me get out of the house from time to time and, although he couldn't curtail my drinking or drug-taking, life wasn't so empty or miserable. He would even introduce me to people.

Long walks on the beach, cliff path or prom, he was just damn fine company. You couldn't stay sad around him. He was always happy and that happiness was infectious. Not just with me but with everyone we met. Chasing a ball or other dogs around the Castle grounds or some other park, there was a lot that I could have learnt from Klint. There is a lot that we can all learn from dogs.

When I was to end up moving back up to London for a couple of years in 2014, aside from my parents, Klint was the only thing in my miserable, pointless life that I wouldn't be overjoyed to leave behind.

Chapter 15

Fragile Mind, Fragile Body

Anyway, back to the chaos. 2011 had started like the previous few. Back to the endless slog. Being fucked about for money. The harder we worked, the less we were respected. Me and my brother against the world. We were the black sheep of the company, drinking and sniffing after leaving all of our energy on site. We weren't respected like the others because we wouldn't dial it in at work so that we had the energy to go to the gym. How fucked up is that?

We slaughtered our bodies at work, carrying fucking passengers every fucking day, doing the long hours to make deadlines when no other cunt was prepared to weigh in. We might have been massive mash-heads, but we got the fucking job done. We might be late occasionally, but we would always do a proper days' work. We weren't afraid to get our hands dirty.

Around the end of February, I had started to suffer from flu-like symptoms. I don't know if it was a case of misplaced loyalty, the need to earn money to continue using or a total disregard for my own health, but I just ploughed on, never even thinking of taking a day off.

A couple of weeks later, I asked for some of the money that I was owed so that I could pop for a pint on the way home, nothing felt untoward. No money was forthcoming, so I just jumped on the bus home. By the time I got home, I had a thumping headache, and any movement of my head caused it to throb, as if my brain was trying to escape the confines of my skull. I was also shivering and couldn't get warm.

I went indoors, made a cup of tea and ran a warm bath. After a while in the bath, I went downstairs to try and eat my dinner. Nothing doing, so around eight, I dosed myself with painkillers and took a cuppa upstairs to bed, checking before I got under the covers that my alarm was set for the following morning. I got off to sleep quite quickly.

I slept deeply for a while but woke up at some point with a raking, chesty cough. I couldn't swallow too much of what I was coughing up, and so I started spitting in my bin. If I lay down, my chest would fill up and I would start coughing painfully. It felt as if every cough was ripping more of the lining of my lungs. The only way to stop the coughing was to sit up. This just led to me getting freezing cold and shivering uncontrollably. I settled into a pattern of a little time curled up on my side followed by a period sitting up while I coughed the contents of my lungs up.

After what seemed like hours of this, I turned on my bedside lamp to see how long it would be until my parents were getting up. It couldn't be long; I had had a decent sleep and I had been awake and coughing for a long time. My clock showed 00:40. How the fuck was that all that it was? I had been in this state for fucking hours, hadn't I?

I then decided to look in my bin at what I was coughing up. My head started to spin as I realised that I was coughing up blood. I am thirty years old! I shouldn't be doing this! I've got fucking TB! No, it can't be that; I had my BCG. Must be lung cancer! At least, it's a way out! I hoped that I would find a quicker, less painful way to die, but I had my reason to totally give up. How fucked up is it that I was glad about the prospect of having lung cancer?

The rest of the night was agony. Minutes felt like hours, as I was almost constantly hacking up whatever it was. It was just me and my thoughts. I deserved what was happening to me. It was my fault, through the lifestyle that I had chosen to live. It would all be over at some point. Hopefully, I wouldn't draw it out too long. You hear about people or animals who give up and drift away. This could be me. It may not be close, but that final peace was on its way.

When my father came into my room in the morning, after what seemed like an eternity, they were well aware that something was wrong. When he saw the scene, Mum was straight onto the doctor's and I was given an emergency appointment. I had pneumonia. Still, that could be a killer. It had killed my grandfather. People have asked me what type of pneumonia. I have no idea, when all of this was going on, I was absolutely fucking delirious. Unfortunately, he seemed confident that it could be treated and he phoned the hospital to let them know that I was on my way and I was admitted immediately when I arrived.

I had to wait a little while to be seen, and I huddled up in my fleece, thick coat and hat. Even though I was sweating and my temperature was racing, I still couldn't get warm enough, but the nurse said that I had to lose the coat and hat, as my temperature was spiking, and that wasn't good. I was very quickly started on intravenous Amoxycillin and almost instantly started to feel some relief. I felt better and was able to get comfortable, and then it dawned on me that my condition wasn't life-threatening. Although the pain was eased a bit, I found no comfort in this. I would have to go back to work at some point.

I was to spend six days in hospital and received excellent treatment, apart from one cocky doctor. It turned out that I had a Vitamin D deficiency and he asked how that could happen when I worked in the building trade and should get plenty of sunlight. *Look, you utter prick! I leave home in the dark, I spend all day in dark, dank, dusty fucking shitholes, I go to the pub and I get home after dark!* I thought.

"I do a lot of inside work," I said.

What really pissed me off was when it came time for me to be discharged. I asked him if the shortness of breath would pass. "You're a smoker, aren't you?" he replied with a smug grin and looked around to accept the fawning laughter of the student doctors. *Listen, you cunt. I would have you for absolute fucking fun on site. I would break you in under an hour with that fucking attitude. I work in a physical job and I need to know that at some point, I will stop getting out of breath brushing my fucking teeth because otherwise, I can't return to my job and that will be game fucking over for me!* I thought. I didn't say anything. *Just get me home!*

When I was younger, I had always had a thirst for knowledge and was a voracious reader. This had gone by the wayside, as I slipped into depression, and getting into hard drugs just allowed that to disappear further. I had come to view knowledge and intelligence as a weakness and something to be hidden. I wasn't interested in learning anything new. I had allowed my mind to disintegrate with my mental health. What was the fucking point? I was never going to do anything with it. I was just getting through one day at a time until the day came that I wouldn't get through and I would be free. It couldn't come fast enough.

With nothing else to do in the hospital, I started reading again. Two or three books a day, my mum regularly having to go to the library. I really enjoyed the escape to a different time and place, and it passed the time. I spent six days in hospital and was discharged on a Monday morning. I stopped reading almost immediately.

It would be more than a week after leaving the hospital that I would finally be able to sleep lying down, and a further week before I returned to work part-time. The Sunday after getting out, I decided to pop across the road to the pub for a couple of orange juices. Yeah, like fuck!

I hadn't smoked since I went to bed on that first night. Two weeks later, the habit was broken. I hadn't thrown my cigarettes out, and so, I sat out the back of the pub with my pint and lit a salmon. Well, that was a good opportunity wasted.

I stayed in the pub most of the day, and then the urge for a fat line came. I called a couple of people, but no dice. My most reliable source was away, so I thought that I would jump in a cab to a mate's house. He didn't answer the door, although the lights were on, so I thought that I would just go and knock on the door of the person that he usually got it from.

I don't know whether I knocked on the right door or not, but, looking back, luckily there was no answer. He didn't know me from Adam and wouldn't have been too happy with me just turning up and enquiring if he had any drugs.

I started walking pretty aimlessly when I saw a lad in his late teens sitting on a wall. I asked if he knew anyone and he was able to sort me out. He even got a mate to give me a lift home. I paid him with a gram and a score for his troubles. Two weeks after having a major health scare, and still suffering from the after-effects, I was back to all of my old habits. I had found my belief system. I was a nihilist. I really didn't give a fuck about what happened to me.

Chapter 16

Out-of-Town Troubles

I returned to work full-time on a big job on the Surrey border, not far from Ascot. Still working for that Swansea cunt but living in the house we were working on. We were in the smallest house on the road, with a house built by Telly Savalas down the road. Across from us were, apparently, Brian May and the Crown Prince of Dubai. His estate was massive, and he only used it for about six weeks a year around Royal Ascot. This came soon after our arrival.

With no television signal in the house, we bought a small satellite system from B & Q and fixed it to the roof of one of the vans for a better signal. This brought a knock at the door from the security over the road. They were a bit concerned about who we were, but nothing came of it.

For the first weekend, there were just three of us there, my brother included. On Friday night, we went into a nearby town on the piss, as boys working away do. We got smashed, and my brother's attitude always changed towards me when there was somebody to impress. I ended up walking off on my own, looking for a rock bar if one even existed, in order to find some cocaine. My drunken thinking was that, because I could score at a rock bar in Swansea, I would be able to here.

I never found that mythical rock bar and somehow found a cab to take me back to the house. I was first back to the house. As I didn't have a key, I broke into one of the vans somehow and fell asleep on the front seat. Sometime later, my brother appeared and woke me up and let us into the house. Our 'colleague' arrived shortly after in a separate taxi.

The next day, we were all meant to work, but by midday, I was the only one up. We hadn't bought the satellite yet, and so I was at a loose end. Only one thing to do, have a bite and go down the pub. After making bacon sandwiches, eating only the bacon and throwing the bread away, I showered and went out feeling rough as fuck.

It was about a ten-minute walk to the nearest pub, and it was a beautiful day out. We had been to this pub the previous couple of nights, so the barman knew my face. I sat on the corner of the bar and chewed down my first pint. As some of the Saturday afternoon regulars started to drift in, I ended up in conversation with a couple who were horse-racing enthusiasts. One thing led to another, and I entered a sweepstake with them, ultimately winning. Now I was duty-bound to stay for a couple more.

I proceeded to get absolutely cunted, and slowly my company dwindled. At some point, it must have occurred to me that it was time to go home, so off I staggered.

Fuck knows what time it was, this was a sunny April day, and the evenings were starting to draw out. I made it back to the house, and the other two were lounging about eating pizza. I was absolutely legless, and it turned out that the client and owner of the house had popped round and only recently left. Lucky I had those extra pints then.

More boys came down throughout the next week, and the place became quite crowded. It was decided that I was the one to clean up after everyone in the communal areas. I managed to say something about doing it during the working day, not in my own time, and the boss sort of shrugged his agreement. I really thought that I was the shit on his shoe.

Everybody went back to Swansea for the Mayday Bank Holiday weekend except for the two Walders. We decided to stay up and work. The going was good and, to be honest, it was nice to have the place to ourselves. Nobody would return for a week and a half. We had a few drinks each night, and on Sunday, we finished a bit early and headed off to the local pub.

This would be the last time that we would go to this pub. We had a fucking skinful and neither of us remembered much, but somewhere on the walk home, in some woods, I must have fallen and passed out for a little while. I just remember struggling to get up and then waking up in the morning without my phone or my glasses.

My brother called my phone and a lady answered. She had found it, and after speaking to me, she left it somewhere safe for us to pick it up. My glasses never did come to light, and so, we went in to Windsor where I visited Vision Express, and we had lunch while we waited for my lenses to be prepared. I have particularly bad eyesight, and so I have to pay for special thin lenses. Even with the cheapest frames, the whole thing cost me over £200. An expensive night out!

One Thursday, that we were up there, Swansea City were playing Nottingham Forest in the Championship play-offs. A night out was in order. We all jumped in the back of one of the vans, and we were off to Ascot. We found a bar right by the racecourse. Beers were bought and tables found to watch the football. By the final whistle, we were well on our way.

More pints, loads of shots and soon minds turned to cocaine. People would think that Ascot wasn't prime hunting ground for narcotics, but we really didn't have to look far. It was good shit as well.

I think that there were six of us out that night, and according to what people said, we spent over a grand between us. I know that I came home at least £200 lighter, and that my brother spent similar, but I'm pretty sure that the others didn't dip in their pockets anywhere near as much as we did. They were happy to take their fair share.

When we got back to the house, the remaining Charlie was doled out and the rest of them disappeared upstairs, most probably for a wank while my brother and I sat down and drank for a couple more hours.

The next morning, the boss was first up, trying to make a point. As soon as we heard him, I got up followed by my brother. A quick cup of tea and a cigarette, and we got to work. The other four didn't lift a finger, too fucked from the night before. Fucking amateurs!

About ten, our boss announced that he and his mate were leaving and that we were to finish the day's work, then I was to clean, and then we could go home. It would have taken the other two a fucking fortnight to do a day's work, so we sat down for an hour, drank some tea, quickly boshed in the cleaning and got on the road.

We got back to Swansea mid-afternoon, and my brother and I went for a couple of pints before I was to head home to my parents' for the weekend. To this day, my parents don't even know that we were back that weekend. It was only one or two pints and we fancied a stripe, so we went back to my brother's house, ordering on the way, picking up a shitload of beer and settled in for a good night. We had the rest of the weekend to catch up.

A mate came round and we decided to play FIFA. We had taken the Xbox to Surrey with us, and it had obviously got damaged on the journey back to Swansea. There was an Argos about five minutes down the road, so I went down to buy a new one while they waited in for the drugs. Fuck it, I was earning good money working away. I got back just in time for our delivery, and we settled in for a very pleasant evening.

Not surprisingly, we carried on for the next 36 hours and got right off our boxes. In all fairness, it was a cracking weekend, but it wasn't about relaxation and recuperation. My brother and I chilled and dozed on the sofas and then on Monday morning, headed back East.

A fairly routine couple of weeks later, and everybody returned to Swansea, as the Swans had reached the play-off final. A few of the boys went up to Wembley, my brother included, but I stayed in Swansea. It wasn't my party. I just had a good drink with a couple of mates and then a sniff at home. We travelled back to Surrey on Tuesday afternoon, and my brother and I wouldn't return for over six weeks.

The money was good, people spoke a bit more like us, and we would have the weekends to ourselves. We worked every day and we drank in the evening, quite often having a sniff too. It became routine for it to be just the two of us most of the time, but there was a couple of weeks where we had a decorator up there with us.

He was a top bloke, and the three of us got on really well, and it was a genuinely good atmosphere. We would do a day's work, pop out for a couple of pints, have a spliff or two, and then go and see what we fancied in the Co-Op. Always fun after a joint!

Things started to get a little hectic for the last couple of weeks on the job. The house was full of boys and things would get fractious at times. It came to what was to be our last day up there, and I was more than ready to go home.

Late in the afternoon, Cunty said that I would have to stay up with my brother and put the final coat on the floor. We weren't happy with this. We were the ones who had put the long hours in, stayed up at weekends and had only had one day off in the previous six weeks. My brother, with a little persuasion from the sparky, told him in no uncertain terms that we were on our toes that fucking night. We hadn't travelled very far when I got a phone call. Our sister's IVF had been successful and we were to be uncles. A great day.

The first job that we had back in Swansea was to fit a new kitchen for our parents. They went away for a couple of weeks, and my brother basically moved in. Fuck me, did we make the most of being back in Mumbles.

It was a lovely summer, and we had plenty of money from working away. Every evening was spent on the piss, and then more often than not we would get on the barley. Occasionally, we would even go out for a meal! Well, maybe once.

After about a month, we were sent back up to Surrey, just the two of us for a few extras. We travelled up midweek and had to find digs. The first place that we tried was a pub that we had used regularly during our previous stay. They had a room, dirt cheap, and we were away.

Friday night was one hell of a good piss-up, and the bar staff knew us well enough to introduce us to a dealer. That was that then. A big session commenced. Saturday morning came, and we weren't in any fit state to work, so my brother sent a text to let the client know that we had to go back to Swansea for the weekend and would be back to work on Monday. Did we go back to Swansea? Did we fuck?

I phoned my sister and we arranged to meet up at The Valley for Charlton's first game of the season. The timing was good, as she had lost her baby and we were able to have a good chat about that. Charlton beat Bournemouth 3–0, and we would go on to fucking shit on that division and earn promotion with 101 points.

After a couple of drinks, once the game had finished, we went our separate ways and I headed back to our digs. My brother hadn't moved too much and was in our room. I stayed in the bar for a couple of pints and then went up and chilled in the room with him.

The next day, we were both feeling great. We got up and went downstairs late morning. The idea was to have a good bit of scran and then a couple of pints watching the Community Shield in the afternoon.

When we went downstairs, one of the bar staff was in cleaning and offered to pour us a drink even though they hadn't opened yet. Why not? We've got plenty of time. Well, that was that. We didn't move from there all day. I'm pretty sure that the tequila was out before the football even kicked off. A ridiculous amount of drinking and many lines later, the pub was closing. We bought a load of bottles and got another good whack of chop to stave off the hangover and toddled off upstairs.

We woke up on Monday morning, feeling no better than we had on Saturday morning, but we went to work. We were up there for most of that week, carrying on in the same vein. The work got done to a good standard and we returned to Swansea.

There would be one more stint up there later in the year, and we would be back in the house as the client was abroad. We had a little chavvy cunt with us this time. We fell back into a very similar routine, and one night, we went for a drink in Ascot.

After ramming a few down our throats, the thought inevitably turned to coke. We struck up a conversation with the first likely source, and it was game on. We picked up a nice bit and went back to the house, picking up a load of beers. My brother and I did like to row at times, but I really struggle to remember one time when we have fallen out when we have been on the nosebag.

This chavvy little cunt obviously fucking riled us somehow, and over time, the atmosphere dropped and we ended up having an argument. Somewhere between four and five, I packed my bags and walked out. The closest station was about three miles away, so I made my way there and sat down for over an hour until the first train to Reading arrived, and then I went back home to Swansea.

I ignored any effort of my brother to get in touch for the next few days, vowing that I would never return to work with him. Eventually, he turned up at the house with the money that I was owed from the work that I had done away. We went for a couple of pints and everything was fine again, and I would report for work on Monday. That was it; by now we had settled into a dysfunctional, interdependent, mutually destructive relationship. How fucked up could it become? On the bright side, we both had someone to blame for the way we were and our behaviour. Every cloud, eh?

Chapter 17

'Tis the Season to Be Jolly

Life carried on very much as before. Long working weeks with plenty of time for R & R due to the amount of Charlie we were sniffing and the lack of sleep that provided. Money was always coming in, and money was always going out. Most of the time, things were pretty harmonious; there was the odd eruption, always at work, mainly borne out of the utter frustration at the efforts of our bone-idle supposed colleagues.

We wouldn't down tools and could work in tandem, calling each other every name under the sun. I wouldn't usually row in public, as I know that it creates an atmosphere, but I didn't give a shit about these useless cunts. We were constantly carrying passengers and pulling the firm out of the shit.

The subbies were great. All good boys who had a graft in them, and they would stick up for me because they could see that I was a good worker. I wasn't going to stick up for myself.

In the run-up to Christmas, we were working on an extension and the snow came down. This meant a few days off work, and I stayed at my brother's so that we could gauge the weather each morning. The long days were filled in the usual way. A little bit of time monging in front of the telly with a cup of tea, then down the pub before we went stir crazy. A good afternoon/evening in the pub and then home with a few beers to make it snow indoors.

We really hoped to return to work on Monday of the following week but woke up to see some fresh snow. A bit more time in bed, and then up to try and see out another day. It's clear to me now that that is how I have spent most of my adult life. Just trying to see out each and every day, something to be endured rather than embraced.

We were in the first pub, as it opened, and settled in for the day. Now a little bit of snow and Swansea seems to come to a complete stop, so the pubs were always busy, usually with a decent atmosphere going. This was no exception, and we stayed for hours even winning a couple of quid on the quiz machine. We visited a couple of other pubs and made our way home.

My brother received a call inviting him out for the evening, and I was going to stay in the house. For the life of me, I can't remember how, but it kicked off between us. A couple of punches were thrown, and I was told to pack my bag and fuck off.

I phoned home and my father came and picked me up from the 24-hour garage across the road where I had to wait for half an hour or so, freezing my bollocks off. I was never going to work for my brother again. I was done with work for the year.

The day before Christmas Eve, my brother came around. He needed a hand the following morning, only for a couple of hours, and I would get a full day's wedge. Be stupid not to, wouldn't it? To make it easier, I went back to his that night, and after a couple of beers, we got some white in, and everything was alright between us again. I was back in the fold.

Into the new year, and things carried on as it seemed they always fucking did. When asked by my boss what I planned to do with the extra money that I had earned working away, I had stupidly said that I would get my driving licence.

I had passed my theory test before Christmas, and I thought that the least disruptive way to learn would be to do an intensive course. In March, I took a week off work and had 30 hours of driving lessons over 5 days, followed by my test. My instructor was late every day and, although I never lost any of my time, waiting for him to turn up would cause my anxiety to spike.

When it came to the day of the test, I knew that I was never going to pass, and about five minutes into my test, I went looking for third gear and found first. There's a few hundred quid I won't see again. Fuck it! I never wanted to drive anyway. *Pint anyone? Just me? OK!*

The drudgery continued unabated. *Work, fucking miserable. Drink, fucking getting there. Powder, fucking alive? Sleep? I'll sleep when I die. I fucking hope that it won't be long!*

To show willing, I resumed driving lessons, but my anxiety meant that I was an absolute fucking wreck behind the wheel. My financial reserves were gone, and I hated getting up. But for once in my life, I kept on getting up.

One day, I had worked on with a Chechen labourer, and neither of us drove. My boss never turned up to pick us up, and I didn't even have enough money on me to catch the bus home. My brother called to find out where I was and offered to come and pick us up.

Once we had dropped the labourer off, we got into a massive barney about me not having a licence. By this stage, our boss was paying us as one entity and I hardly ever saw any cash. His point was that he earned more than me. He did and rightly so, he had the experience and the know-how. My argument was that I was basically at his beck and call 24 hours a day, 7 days a week. What more could I do if he wanted me around all of the fucking time and also to get off his fucking box?

We both had good points. We were both right. We were both wrong.

This was again forgotten after work the next day, and it wouldn't have been long until the next lost weekend. Charlie and beer. Beer and Charlie. We weren't fucking fussy, as long as we could escape from time to time, i.e., most days, we would get through. Regardless of how much we worked, funds were dwindling, we weren't getting what we used to from using, and yet, we had nothing else. We were at each other all of the time. Things were beginning to seriously unravel.

Chapter 18

Like a Hamster on a Wheel

Things carried on as they always did. Work, drink, sniff, repeat! What more could you want? Purpose? Fuck that for a laugh. I had no purpose. I was just trying not to do too much damage until my time came. In reality, I was causing chaos and hurt all over the place. Without realising it, and definitely without meaning it, this was what I did, and I was getting very good at it.

The two of us continued to work long and hard, but on-site arguments were becoming the norm. Private jobs were a different matter. I suppose when you are earning a decent crust and you know that the people you are working with are pulling their weight, then you will always have a good atmosphere on site.

One weekend, we had a two-day job building block steps in somebody's back garden. The first day was the key. We had to get the delivery up a steady incline of approximately 150 metres. Once up there, we had to pass everything down an eight-foot wall, mixer and all.

It wasn't a huge delivery, but it was shit access. We also had to dig and pour a footing in order to come back and lay the blocks on Sunday. My brother got our friend who played FIFA with us in for the day. He was a hard worker and we all got on well.

We had a long day and got to where we needed to be. It was a proper graft, and we all left absolutely everything on site that day. I love days like that, where you literally work yourself to a standstill. The satisfaction of having put in a proper full-on shift was all the satisfaction I got at this time.

First stop after work, the pub. We had earned it; that was a good day's work by anybody's standard. A few pints to take the day off, and the decision was made to get on it. Let's be honest; that decision was made before we even lifted a finger. This was going to be just like any Wednesday night.

Well, we ran out of gear later that evening, and after a little while of nobody bringing it up, we started the complicated procedure of finding narcotics in the suburbs of Swansea after midnight on a Sunday morning. This was never a problem in Bromley. Anything and everything on tap.

Our mate spoke to one of his mates, and I went off with him in a cab. My brother didn't trust him to come back if he went on his own. We got back and we did a line. It turns out that he had bought Meow. My brother wasn't too happy; we had work in the morning. I didn't really give a fuck. I would work in whatever state I ended up in. Our friend wanted to stay up and play FIFA. My brother didn't. I didn't really care. Nobody was going to sleep for a while.

My brother got fed up eventually and threw the pair of us. There was a pile of rubble to one side of the drive, and our friend decided to pick up a couple of large pieces and throw them at the van, smashing the windscreen in the process. This was a courtesy vehicle as the van my brother usually drove was in the garage for some reason or other. Our friend fucked off, and eventually, my brother let me back in.

The next day, after a grovelling call to the customer, a mate, to come and pick us up, we slowly got the rest of the work done, but it wasn't long into the day that the threats started coming.

The boy who had been with us the previous day was threatening all sorts if anything got to the police, not just against us but our boss and his family. We were in absolute pieces and somehow got through the day. I went home to my parents, and my brother stayed with his ex-wife for the night, giving the house a wide berth, just in case.

We (my brother) paid to have the windscreen replaced and a bullshit story about a brick falling off some scaffolding seemed to do for the dent in the front wing.

A long, hard weekend's work for absolutely fuck all!

The following week went as any other really, except without club night on Wednesday. The weekend arrived as usual, and it was time to think about drugs. For whatever reason, none of our regular sources came up with the goods, so my brother called our mate from the other weekend. He came up with the goods, and it was actually something approaching cocaine. He was back in the fold. My brother had little more respect for himself than I did when it came to getting off it.

Days turned into weeks, weeks became months, and fuck, all changed. Our existence was clear. As long as we could escape for a little time each evening, we would just have to put up with the misery that was the rest of our waking hours.

At the end of that year, my brother moved house, leaving a sizeable shed full to the rafters of sacks of crushed cans and empty bottles. We started renting a house from one of the useless cunts that we worked with. It was cheaper, in a different part of town, away from some bad influences.

I helped him move in and we set about redecorating. They were going to order a new kitchen, the old one was fucked, and we would fit it for them. We had kitchen fitting down to an art form, often fitting a kitchen in a day. That kitchen never came.

This felt like a new start, and although our behaviour didn't necessarily change, our mood definitely picked up. Monday to Friday was still the same old shit, and so were the weekends to be honest, but sometimes, a change of scenery is a boost in itself. I was spending more time than ever with my brother, and things were OK for a while. Always the odd disagreement at work, but in our spare time, we got on, even if we didn't really enjoy each other's company.

Most of the year carried on predictably. The slog facilitated our crutches. We tolerated each other. I offered him all of my time, foregoing any money for payment in drink, drugs and fags. He paid to medicate me safe in the knowledge that I would work all of the hours that God sent. We were both taking the piss out of each other, and this would lead to the odd barney, but mostly we had both given up. We had both resigned ourselves to the fact that this was our life from now on and we were probably better off sharing it than walking it alone.

We did nothing remarkable, or even noteworthy, and I would make myself throw up occasionally in the morning to get a day off when it became too much, and I would just curl up in bed, contemplating absolutely nothing. No ambitions, no aspirations just to wake up each morning breathing and to get to bed each night still breathing. Whatever happened in between was purely incidental. One day, I was going to stop breathing; I knew that I wasn't able to make this happen myself, being so fucking useless, but each day, I got to the end of was one more day that I wouldn't have to live through again. My time was counting down slowly, but it was counting down all the same.

Around October, our cunting boss started telling my brother that I wasn't needed so much, and this totally tailed off eventually. I didn't really care. I was going nowhere. I was on the scrapheap. I had worked myself into a hospital bed and to near insanity for a narcissistic, bone idle cunt of a man.

I still helped my brother out with his private jobs and enjoyed those times, taking the opportunity to have a drink and a sniff with my brother, more relaxed around each other now that we weren't always in each other's pockets. I needed more money, however. So, it was time to start looking again.

I have looked back on this time working and living with my brother as an extremely tough time in my life and with little fondness. The fact is that we were both miserable; life was shit for both of us. It did take its toll on us both, and we definitely needed some time apart from each other after this. However, recounting my experiences, I have come to realise that this was the longest continuous period of my adult life where I didn't attempt to take my own life. I don't really remember suicidal thoughts being around much at that time.

Although we didn't get on brilliantly, there was a definite loyalty to each other, even if from an 'us against them' stance, that has become the basis of the close, strong relationship that we enjoy today. I can see now that, probably more by luck than judgement, my brother kept me going. He kept me safe. He kept me alive.

Chapter 19

On Your Own, Son

I registered with the Job Centre and started looking for jobs to apply for. I didn't have a clue about what I could do. I didn't particularly want to go back into the building game, and I knew that I wasn't going to find work in accountancy. My CV was a fucking mess, but I could at least get some advice on that from the Job Centre, right?

I began applying for anything and everything in the admin. By the time that I had my meeting with the Job Centre, I had dozens of applications out. The Job Centre said that they wouldn't be able to help me much as I was finding plenty to apply for. Well, that makes sense. Somebody who is keen to find work, just leave them on their own and concentrate on protecting the benefits of people who don't want to work.

Any advice on my CV? I was told that there was no wrong or right way to have it.

Well, thanks so much for the fucking help, I thought. I felt so let down and hung out to dry.

Anger would be too strong a word; I wasn't worth getting angry about.

Shortly before Christmas, I did get a reply and went for a preliminary interview for something with a very vague job description. I was asked back for an assessment day. The day before that, my first dole payment hit my account, and so, I met up with my brother for a couple of pints and then the obligatory sniff back at his.

I got up the next morning, travelled into Swansea and bottled it as far as the assessment day was concerned. As it turned out, this was an opportunity I would unwittingly revisit at a later date. It was no great loss.

Christmas passed off without incident, and we entered another new year full of expectation and optimism. Only joking; I just didn't want this year to hurt too much. I carried on applying for jobs, more out of duty than hope. Going through the motions.

My Job Seekers' Allowance allowed me to have a drink and some bugle from time to time, and I would still do some weekend work with my brother. Always a good excuse for a session. Were things actually that bad?

Around March, I was invited to an interview day at a call centre in Swansea. I went along, and after taking part in many ridiculous activities, I found out that I was successful and would be starting soon, commencing with four weeks' training. A nice easy start. I was going to apply myself and I would soon progress. I couldn't concentrate during the training room but knew that I was taking in enough to muddle my way through.

My first paycheque came in while I was still in training and just before the end of the football season. A flying weekend visit to my sister's was hastily arranged, and I went back for Charlton's last game of the season, at home to Bristol City. Charlton had had a decent first season back up in the Championship and were finishing very strongly under club legend Chris Powell.

We ran out comfortable winners, and The Valley was bouncing again, like the good old days. If we took this form into the new season, then we would be in good stead, and we might just surprise some people. After the match, Chris Powell made an emotional speech, and I couldn't remember the last time that I felt so alive.

After a pleasant evening with my sister, I travelled back on Sunday, ready to continue my tuition on Monday. A couple of pints at Paddington and westward ho! Usually, my father would pick me up from the station, but I said that, as they had church, I would make my own way home. This allowed me to have a couple of pints in town and then pick up some Charlie. Everyone's a winner!

I completed my training and went on to the floor to take some calls. I was barely prepared, mainly due to my own perfunctory attitude during training, but found that I could blag it. I was in Customer Services, so a large part of my job was taking the flak for other people's fuck ups. This was no problem for me; I had spent years in similar situations, and even longer blaming myself for shit that wasn't necessarily my fault.

It was a weird place to work. One of their core values was fun! This turned out to be fun according to their interpretation of the word. They loved fancy dress. I didn't. I had to catch two buses to and from work, and we hadn't been allocated lockers, so I would have had to travel in costume. Now, I'm not sure whether it has come up, but I can be a tiny bit self-conscious at times, so I wasn't prepared to do this and just came in my civvies.

On the interview day, they made a big song and dance about all of the facilities and breakout areas that they have, but once we were on the floor, we were told that it seemed strange to people on the other pods that ours seemed to empty and we stayed away from our desks during our breaks. It was implied that we were alienating ourselves from the rest of the workforce. *I'm sorry, but I'm a fucking smoker, and I am going to spend my breaks fucking smoking!* I told myself.

One day, there was a pyjama and pizza day. Come in and work at your desk in your pyjamas. I don't own any pyjamas and tend to sleep in my pants. There was no way that that was happening, so I was excluded from having pizza, along with a couple of others. It wasn't the denial of pizza that annoyed me, but I had mentioned in my interview about my history of anxiety and depression, but there seemed to be no understanding for people who might find certain things out of their comfort zone.

You were either one of them or you were on the outside. It was happening again.

That night, I popped to my local for a couple of pints and ended up staying out all evening and also having a sniff when I got back home. Somewhere along the way, I managed to lose my bag with my headset and all of my literature for the job. The headset would cost me £85 to replace.

If they had given us lockers, like they had promised, I wouldn't have been carrying my bag around and I wouldn't have lost it. This was in no way my own fault for going out and getting absolutely rat-arsed straight from work, rather than dropping my bag off at home, two minutes from the pub. No, for once this wasn't on me!

I used a bit of nous the following morning. I travelled into work as usual and met a couple of my colleagues in one of the breakout areas for a cuppa. I made a big show of feeling unwell and disappeared off to the toilets for a while. When I came back, I said that I had been up half the night. I made my excuses and went to speak to our team leader. He told me to take the day off. Result! I would recuperate in a pub in town.

The next day, it was phase two of my plan, and I called in sick, promising to be in the following day. Now for the coup de grace. I went in on the third day and started asking around to see if anybody had seen my bag the other day, as I had got home without it. I actually garnered some sympathy; people related how it was easy to misplace things when you weren't well. I said that I had been in touch with the bus company and the police to see if it had been handed in anywhere. Weirdly enough, it hadn't and it would never turn up. A temporary replacement headset was found and I returned to work.

I had started taking driving lessons again and would either have one from work or, on later shifts, get picked up at home and drive to work. Punctuality was still a problem for my instructor, but that didn't matter, I had no outside interests.

My parents went away for a week a little while later, and I was left to my own devices. No problem, I enjoy a bit of time to myself. I had a driving lesson booked before work one day, but I was still suffering from the anxiety that had blighted my previous attempt.

We also had a fancy-dress day coming up at work, and the decision had been made that everybody at our pod would dress up as a Disney character. I didn't have money going spare to hire a costume, so I wasn't looking forward to this either.

I was waiting for my driving instructor, getting more and more anxious, shit whirling through my head. I didn't enjoy driving and didn't have any particular need to drive at this point. I was in a job that I could do, but it was low paying, and I was forever going to be on the periphery, never fitting in, never conforming to being 'fun'. I brought on the biggest panic attack I had ever had up to this point and locked up the house and went up to my room where I curled up tightly on my floor, shaking and hyperventilating for a couple of hours. I had turned my phone off, but I knew that my driving instructor had gone by now, so I crawled into bed and waited for it to get dark.

Once it was dark and I could legitimately shut the world out, I ventured downstairs. I went and stocked up on cigarettes just before the shop closed and shrunk back indoors, sitting there with no lights on, curled up on the sofa. I had fucked everything up again. I was still on probation at work, so that was quite clearly gone. I was unemployable now, surely. I didn't know what to do. There was no explaining away what I had done. I was just a fucking weak, spineless individual. What the fuck could I do about this? I can't succeed by slitting my wrists, and I don't have a strong enough constitution for an overdose. I pondered with the idea of taking a walk along the coast path and throwing myself in. This was something that could wait until tomorrow. I knew that I wouldn't be disturbed for another three days. As the sun began to rise, I went upstairs to bed and waited for it to set again.

I don't know why I wasn't drinking during this episode. Did I revel in the terror of anxiety? Did I want to experience the despondency undiluted by alcohol? Did I just feel that I deserved all of the torment without easing my pain? I just don't know. I do know that I spent the entire time coming up with ideas of how to end my life, shouting each and every one down with a sharp *'No, you'll only fuck it up, like you always do!'* I went downstairs in the dark and braved turning the television on, just sitting in the dark with the flickering blue light and my thoughts for company. I don't know what I had on the TV that night; I was creating my own entertainment.

As the sun came up, I knew what I was going to do. I went out into the back garden for a cigarette and then went upstairs. I got into bed and I tied a carrier bag tightly over my head, curled up under my duvet and thought that I would just slip away. This was a fantasy.

The reality of trying to suffocate yourself is that breathing gets harder and harder with each breath, as you would expect, but your instinct is still to try and fill your lungs and all of your muscles tense for this, but you can't find that air. Your lungs don't inflate, they burn. It's excruciating. Your instinct is to gasp for breath, while your mind is trying to convince you that it will all be over soon, but even though you never seem to be breathing anything in, you also never fully seem to be able to empty your lungs.

Eventually, I just ripped the carrier bag off my head and took the biggest breath I had ever savoured. *I knew that I would fuck it up again!* My chest was fucked, my head was spinning and my spirit was dead. But I wasn't. I curled up to wait for it to get dark again, and I would come up with another plan.

That evening, I did very much the same thing. Drinking tea and basically chain-smoking. Thoughts and ideas rushing through my mind. I know at one point *The Deerhunter* was on. A gun. That's what I needed. Where could I find one? I know who I would call if I was at home in South London. I could think of nothing and went back to formulating ideas for my demise.

Jump in the sea! No, you'll float, you cunt. Hanging? With what? You can't even tie a proper knot, wanker!

Everything seemed out of my capability; there was nothing that was guaranteed, and then it struck me.

You know what to expect this time. You won't take yourself by surprise. You won't panic. You will be able to handle the pain this time.

That morning, I went to bed with a carrier bag over my head again and tried to gaffer tape it closed. It seemed like a lot longer this time, and I knew that I wasn't breathing at all. My lungs were on fire, unable to inflate, and my diaphragm was in agony, as my brain told it to make me breathe, but it had nothing left to find, yet I was still alive. Why couldn't I die? Surely, just a little while longer. Any second now. Again I bottled it and tore the bag from my face.

You completely fucking worthless piece of shit! You're not even strong enough to die! All you had to do was wait. You deserve all of the pain that life is going to throw at you. Cunt! I told myself.

I would only leave my bed to use the toilet for the next 30 odd hours until my parents returned. Mum came up and found me in a state. I eventually joined them downstairs and explained what had gone on.

After the weekend, I got in touch with work and said that I had been struggling with anxiety. I went to the doctor to get signed off for a while, and I was given something for the anxiety. I can't remember what; I didn't take them for long, as they weren't compatible with alcohol, and I knew that alcohol was a lot more beneficial for anxiety than anything else possibly could be.

I was off work for about a month, and then it came time to return. I left the house that morning and headed into town where I stayed. God Bless Wetherspoon's! I went straight in there and sat with a magazine until the other pubs opened and moved somewhere quieter where I could sit alone, without fear of having to interact with anyone other than the bar staff. I wasn't drinking quickly, for once, but I was drinking long, and after having a slurp for about ten hours, it was time to pick up some Charlie and go to see my brother. I never liked taking drugs in public.

I turned up at my brother's with some beers and some toot, saying that I had had a couple after work and his place was closer to work anyway. He didn't mind; I had brought the entrance fee with me and we had a pleasant evening.

In the morning, he left before me and I just lay in bed for hours until I thought that I should scarper as I was fairly sure that the news that I had fucked work off was going to break at some point. I headed into town, switched my phone off and found a little pub where I knew I wouldn't be found and stayed there for far too long.

When I left, I turned my phone back on, and I knew that the game was up. My brother had been in touch and his home would no longer be a refuge for me. I had to return to my parents.

I felt bad for the worry that I had caused them, but I was angry with myself that I had passed up another chance to do myself in. I had been scot-free and could have done anything to myself, but I had returned home. The decision to leave the call centre job wasn't a difficult one to make. Another chapter of failure was over.

My brother had left his previous job in the meantime and was working with a mate, doing their own thing. They said that they needed a pair of hands, so I joined them. The three of us all got on and my brother was much happier. There was always a good atmosphere on site and we had a right laugh, all earning OK from it. It was going to be different this time.

Chapter 20

Feeling Nothing Is Still Feeling

Work was fun for once. I was back to spending a lot of time at my brother's, as he lived just around the corner from the fella we were working with, and most of our work was up that end of town. We were fairly busy and were bringing in the money, allowing us to carry on as usual. The weeks passed much as they had previously except that the sun seemed to be shining a bit more.

Towards the end of the year, we moved out of the house due to a dispute over the rent and we were back with Mummy and Daddy. This was par for the course for me but was all a bit alien for my brother. He didn't like thinking that he had to rely on anyone, and his mood started to drop.

Work started to dry up, as it often did this time of year, and as we were back with our parents, we took our drinking outside a lot more. We were in a place where I knew more people, and I think that this brought out some sibling rivalry in my brother, and he would always try to put me down and assert his dominance over me. We were soon back into the old routine where he was holding the purse strings and he loved to lord this over me, making a big show that he always had money and that I didn't. I was his fucking bitch!

In the build-up to Christmas, our drinking accelerated, and whether it was that we were out in the open or whether it was because my brother was becoming more and more unhappy, but we started to fall out on a regular basis.

Christmas wasn't the happiest time for any of us that year. My sister had become pregnant through IVF again earlier in the year and was heavily pregnant when she arrived at Christmas. They went home for New Year and we would see them when the baby came in February.

My brother and I had sporadic work to go back to in the new year and any money that came in was put straight behind the bar. We were both really beginning to withdraw from life as well. If either of us weren't working or drinking, we would be in our respective rooms alone, passing the time doing whatever the fuck it was that we were doing.

One day, early in January, our father received a call from our brother-in-law. They had been for a scan and were unable to detect a heartbeat. My sister's baby was dead in the womb. My sister was to have labour induced and her baby would technically be stillborn. My parents were to travel up the next day and stay while they were needed. We were going to stay in Swansea and continue our parallel, solitary existences.

Hannah Esther Boyden was born on 12 January 2014 but was never to take a breath. My sister's daughter, my parents' granddaughter and my niece, yet I felt nothing. I honestly felt some sadness for my sister and her husband, my parents too; it was most probably their last chance to be grandparents. I was never going to provide them with grandchildren. Towards Hannah, my fucking niece, I felt no connection, no loss, nothing. I was a complete shell. Empty, emotionless and dead.

I travelled up for the funeral while my brother stayed in Swansea, and it was a big occasion. Even the sight of a solitary pallbearer carrying her shoebox-sized coffin couldn't evoke any reaction of true feeling. To be honest, I was just grateful for a change of scenery, whatever the occasion.

How wrong is it to envy a child that never took their first breath? I knew that I would have to return to the endless purgatory that was my life. I had exhausted all options open to me, and I just had to keep on waiting for the end. It was coming, but it never felt like it was getting any nearer. I had no way out.

I had started signing on at the start of the year, and so, this brought in a bit of income. This would usually go within a day or two either on a bender or I would pay off my brother's tab and then a bender. The two of us were hardly doing any work together now and were spending next to no time together anymore.

He had won. He was the boy, and everybody looked on me, as if I was the biggest piece of shit on the fucking planet. That was my perception anyway. Who knows how close to the truth it was. We had no relationship; it hadn't so much snapped or exploded; it had imploded, dissolved. We didn't want anything to do with each other. I had lost my brother.

I eventually heard back from one of the myriad applications that I had submitted. It was for the same sort of thing that I had passed up over a year ago, except this time based in Cardiff. I went along to the assessment day this time and found out that it was for door-to-door sales. Self-employed, so you only earned what you sold.

I spent a day tramping the streets with an agent, and at the end of the day, I had a meeting with the boss, and I was told that I had the job, when could I start? Straight away, the next week. I popped into a pub near Cardiff Station for a pint or two to celebrate. I was excited even though it wasn't something that I had ever wanted to do, and I had no confidence whatsoever in my ability to do the job. Another new start. Another false dawn? Too many false dawns.

I reported to work on the following Monday and was given a bit of a briefing and taught 'The Pitch'. Broadband for £1 was the big selling point, and we were to push this. That was a barefaced fucking lie. You needed a phone line with the company that cost £15.99 a month, but the idea, it seemed to me, was to con people into signing up through all sorts of chicanery and half-truths. This just wasn't me. I was honest, wasn't I? Who was I fucking kidding? If I could have applied the enthusiasm and fervour that I had when it came to duping people out of money for drugs, then I would be retired now. Just another hypocritical double standard that I have held for all of these years. Part of the dichotomy of me? *Shut up, you pretentious prick.*

I did this for nearly a month. I would get up at 6:00 a.m., jump through the shower, make some lunch and then straight out of the door to catch a bus to town. A short walk to the station, and then an hour on the train to Cardiff followed by a short hop on another train at the other end and a walk of about five minutes to the office.

There was a weird sort of morning meeting to get us all psyched up for the day, and then we went off in our small groups to various parts of south-east Wales.

Now, I was never cut out to be a salesman. If there is something that I am passionate about, I can wax lyrical all day and all night. Bog standard telecommunications at no special price was not one of these things. I would make the occasional sale, never really covering my outlay, but it was getting me out of the house.

The hardest part of the job was dealing with repeated rejection. This was no hassle for me. I had repeatedly rejected myself before anyone else could. Strangers telling me that they didn't want something that I had to offer when I knew that it was all fucking garbage, really was water off a duck's back to me. I think that over my time here, I most probably had more cups of tea with lonely, elderly people than I did sales. In all honesty, this gave me a greater feeling of self-worth than getting someone to sign a contract that would, more than likely, be cancelled long before I received any commission.

Each day ended up with a meeting with the head honcho to let him know how you had done. I never made more than two sales in any single day and this obviously pointed to me having an attitude problem. Sorry, this isn't fucking hard work. I had done longer days pushing wheelbarrows the whole time, or on the fucking mixer. You lot aren't fucking special. Just because I wasn't comfortable with stretching or bending the truth, and I was never going to be the person who could take control or put someone on the back foot in their own house, didn't mean that I had a bad attitude. It actually meant that somewhere deep inside, hidden away, I may still have had the last vestiges of morality. Maybe.

After these meetings, I would go back to Central Cardiff, grab an hour in the pub, well, I had done a day's work, and then jump on the train back to Swansea. I would get in somewhere around one in the morning just to get up five hours later to do the same shit again. This was my routine six days a week. On the seventh, I rested. Usually after some coke the night before.

One evening, I tired of having my attitude questioned and said that I would take the next day off in order to recharge my batteries. I never went back. I owed them nothing and they would be better off without me. Just like everybody else would.

About a week later, I made the excuse to my parents that I had a meeting with my boss in Cardiff to discuss my future. This was bollocks. I was straight into Swansea where I bought a couple of magazines and settled in for a day's solitary drinking. My favourite kind.

Late afternoon, my funds were dwindling and I fancied some chop. I applied for a loan on my phone, and after some bullshit, I had £300 in my account. This really was too easy. It's not difficult to see how people get into serious financial trouble. I had no proof of earnings whatsoever. I didn't even know when I would earn again.

My regular dealer was out of the country, so a little bit of a magical mystery tour ensued. Seriously, the resourcefulness of a substance abuser when searching to score, if channelled correctly, could solve all of the world's ills. I owed my regular dealer some wedge, and this loan would allow me to pay him off when he came home.

I found Charlie that night, and the next, after another good day's drinking, and it was gone. My dealer would have to wait.

Around this time, my brother found work back up in the south-east and he headed off. Almost as soon as he had gone, we started talking regularly and all seemed well again. We had cast off the shackles of our mutual misery, and we were free to be brothers again. We remain close and extremely loyal to this day. Was it all worth it? To have the relationship that I have with my brother now? Of course, it fucking was!

I started doing a few bits with the mate that we had been working with previously, and this provided a few beer tokens and the occasional sniff. Nothing special, but comfortable.

Come July, Mum, Dad, Klint and I went up to visit my sister and brother-in-law for a fortnight. While up there, a couple of family friends wanted various little odd jobs to be done, so I ended up staying for a while.

I once again did the rounds of the employment agencies in Bromley and actually managed to get some advice on my CV. Basically, it was fucked, but at least I was given some idea of how to format it. I was desperate now to leave Swansea. I had a new lease of life back here. I needed to come home.

It was towards the end of September; the private work had dried up and I hadn't managed to find anything else, so, with the proverbial heavy heart (did I still have a heart?), I booked tickets back to Swansea for the following Monday. I had a lovely day at my sister's that final Sunday, just chilling out with a couple of beers, and I got myself ready to return to my own personal hell.

My brother-in-law received a call from a fellow director of his company. They needed a pair of hands on one of their projects, preferably somebody with some building experience. His boss was reticent to hire me, as I had let them down badly before I left Bromley when I was doing a bit of bookkeeping for them. However, for want of a better offer, they agreed that I should be given a chance. I had got lucky again. I was staying.

Chapter 21

The Bright Light of Another False Dawn

I got up at 5:00 a.m. the next morning with fresh impetus. This time would be better. It would for a while too. Strangely enough, I have never really struggled with nerves or anxiety when it has come time to start a new job. Maybe this is because it has always seemed like another last chance after I had thought that I was lost. Possibly, I was grateful that I would be earning and soon be able to start using regularly again. I don't know, but excitement always outweighed trepidation on these occasions.

My brother-in-law accompanied me that first morning in order to make some introductions. The first job that I was on was fitting new toilets and kitchens in an office building just across from Covent Garden. It was only a fetch-and-carry remit for me, so absolutely no pressure or responsibility.

I started on a very good day rate, and after a couple of weeks, I was on really good money for the work that I was undertaking. Overtime and out-of-hours work was paid at time and a half, and things soon got very busy.

I started being given more responsibility, and with their faith in me, my confidence grew. Gratitude abounded. I felt on top of the world. I was earning good money, I was working independently when required to, and I had growing belief in my own ability. I had fallen on my feet this time.

The run-up to Christmas was extremely busy, and I loved every moment of it. Working seven days a week, with the days getting longer towards the end, I was raking it in and had little time to spend it. I was really enjoying my work and was happy to pop to clients who I had never met in order to carry out basic maintenance tasks. I could be working on site with the boys and then receive an email, and I was on my toes across London somewhere to do whatever was asked of me. Christ, I could make it work in the building industry after all.

The boys that I worked with regularly on site were sound as fuck, and we had a good laugh every day. Sometimes, there would be a bit of friction, but this never really affected me, as it all went on above me on the hierarchy of command. On weekends, I would often be painting somewhere on my own, and I was told that it was OK to jump the Thames to watch Charlton on a Saturday as long as my deadlines were met. And they always were. I was home in person and at The Valley, I was home in spirit. We're on our fucking way now, boys!

For once, I got to Christmas with a decent bit of bunce in the bank. I was going to make up for all of the special occasions that I had missed, and it felt good that I would be reciprocating some of the generosity that I had received over the years. I worked up until the 21st of December, and on the 22nd, I had a day with my sister and brother-in-law and we went out bowling in the afternoon followed by a nice meal at home and then a few beers.

I caught the train back to Swansea on the 23rd and was looking forward to returning to regale people with stories about my modicum of success, even if it was based on an incredible piece of luck. They didn't need to know that. Christmas Eve was the day to reveal the new, affluent me. First things first, I still owed my dealer his cash. After offering him a ton for a £40 debt, he was obliging enough to put me back on his delivery round.

It's nice to pop back to a place that you have lived soon after leaving. People still remember you and even those that you weren't close to seem to show more of an interest. Over time, though, the world keeps turning and people move on with their lives. You eventually become a distant memory, a footnote if you're lucky. I still had a cracking night, and it was back to being a dutiful son for the festive period.

My sister and family came down after Christmas, and we saw the New Year in as a family. The first job back was to fit out my brother-in-law's home office. They stayed in Swansea and I headed back to prepare it.

The night before I travelled to Bromley, I had a decent drink and picked up some Charlie. When I was running my bath the following morning, before heading off, I went dizzy and blacked out in the bathroom. I managed to convince everyone that it was nothing, and I was on my way with them none the wiser.

I got back to my sister's house and ordered a pizza after a couple of pints. The plan was that I would work the Sunday, stripping wallpaper and getting the polystyrene tiles off the ceiling, ready for Monday morning. I was feeling rough and didn't have much to drink on that Saturday night. I got on with the monotonous work as planned.

I have never minded doing the mundane. As long as I have got some music, I can happily spend hours doing the most menial of tasks. I realise now that this hasn't always been the best for me. Anyway, I didn't make the best progress, so I popped down the pub for a couple of hours. I couldn't do any damage doing what I was doing. I took some beers home, and I ended up working until three o'clock in the morning to make my deadline. But I did.

It felt as if I had only just fallen asleep on the sofa when there was a knock at the door. It was the boys ready to start work. I let them in and made my excuses to have a quick dip under the shower, and then I was down to help them. The room we were working in was tiny; it had actually been my bedroom from ages 12 to 18, and so, there certainly wasn't room for three of us in there. I was on tea duty which suited me. I knew that I could make tea.

My sister and brother-in-law were due back on Wednesday morning, and we had made good progress. I arranged to meet up with my brother on Tuesday evening, and after work, I popped over to his local for a couple of pints. Well, fuck me, you can guess what happened.

I had gone out with a decent amount of money in my pocket, and I woke up free of cash and with a debit card receipt for over £120 from his local pub. Fuck me, we must have gone for it. I knew that he hadn't spent much. He had bills. We had countless pints, and it turned out that we had drunk well over a bottle of Jameson between us. Well, it was a special occasion. It was a Tuesday, after all. No cocaine; I was determined to stay clear of that up there.

The office was finished that week as arranged, and we were back up in Central London, and I have to say that I was genuinely enjoying my life. I loved what I was doing for work. I was seeing loads of my sister; we have always been close, and she and her husband have always been there for me. I could see Charlton whenever I wanted and had reconnected with a couple of very good friends. This was a very prosperous path that I was on, and it was up to me to maintain it.

Work was constant and busy. Long days and weekends suited me. The rewards were there in terms of money, gratitude and self-esteem. Was I actually good at what I did for once? It certainly appeared that way. I remember that my birthday was a Sunday that year, and I worked and then settled down to a pint outside a pub on the South Bank.

As I took stock, I felt genuinely happy. I had hope and optimism for the future. Things were bound to work out for me. I just had to keep my head down and keep doing what I was doing. My confidence was at a level I had never experienced before, and I was able to deal with a bit of responsibility for the first time in my life. Through work, I was asked to undertake things that I never would have felt comfortable doing before, I knew that I had the support and could ask for assistance if I needed to. I very rarely decided not to take something on. I trusted my ability.

This was new territory.

I sat there drinking alone for about an hour, but it was different now. Life was good. I supped up and made my way home. We had a lovely evening in for my birthday. There was a roast waiting for me, most probably lamb, and we just had a chilled evening in with a couple of drinks and then to bed, ready for work the next day. All very civilised.

A week later, and it was my sister's birthday. A few of us went for a pub lunch and then back to theirs for a few drinks. It was a good day, and in this company, I was in complete control of the booze, stopping when everybody else did, or earlier so that I could go to bed, ready to get up at five the next morning.

It was time for me to move on. Very gently the idea was put to me. I knew it was coming, and it was the right thing to do. No real pressure just to start looking. I decided that I only needed a room, as I worked so much, I only really needed a place to lay my head. Besides, rents are so high in that part of the world that it is a fair bit of change for a single person to rent a flat or house. Somebody said that I should go on the social, but that wasn't for me. I didn't need it.

I enquired about one room only to be told that the advertised room had been let, but they had another room for an extra £70 a month. *Fuck you, I ain't no mug!* The second room that I found would be available in a month's time. I went and had a look at it and put a holding deposit down straight away.

It was within five minutes' walk of the station and Bromley Town Centre. It was a ground floor room, and there was also a ground floor shower. These were essential in my thinking, as I knew that I would be the first up, and I didn't want to get off on the wrong foot with my new housemates by waking them up at dawn's crack.

Financially, it made sense. All of my bills would be covered by one week's work, after that just travel, that I only needed to pay for on days that I worked, so that was covered, and then food. After that, everything was gravy. I was 34 years old and finally ready to launch. About time, but I was ready now.

Chapter 22

Fear and Self-Loathing in South London

Sunday, 8 March 2015. The day that I finally became an adult. I caught the bus to my new abode to meet the landlord. I read and signed the rental agreement, and then he gave me the keys.

There were a few things that I had to pick up for my new life, so I headed into Bromley Town Centre and spent a couple of quid. After that, it was round to my sister's for Sunday lunch, and then we took the rest of my belongings to the place that I was to call home.

I met the first of my new housemates that evening while I was having a cigarette in the garden. We didn't get off on the best footing. We chatted for a bit, and he said that he was a geophysicist. He didn't seem to like the fact that I had an idea what this entailed, obviously thinking that he was something special. He proceeded to give me a textbook definition, trying to make himself look more important. He said that his current job required him to collate results on a computer database. "Oh, a data entry position then," I said. We didn't have too much to do with each other after that. He would ignore me if our paths crossed in public, especially if he was with anyone. I would make it incredibly obvious that I knew him. It became a game to me. Still, it was his loss, the hoity-toity, jumped up, little cunt.

I settled in quickly, and work carried on much as before. My other two housemates were pretty sound. All four of us were on different routines, so we never saw much of each other. I found a sports bar in Bromley that I could have a quiet drink in after work. It was huge with plenty of booths and always nearly empty when I was there. I could have drunk there for years without ever having to engage anyone bar the employees. I only really went there for a couple of hours a night to read a magazine, then home to eat.

The kitchen was almost always in a tip, nobody seeming to clear up after themselves, so I battered the Just Eat app. I would usually eat at my sister's one evening a week, and there was always a Sunday roast there for me. Life was busy, and this suited me. I still enjoyed work and didn't have too much time to myself, just about enough.

Over the next couple of months, nothing much changed. I perhaps started spending a little more time in the pub, and after a long day, I would pop for a pint in London, just to let the rush hour die down, of course. This soon became a habit of a couple of pints in London, regardless of when I finished work. I knew the train times, and so, I was happy to miss a couple. I had nothing better to do.

Getting off at Bromley South, I would pop into the Wetherspoon's that was on my way home, honest, and then go home to drop my work bag off. I didn't want to lose my tools! After that, back into Bromley and Burger King. I was eating mountains of XL Double Bacon Cheeseburgers at this time, but this then meant that I could have another half a dozen pints before shower and bed.

I was blind to the fact that my drinking was increasing, again. I was up every morning at five, fresh as a daisy. OK, so I wasn't in bed until around 11 or 12, but I had never needed 8 hours' sleep a night. Fucking hell, for large swathes of my life, zero hours did for me.

We were doing some insane hours at work at times, but, as I said, the rewards were there. I knew from previous experience that time off wasn't always good for me. Seven solid days of work were good for me. I had the cash flow now to allow me to run up some quite sizeable expenses claims, and my bank balance was incredibly healthy.

Just before Easter, I received news that my father had been diagnosed with prostate cancer. It was a non-aggressive strain and the prognosis was very good, but that word is always a tough one to digest. My boss persuaded me to take a week off around Easter to visit my parents.

My father was in good spirits when I arrived in Swansea, and we had a lovely week. I didn't go out drinking a lot and only took coke once. Well, I wasn't using it in Bromley, so where was the harm? The couple of times that I did go out, I enjoyed telling people how well things were going for me, and that I was in danger of being happy. I honestly thought that this was the truth. This trip also gave me plenty of time to reconnect with Klint. Some nice long walks finished off with a pint or two, never anymore. Christ, I missed that dog.

I returned to work midweek and was straight back into it, working on a building in Notting Hill. After a couple of weeks, we had a crazy weekend where I worked nearly 50 hours between Thursday evening and Sunday morning. I left that Sunday morning dead on my feet but had summoned up the energy by the time that I reached Bromley to go for a couple of pints.

We also had a big job going on in Boreham Wood. This was quite a commute, but I only needed to make one change of train, and I didn't have to get up much earlier. I found out that I was to paint the interior of the building in Notting Hill on my own. This would be three weeks of long, out-of-hours shifts. I would be earning about two and a half days' money each and every day that I was there, with very little chance of spending any of it. I would be fucking drowning in Sovereigns when I finished! I got my start date; I would be starting at close of play on a Friday night. I was to carry on working in Boreham Wood until then.

Thursday was to be my last day on site, allowing me Friday to get ready for Notting Hill and to try and flip my routine on its head, as I was to work nights. After work on Wednesday, I popped to the bar as usual and had a decent drink on my own. I carried on longer than I usually would have, but then I only had tonight and tomorrow night in order to drink, then that was it for a few weeks. Eventually, the little Charlie urge crept up on me. This wasn't a problem. I didn't have any Bromley contacts, so I wouldn't be able to get any. No danger.

I spotted a bloke sitting at the bar and made a point of standing next to him while I ordered my next pint. I struck up a conversation and bought him a drink. We chatted for a while and I brought up the subject of cocaine. He was meeting a mate here shortly, and his mate would know someone. Sorted. It really is a piece of piss to find drugs when you fancy it.

His mate turned up and made a phone call. Soon enough, I had two grams of Colombia's finest, hardly, in my sky rocket. I sorted the boys out a couple of lines and a few drinks, and then we went back to my room. After a while, there was a decision to make. Two grams doesn't go very far between three, so another two were ordered, and we were still sniffing as the sun came up.

I was already late leaving for work when the first boy left.

What to do? What to do? I've fucked things up again.

By this stage, the other boy was asleep on the sofa in the communal living room. I switched my phone off and curled up in my bed.

I stayed like that until I heard knocking on my window. It was my sister seeing why I hadn't turned up to work. I made a big thing about how I must have fallen asleep without putting my phone on charge.

I got up, showered and was straight out of the door, calling my boss on the way to the station. I couldn't be arsed to deal with the other boy, so I just left him to sleep on the sofa. I left someone that I hadn't known for more than 12 hours in a house that I shared with three other people and their belongings.

My boss swallowed the story and was great about it. He said that I was well in credit with the way that I had worked for them and not to give it another thought.

This final day of regular hours was now a nice, short day, and I was heading straight round to my sister's afterwards, and we were going out to the local pub for dinner, as I didn't expect to see them much in the near future.

I phoned the boy who I had left on the sofa, and he was still in my house, so I had to take a small detour. I went home and we left together. He didn't have any money to get home, of course, so I lent him more than enough to get home. I knew that he wouldn't pay me back, but he had sorted me out last night, and I might have some use for him in the future.

I hadn't felt like drinking much that day, but as soon as I was back in Bromley, I soon developed a taste. I had a couple with my new mate, and then we went our separate ways. I then headed off to meet my sister and brother-in-law, and we had a nice couple of hours in the pub before I jumped on the bus back to Bromley.

Oh Shit! I've missed my stop! Oh well, I'll just get off outside my regular haunt and pop in for a nightcap. I stayed until about midnight. What was the problem? I didn't have to be up early in the morning, and I wouldn't be drinking for a while anyway.

I got up about lunchtime on Friday and leisurely got myself together. I headed to Notting Hill with all of my tools and made my rendezvous. I stored my gear, collected the keys and went out for food before starting work once I had the run of the place. I could get used to this, a nice sit-down meal for breakfast before starting the day's work after everyone had gone home. I had my radio and gallons of paint all to myself. Who could ask for more?

The first few nights went like a dream. Painting the smaller rooms, white ceilings white walls, I was in my element. Absolute Radio keeping me company; I smashed into it and was well on schedule.

It was Wednesday of the next week that my boss called and asked how I was getting on. I informed him that I was making great progress and we were bang on schedule. I knew that there was plenty of work on elsewhere, but I wanted to do as much of this on my own as the money was there to be had. He said that he would get me an agency painter in, and so, the next night, I had someone to work with me.

He seemed like a nice bloke.

I had been having trouble sleeping in the days. It was the middle of June, and so, the sun was up the whole of the time that I was in bed. Coupled to this, there was a primary school opposite, and so, the kids were out in the playground three times a day, running around and screaming when I should have been slumbering.

I began stopping off for a couple of pints at my local Wetherspoon's on the way home. Just to help me sleep, of course. In there from about eight or nine until elevenish, then to bed and back up at about half past five to get ready for work. Just a normal routine, only 12 hours out from everybody else.

The agency worker was good but painfully slow. He spent his first night masking up and little else. I had a word with him about his rate of work but wasn't very assertive. I wasn't there yet. I had given him the woodwork to paint because, well, because I could. This left me the emulsion. Piece of piss.

There were two huge rooms that were used as call centres, and I decided to paint the ceilings first, get the tricky bit out of the way. The walls weren't going to be a problem.

I worked one whole 12-hour shift on a Friday night, and my arms were aching badly as I left the following morning, and this was compounded by the fact that I was sat on the Circle and District Line platform at Notting Hill Gate tube station, waiting for a train that never came. That part of the line was closed that morning, but there were no announcements or notices anywhere. When I say that, I did find a notice by the entrance to the Central Line platform, that you came to after the Circle and District line entrance. Very fucking useful. By the time that I got back to Bromley, I was suitably pissed off, and I went straight to the pub and sank a good few in a couple of hours.

After a few hours of restless sleep, I headed back up to Notting Hill. I had finished one of the largest ceilings the previous night, and I was confident that I could get the other one done in the same time frame. I severely underestimated the toll that working exclusively above your head can have on your shoulders, and approaching midnight, I was done in. I had bought some painkillers, but they had had no effect, and so, I sent the agency painter home and left.

I popped to the shop and bought myself eight lagers and headed to the Underground station. I had just missed the last tube on the Circle and District, but this was no problem, I could jump on the Central Line to Oxford Circus and change onto the Victoria Line for Victoria. I should make the last train. I just missed it. If I hadn't stopped to buy beer, I would have made the tube at Notting Hill and definitely the train at Victoria. I had worked myself to a standstill. I deserved my drink.

What to do? What to do?

I walked out of the station pretty aimlessly and ended up heading towards Westminster and luckily realised that from there, it was only a short walk to Trafalgar Square where I could catch a night bus home.

Anyone who has never been on a London night bus, well, they are quite an experience. Usually, a fight at some point, quite often you can pick up drugs if that is what you are after. This wasn't what I was after. I was acutely aware that I was falling behind schedule, heaping pressure upon myself that wasn't coming from above. I had serious reservations over whether I would be physically capable to work the following night, let alone mentally. I had no clue how to rectify these things.

On the long journey home, my head started racing. Suicidal thoughts again.

Well, Hello my old friend! Fuck off!

Things are good; I don't want to die!

I only needed a way out of this situation, a way that would allow me to skip out of the responsibility and allow me to continue later back in my previous role of general dogsbody and maintenance man. Then it came to me. I Googled 'How to induce a coma' and began to read.

By the time I got home, I was dead on my feet. I had found no useful information, and certainly, nothing that I could do anything with, at half-past three on a Sunday morning, so I tripled up on my painkillers and got my head down. I slept better than I could remember, not knowing what was in store for me later that day. All I knew was that work wasn't on the agenda.

I woke up about four that afternoon. I didn't feel too bad and could probably have worked, but straight away, the thoughts started. *You've let everyone down, again! You've fucked up another job; they'll definitely bin you off now! Why do you always do this? Why are you just a useless waste of space?* Before long, I had catastrophized to the point that I knew that not only could I not return to the job, I also had to go somewhere where nobody could find me. Somewhere where nobody would know me.

What to do? What to do?

First things first, I needed to be able to think straight, but how could I gather my thoughts? I know what works: a couple of pints. I couldn't go anywhere locally; people were most likely already looking for me. This was before I was due to start work, nobody would know that I wasn't there for hours, and besides, the only number that the agency painter had was mine. He couldn't alert anybody to my absconding. This never occurred to me, so I jumped on a train to Victoria in my work clothes, just as I would have done if I was going to work. I wouldn't have to answer any tough questions then. I was just on my way to work.

I got up to Victoria and was straight in the bar on the station. A quick couple of pints, and then we would formulate a plan. First things first, I put my phone into airplane mode. I stared long and hard at every pint. None of them lasted very long, and it's not true what they say. The answer wasn't at the bottom of any of them. The answer was within me, and the answer was Camden! Fuck knows why.

I went to Burger King, grabbed a bite and bought some magazines and hopped on the tube heading north. I found a quiet corner in a quiet pub and sat down to read and drink. This would do. Yeah, sure the pub would be closed in a few hours, but by then, I would have drunk enough to be able to think clearly and plan more long term.

Last orders came, and I ordered three pints. These set me up for an adventure.

I drank those, picked up my magazines and headed out into the night.

What to do? What to do? I know, I'll call those boys; at least, I can get some Charlie then. Everything is alright with Charlie, I thought.

The first boy that I called didn't answer, and so, I tried the other number. This was the boy who couldn't get the old nosebag direct, but I was sure that if I met him, my expedition would be fruitful.

I managed to get back across London and jumped on the last train, and we met up. He introduced me to a friend who made a call, and we hopped in a cab. Fuck me! We only ended up two minutes from my sister's house. We picked up our cargo and called another cab to take us back to one of their flats to get on it.

The boy whose flat it was didn't actually sniff at that time. He would come to love the toot over the time that I knew him. He said that it was inevitable that he would end up on it, but he had made it this far without that happening and had always been around it. I don't know. I never forced it up his hooter, and after that first occasion, I never offered it to him, but I certainly made sure that it was regularly available to him.

About ten, the following morning, the other boy and I decided to go out for a drink. We headed to Beckenham; nobody would know me there. It was a good couple of miles from where I lived, practically another planet. What a fucking helmet! He met up with his cousin and went to his aunt's grave as it was the anniversary of her death. I holed myself up in a pub, out of the way. They never returned; that didn't bother me. I sat in that pub for a good four hours, trying to work out my next move.

What to do? What to do? I know, the last place that they would look for me. My dark, stinking hole of a fucking pit. Home sweet home! I thought. I jumped on the train for the short journey to Bromley South and then just put my head down, hoping not to be recognised by anyone during the stroll home. I walked straight past the pub. I never knew that I could do that. I got through the front door into my room, locking the door behind me, pulled the curtains and curled up under my duvet. I was safe, for now.

It wasn't long before there was a knock at the window. I knew it was my sister and brother-in-law. The anxiety went through the roof as the adrenaline started coursing through my veins.

Why don't they just fuck off? I thought.

"Steve, you're not in any trouble. We just want to know that you're all right." *It's a trap! The devil's greatest trick was convincing the world that he doesn't exist!*

I can't let them know that I am in here. They just want to fuck me up!

What a way to think! The noise finally subsided, and I didn't dare move for a good time afterwards. The anxiety never really abated. At times like this, it never did.

I became nocturnal again. I would allow my active hours to be between two and five in the morning. The rest of the time, I would be curled up under my duvet, not sleeping, not reading, not living but not dying. I spent the next three days like this, petrified in the safety of my home.

My sister or her husband would come around occasionally and once managed to speak to one of my housemates, who knocked on my bedroom door. I thought that my heart was going to smash through my ribs. I was hyperventilating as quietly as I could, trembling uncontrollably, but I managed to keep it together long enough to be left alone again. They meant me no harm, and I was absolutely oblivious to the pain that I was causing.

My food had run out early on Wednesday morning, and by Thursday evening, I was having serious hunger pains. *Could I just wait them out? Was this a viable option, starve to death? How long would that take? I'm strong enough to do that, aren't I? Fuck it, I've got plenty of money in the bank. If I'm going out, I'm going out fucking skint!*

I picked my moment to head through the shower and then sneak out of the front door.

I took a couple of back roads to Bromley Town Centre and managed to get into Wetherspoon's without being spotted. I ordered a pint and had a gulp as the barman sorted out my change. Well, bugger me. Everything was OK again. Why hadn't I thought of this before?

Lager was an instant relief, and I necked that first pint, enjoying the taste of serenity that it brought as much as the refreshing qualities and just the feeling of having something in my stomach. A couple more pints, and I ordered a nice big steak.

I knew that they would come for me at some point, and so, I had to Foxtrot Oscar.

What to do? What to do?

I jumped on the next train to Victoria and went straight to the bar again. I thought about Camden but decided to stay put. I was anonymous here, and I wasn't going to be bothered. After a couple of hours, I got in touch with my new best mate and arranged to meet up. I was back on the train and just stayed on for a couple more stops to reach my new destination. I would get used to this journey.

As the train was pulling in, I got on the blower and had just enough time for a salmon before my boys came walking up the road towards me. "What's the plan, Steve?"

"I'm getting royally fucked. Do we need to get a sherbet to pick up?" They tried a couple of numbers, but no dice. Just then one of the boys spotted someone that served up. He sorted me out a nice bit and gave us a lift to a flat that I had never been to before, picking up a couple of crates of beer on the way.

We entered this poky little flat, and there were about eight people there. Word got round very quickly, and everyone was around us in the kitchen. They seemed like a good bunch, and they seemed to like me. Somebody stocked the fridge while I chalked outlines for everybody else and one fucking massive hooner for me, the doctor! I booted it straight up. Fucking lovely drop!

A few people seemed to have their own Charlie, and so, it seemed that everything was communal. This was my way of doing things. After a little while, everybody had run out and we still had loads of beer left, so I got someone to order up. "Make it a fucking proper sized bit this time!" I said. Old Charlie Big Potato was back, and I fucking loved it.

It was a good atmosphere, but the crowd started to thin out, and in the end, there were just three of us. Me, my mate and the person whose flat it was. We settled into a nice day of drinking. There was a garage within a hundred yards, so no need for any expeditions, and plenty of Charlie. The early morning gear wasn't of the same high standard, and after that went, I was on the hunt for some MDMA.

A couple of useless contacts, and we decided to get a bit more substandard chang until the good stuff came on the market again later that day. A couple of hours later, we were just chopping up the last line when one of the boys heard the door to the building open. Straight away, he said that it was the police. He was right.

No need for me to worry. I hadn't done anything wrong, and besides, nobody knew that I was there. A knock at the door, my new friend opened it, and the policeman looked straight past him and looked at me. "Stephen, can we have a word please?"

WHAT! THE! FUCK!

I accompanied them outside more dumbstruck than anxious. I had a nice buzz going on, and as long as you didn't count the vast quantity of drugs that I had purchased and consumed, then I hadn't done anything wrong. My sister had consulted with a couple of friends in the force, and they suggested that, because of my history of mental health problems, she should report me missing.

Apparently, she had gone around to mine that morning and got no response, so she called the police. They were there within five minutes and managed to gain access to the property through one of my housemates. They made my sister and her husband wait outside as they forced open my door, as they fully expected to find my lifeless corpse there. But I wasn't there.

They managed to find me within three hours. It couldn't have been difficult. I had a couple of new Facebook friends, and I had been smashing my card in at the garage. They asked me if I had taken anything. "A little smoke last night," I said.

"It looks like a bit more than that!" came the reply. They managed to get me to agree to speak to my sister and called her. I couldn't really figure out what all of the hassle was for. I was in my own little bubble of self-disgust and self-obsession. I spoke to my sister and felt bad that she was genuinely worried and said that I would see her soon.

The police tried to get me to leave with them, but I wouldn't go. I couldn't go after this. "Steve, you don't belong here." *Oh, but I do,* I thought. *This place is probably actually too good for me. I am worse than these people.* If these boys were scumbags, then I was the detritus that they shat out every morning. I was just grateful that they were happy to spend time with me. The police left, we went back upstairs and I said, "Somebody get some Charlie around here sharpish." The whole episode was forgotten very quickly, and we carried on with the serious business of getting totally fucked up.

People came and people went. The three of us that had been there from the start just carried on as before. Different people in different altered states can often cause friction, but the two boys that I had spent the day with were like me. Really chilled on drugs. It was Friday night, so a lot of people used this flat to have a drink and a sniff before heading out. The flat got quite busy, and then it was just the three of us again. Perfect.

After the pubs kicked out, a couple of boys came back and they were pissed. They had no money and were just on the ponce. Yeah, I know. I kept my gear and beer to the three of us, and the other two eventually fell asleep. The owner of the flat took umbrage with this, and so, he pissed on them to wake them up. I didn't find this particularly funny, but I understood his point of view. They came round expecting a free lunch, and he didn't want pissed up people asleep on one of his sofas.

They did go back to sleep, and one ended up having his head shaved. This was just par for the course. If you fall asleep in these situations, then you get what is coming to you. Another boy popped in on his way home from work as the lad that I had arrived with left. He brought some beers and we (I) ordered up more chop. The sun was coming up now, but I was still enjoying myself and had no plans of leaving and confronting the consequences of reality. Over the next couple of hours, we did the last batch and I did another beer run.

The two boys that were there then started to pre-empt me to get more drugs in. Now, I'm nobody's fucking mug! Yeah, I know. I would have happily carried on buying drugs for hours, possibly days to come, but the moment people think that they are getting the upper hand and conning me into doing it, even though I have been totally willing, that's when I pull the plug.

Soon after, I made my excuses and left. I must have looked a fucking mess. I picked up some beers from the garage and strolled to the station. I was to find out that within two hours of my departure, heroin was taken in that flat. Armed with this knowledge, I would still visit this place on a regular basis over the next 12 months. Maybe I was looking for an excuse. If I had been there, at that stage of my life, I would have tried it. I would have taken to it in a big way and developed a full-blown habit. No doubt about it, and I'm pretty sure by now that I would have taken an overdose, whether intentional or not.

Chapter 23

The Misplaced Faith of Others

I got off the train at Bromley South with a four-pack left. I walked straight past the pub and went home. I didn't know what state the door to my room was in. Would I still have the sanctuary that those four walls offered me? All I wanted to do was to lock that door behind me and drift off into an endless sleep. I knew that I wouldn't, and I knew that I wouldn't do anything to bring about my demise with any immediacy.

I opened the front door to my house and saw that my bedroom door was intact. When I unlocked it, I saw that the door lining had taken the brunt and had been bodged back together. At least, I could lock the world out.

I finished my beer and was going to go out for a couple of pints, but I had promised my sister that I would be around for dinner that evening. I ordered some kebabs, ate those and fell asleep. It was Sunday afternoon when I woke up and I showered and jumped on the bus to my sister's.

I turned up full of apologies and contrition. There was very little sincerity even though I knew that I had really fucked them about this time. I had let everybody down, and I was no good to anybody. Things were said and everything was smoothed over. There was still work for me, and all I really had to do was apologise to the boss and show by my actions that this would never happen again. I was so lucky. After all of this, I still had a job. A good job.

If my memory serves me correctly, I spent a lot of the following week at my sister's. I was more relaxed there. I was to return to work at the weekend, on the same job in Notting Hill, this time accompanied by the boys that I usually worked with. I definitely stayed at my sister's on Friday before going back to work, and I was to return there for Saturday night too.

I travelled to work with a certain amount of trepidation that Saturday morning, but that soon relented once I was back in the fold. There was some light-hearted ribbing, but definitely some genuine concern. The pressure was off. This wasn't just my job anymore, I was part of a team again, and I had a good day painting. *I've got away with it this time*, I thought. I was entrusted with the keys, as I would be the first one there in the morning. The boys had another job to go to on the way. I left feeling pretty good, grateful that there was a future after all.

I decided to have a pint at the station as I had a short wait for my train. I'd done a day's work, so I'd earned it, hadn't I? After getting off the train, I popped for a couple of pints to reflect before I caught the bus to my sister's for dinner and some sleep.

While I was in Bromley, I received a text from one of my new best friends. A couple of them were in another pub, so I went along to join them. After a few pints, the issue of Charlie inevitably surfaced. We ordered a bit, picked up some cans, and made our way around to the flat where I had spent some time the previous week.

One thing led to another, and I was there all night getting off my box. The good thing about Charlie is that after 12-hours' drinking, I wasn't that pissed. I would just go straight into work from here.

I checked the train times and, forgetting that it was a Sunday, was shocked that I had quite a wait. This plunged me into a spiral. I could still easily be there before anybody else on the firm turned up, but in my mind, I had fucked it for definite this time. When the train arrived, I jumped on and alighted two stops later, to go home, rather than stay on and go to work.

I rushed home, making sure that I avoided nobody in particular, and let myself into my house. Once inside, I pulled my curtains, locked my door, turned off my phone and curled up under my duvet, just trying to relax enough that I might be able to drift off to sleep.

Fat fucking chance. I lay there, hardly moving, my head spinning with thoughts of how I had really screwed up this time. There was no coming back from this. God knows how long I lay there. I had got home about eight on a June morning, and I didn't leave my bed until it had been dark for a while. Most probably Monday morning.

I allowed myself a couple of excursions out for cigarettes, but my TV and all lights were off before the sun came up again. I felt that this dark room was where I would spend the rest of my days. Why couldn't I just slip off this mortal coil?

What was the point of my continued existence? I had no quality of life anymore, and I was a detriment to the quality of life of everybody whose path I crossed.

Some point on Monday, there was a knock at my window. It was my sister. She was surprised to see me respond. I passed her the keys for the Notting Hill job and kept apologising, saying that I had lost my bottle on the way home and just come back and locked myself away. This was the rankest of half-truths. She said that when I was ready, I was always welcome around theirs. I didn't think that I would ever be ready.

I can't remember how many days I stayed in my room, just listening to myself breathing, hoping that it would just suddenly stop. It didn't. Eventually, probably through a mixture of hunger and extreme boredom, even bored of my own self-flagellating thoughts, I left my pit, showered and went to see my sister.

There wouldn't be any work for me in the foreseeable future, but my sister and her husband said that it was time to get myself sorted and that they would be there every step of the way. It was time to admit that I had some mental health issues. Up to this point, I had never even thought of this. I just accepted that I was an incredibly weak individual who had no will power or any other way of coping with life than to escape in a torrent of drink and a blizzard of drugs.

Being Christians, they had heard of something called Sozo healing that was done at a church that they knew. I agreed to a session and went with an open mind. I was at the end of my tether and would have tried anything.

The analytical mind that I have would liken this experience to sensory deprivation. Of course, you are going to see visions if you have your eyes closed all of the time. I did, however, leave in a better frame of mind, a little more positive for the future, but I stopped short of speaking in tongues, or pretending to.

I started leading a double life. The dutiful little brother around my family and the flat-out beer and coke monster around my 'friends'. I was earning little bits of money here and there from little jobs for my sister and some family friends. I didn't spend any money on food. Everything that I earned would go on my medicine.

One Sunday, I was absolutely starving. I couldn't remember the last time that I had eaten. I went into town to sell some of my tools, but there was nowhere open to do this. I returned home and looked on the internet.

There was a place that I could get to by bus that would be open at nine in the morning. I just needed to make it until then. I tried to get to sleep, but it seemed like the sun was never going to go down. When it did, it took an eternity to rise again. All of the time, I could feel my stomach trying to consume itself. No doubt about it, when I got some money in the morning, I would be stocking the cupboards. I would set myself up properly with food.

The next morning finally arrived, and I couldn't get out of the door quick enough. I had probably enjoyed brief snippets of sleep, but not much. I knew what I had to do, so I jumped on the bus and would be at Cash Generators in Orpington before it opened. I had my documentation and my goods. I got a pretty fair price for them, on a buy-back deal, and I was off shopping. First things first, I needed some fags.

That first cigarette was absolute fucking heaven scent. Things were going to be alright from now on. I've got a nice little bit of money now, and I had a couple of little earners coming up, so there was no harm in a quick pint before I went shopping.

I bought a paper and found a quiet corner in a pub and settled down for a short drink.

Two hours later, my stomach full for the first time that I could remember, I wasn't hungry anymore. I know what I need now. Yep, you've guessed it. I've never really felt comfortable carrying drugs in public, so I headed home to order up.

I got home and was told that I would have to wait a couple of hours. Oh well, it was a nice day, so I popped back into town, bought a magazine and went and sat in a dark pub to top up my tan. The time passed, and I got a text saying ten minutes. Lovely, just time to sup up and get home. Reliable as ever, my prescription arrived. Well, this was emergency medication, so I served myself up a good dose and decided what to do.

Wow! I'm alive! I was going to need some beer, back to town, leaving my drugs indoors. Well, as I've made the effort, a walk of less than five minutes, I might as well treat myself to a pint or six! I was really enjoying my day, so why rush to the finish line. I returned home at some point and got into the serious business of powdering my nose.

Later on that evening, I realised that I had made a miscalculation. I was going to need more. A couple of texts later, and it was on its way. Just enough time to stock up on beer and cigarettes, and then lock the world out and enjoy a party for one!

At some point in the early hours, the coke horn came on like a good 'un. *What to do? What to do?* First things first, I ordered Television X for the night. This was shit, so I got the laptop out. Not looking for anything in particular, I noticed pop-up adverts for sex contacts. *What's this then? Seems easy enough!*

A couple of hours later, there I was, still sat in my room with Television X on my TV, some non-descript grot on my laptop while I was browsing findamilf.com on my phone to try and find something to dip my wick in. My cock wasn't playing ball, though. *What's wrong with you? Work, you little fucker! I know, I'll have another big boot, then give it a good shake and I'll be laughing. Depravity, thy name is Steve!*

I was still going long after the sun had risen and after all of the drugs had gone, and I had managed a couple of half-hearted five-knuckle shuffles. I lay down to sleep for a while. *Ha-ha! Like that's going to happen, you little prick.*

Only one thing for it. A couple of pints. After a quick shower, I was off to the pub with my magazine. For full details of what followed, re-read the previous four paragraphs. I had spent all of my money and hadn't had a scrap to eat. I followed this up by staying in bed for the next 48 hours. This was living.

During the summer, there were a couple of changes in personnel in the house. The arrogant little prick fucked off and in came a South African fella. He seemed pretty sound, and we got on well, the little we saw of each other.

One Sunday, I was curled up in bed, just trying to get to the end of the day. He had the room above me at the front of the house, and he started shouting out of his windows at the neighbours. Next thing that I knew was that he had run outside and there was an altercation. It's over as soon as it had started, but I knew that I had to escape. I jumped up and rushed to the shower. I got dressed and was just about to leave when there was a knock at the door. It's the police. I told them that I hadn't heard anything, as I was in the shower. I then made my way into town, shaking. I needed a fucking pint. I would fall out with my housemate eventually, but that was much more down to me.

My existing housemate moved his girlfriend in when a room came up, and their relationship was over within 48 hours. She was fucking nuts! I appreciate the irony in me saying that, but she was fucking nuts! I returned home one night and her bed was in the front garden. She called the police on both my housemates, our landlord and the cleaners. I was the only person that she didn't.

Being in the front room downstairs, I always had to answer the door. I was dealing with the police all of the time. She was Spanish and spoke only broken

English, so I had to act as an intermediary. My nerves were shot. I couldn't even take drugs in my room in peace anymore in case the police were called. It didn't stop me, but it always put me on edge.

One day, I had been working and came home, and she had splashed hair dye all over the downstairs shower room. She was in an awful state about it, so I took pity on her. I always had some white emulsion around, and I gave it a couple of coats to cover the hair dye.

Another time, she knocked on my room door. I was in the middle of a cocaine and masturbation marathon. I could see from her eyes that she hadn't taken her meds that day. I had! "I think that you have a plan!" she said.

"Just fuck off!" I wittily retorted and shut the door in her face. I had always tried to be patient with her, but I was toiling in my own personal hell, and she was just adding to it. I was afraid to leave my room in case she went schiz on me or accused me of something and called the police. I needed to be free of her. I needed to be free of everyone.

I slipped into despair for the umpteenth time. Spending my days and nights lying in bed, torturing myself, hardly eating, hardly sleeping. One day, I made a decision. There was no way out. *Stop fighting it, you have used up all of your chances.* The struggle was over. I was going to die at my own hand, and it would be soon. I calmly went about planning my final release.

I went around the town centre buying various painkillers from all of the chemists, newsagents and supermarkets and had an armoury of well over one hundred tablets, capsules and pills. I knew that I had to wait for a few days where I had nothing planned with anybody else, and that would be coming up after an afternoon and dinner with my sister. She actually remarked that I seemed brighter. If only she knew.

When it was time to leave, I headed straight home. I didn't stop for a drink anywhere, as I didn't want anything to make me sick and jeopardise my chances. I got home, had a cigarette while I boiled the kettle, then made myself a cup of tea and retired to my room.

Over the next couple of hours or so, I sat in my room, enjoying my final few cups of tea and my last couple of hours of television. I had a smoke every time that I boiled the kettle, and every time that I got up, my head felt lighter, fuzzier. Something was happening. When I finished my tablets and my final cup of tea, I popped out for one last fag. I was extremely unsteady now and barely made it back to my room without blacking out.

My stomach felt volatile, but I didn't feel like I was going to be sick. I locked my door behind me, turned the telly and the light off and curled up in bed. An incredible calm washed over me. I had done it this time. I had cracked it. Before long, I slipped away.

It was over 30 hours before I came round. I certainly have no memory of regaining consciousness during that time, and it would be several more hours before I left my bed. I had no idea what had happened to me. My surroundings took a while to become familiar to me and my actions leading up this moment eluded me for some time.

I went outside for a cigarette to try and figure things out. It slowly dawned on me that I had tried to kill myself, again, and that I had failed, again. My head was all over the place, everything felt surreal, and I certainly didn't have the relief that I had felt after previous failed suicide attempts.

I spent at least another day in bed, surfacing for the occasional cigarette. In time, it became clear that I had to try and piece my shambolic life back together.

Amazingly, the door was still slightly ajar for me workwise. I was to get in touch to say when I was ready. In the meantime, Charlton had drawn Crystal Palace away in the league cup. Charlton fucking hate Palace, and going to their place was always such a buzz. I knew that I was going to be asked to go by someone at some point, and when I got the message, I replied without hesitation. I would worry about how to finance it nearer the time.

On the day of the Palace match, I had a little gardening to do for my brother-in-law's parents. I had been doing a few bits for them, including some decorating. I finished and got paid, with the little money that I had already and what they had given me, I was all set for a good night out.

I had agreed to go back to work the following day, allowing me to borrow some money from my brother-in-law as well. I had to walk through Bromley Town Centre to get home and decided to stop in my favourite sports bar. A couple of hours later, I needed to get ready to go to the match.

Fuck it, I haven't got any food in. Cocaine it is then. I phoned through my order and then worked out that this was my money for the evening gone. Another phone call to my brother-in-law and some bullshit about bank charges, and my pocket was restocked.

When the Charlie turned up, I had little over an hour and a half until I was meeting my mate. As I have said before, I don't particularly enjoy carrying drugs, especially not around large numbers of police. There was bound to be a good presence at the match. The logical thing in my mind was to bosh the gear in as quick as possible, getting totally off my box in the process, and then get to the pub to drink through it. When I met my mate, I was quite tipsy but wasn't buzzing my tits off uncomfortably any longer. Success.

We jumped in a cab to meet some of his mates at a pub and settled down to a good drink. They had all worked, just finishing a bit early, so they were up for a drink. I would match them, having drunk a week's worth already. I had met most of them before, but I didn't know any of them that well.

I started to feel on the outside again. No doubt, this was all my own perception, but here I was with the bloke I called my best friend, doing what I had always enjoyed, and I had never felt more isolated. This was Charlton, and it felt alien to me.

We got to the ground, and there were long queues outside. The singing had started, and there was the lingering sense of menace in the air that you only get at a derby. I was absolutely smashed and got separated from the boys on the way into the ground. Once inside, I couldn't find my ticket. I had literally just had it in my hand, I never did find it. Not knowing where to head, I just got up into the stand and stood on the walkway. Loads of other fans gathered there, and that is where I watched from.

We were fucking noisy, despite losing 4–1, and attempts to rendezvous were hampered as we couldn't hear each other over the phone. Once outside, I did not have the foggiest idea where I was, even though I had been here countless times before. I picked a direction and walked. My best mate called, trying to meet up. There was some trouble going on, and he wanted to know that I was safe. I told him that I wasn't aware of any trouble and that I was heading home.

Fortunately, I had set off in roughly the right direction and came to a pub after walking for about a quarter of an hour. I went inside, and it was absolutely empty. Smashed as I was, and having lost my voice during the match, I was still able to order a pint and ended up staying for about an hour and a half until being kicked out after last orders. Right then, how the fuck do I get home from here? Pick a direction and hope for the best. Luckily, I guessed right again and stumbled across a bus stop where I could get a bus directly home.

I got through the door shortly after midnight. I had to be up in five hours for work. Christ! I was going to have one hell of a hangover. I know what. I decided to try and head the hangover off at the past my getting some chop. No dice. I was starting to worry about being fit for purpose the following morning and must have fallen asleep, waking up at seven in the morning. Late! Again! Panicking, I turned my phone off, curled up and waited for everything to sort itself out. That usually worked.

Later that day, I decided that it was time to face the music. I turned on my phone to find several messages. I called my brother-in-law and explained how I had had a panic attack shortly before I was to leave. This seemed like a good enough explanation, and it was agreed that we would try again on Monday.

I would stay with them on Sunday night, and he would travel up with me and deliver me to site on Monday morning. This seemed like a plan. I wasn't too worried about making my own way in, but spending the night before alone would have been a problem.

Monday went as planned, and this led to a slightly more settled work routine. I wasn't full time, but I was used as I was needed. Dad had helped me with my rent once over the summer, but now I was back to being self-sufficientish. I carried on much as before in my private life, but not to the same degree and had a short while where I was reliable.

I had been a semi-regular visitor to the flat of disrepute that I have mentioned before, and on a Friday, I met one of the boys for a couple of pints after work; that's me who worked, not him, and we moved on to the flat after a while.

I had told them that I had work the next morning, so wouldn't be staying long, I had as much work for the weekend as I had willpower around narcotics. However, in the early hours, there were only a couple of us left, and it was a good vibe. I said that I would blow off work and get some more Charlie if we could get hold of some MDMA for the rest of the weekend. I was assured that we could, so I ordered up some Charlie, picked up some beer and we continued to get on it. Around seven in the morning, I made a big show of pretending to email work to say that I wouldn't be in for the weekend, then settled in for the ride.

Around midday, after another delivery of cocaine, the search for Mandy began. It was sorted very easily this time. By this time, a couple of others had turned up. I knew them both, and one, I shall call him Ratboy, was really greedy around drugs, but a real lightweight. By early evening, we were all well on our way, and I decided that we should get more provisions for the night early so that we could tuck ourselves away from the outside world.

Ratboy was also a lazy cunt so wouldn't go with us. It took about 15 minutes to walk to the dealer's and the offy and get back. Ratboy had found the MDMA that we had stashed in the kitchen and done quite a bit. He was fucked. He wasn't going to come down for a while!

It was a warm summer's evening, and the best place to stay cool was to sit just in front of him. His fucking jaw was swinging so much that he was causing quite a breeze! Within a couple of hours, he would have a conversation with a wall, lie down in the empty bath, gibbing out, go on to piss himself and spend the next 15 hours or so curled up in the bedroom not knowing what the fuck was going on, paranoid to fuck. Fucking little cunt deserved it.

It turned out to be a great night without Ratboy. I fucking loved Mandy, and it was a cracking group of us that night. We had a brilliant time and just slowly monged out the next morning. Around lunchtime, I was ready to go again.

I fancied a couple of pints. Always a good way to bridge the gap between two sessions. Two of us headed off to catch the train to Bromley. When we got to Bromley, I headed straight past the pub towards my house. "Where are you going?" he asked.

"Trust me," I said. We got back to mine, and I dug out an untouched gram of Charlie. I had stashed it there on Friday night, not expecting to be out so long. We both did a big hooner and took the short walk in the sunshine back to the pub.

Of all the boys I had met in my hedonistic pursuits, he was the one that I really got on with. I think that he actually wanted to change, and I would encourage him. I couldn't encourage myself, but I knew that out of all of them, he wasn't a lost cause. We talked a lot and proceeded to have a really nice day on the piss, quite relaxed, and I sent him home with the rest of the Charlie, minus a line. I had my own plans, of course. Back to Steve's sordid night-time activities.

One morning, I woke up for work and my phone was blocked. In all honesty, I had had some Charlie and was looking at some less than savoury material the night before, but nothing approaching illegal. There was a warning from Cheshire Police that my phone had been used for illegal purposes, possibly to do with fraud, sending bulk spam and indecent material that may or may not feature minors.

Well, I shit myself. I sent the office an email from my laptop saying that I would not be able to be contacted, but that I was going in. On the journey, I was back in Boreham Wood, so I had plenty of time. I read the message over and over again. It said that if I paid £100, all of the charges would be dropped; if not, I could face a fine of £20,000 or twenty years' imprisonment. The fuzzy state that my head was in, I started to fret. Had I stumbled across something that I shouldn't have?

As the day drew on, I could focus on very little else, but as my head cleared, I became more and more certain that it was a hoax. After work, I went to see my brother-in-law and, after a short investigation, he discovered that it was some ransomware and could be fixed very simply. Disaster averted.

Not long after this, I was on my way home from Boreham Wood when one of my new 'friends' called to let me know that his dog had died. I agreed to meet him for a pint when I was back in Bromley. There were a couple of others there, and a session started to ensue. He actually left quite early, but the rest of us tucked in.

Towards the end of the night, there were just two of us left. There was an older woman that he knew, and we sat and had a drink with her. When the pub closed, the three of us made our way back to mine with some takeouts. I made my usual phone call and soon had a nice big bit of Charlie.

At some point, I popped out for a cigarette, and when I came back in, they were under my duvet. I think I was being very naive, but I definitely hadn't expected this. Well, if you can't beat them, etc., etc. What followed was something so far from being erotic. I just have no words.

When the time came, I had to send an email to work, something about a dodgy kebab. We all messed about for a bit longer, and then the romantic mood was ruined when she was sick in my bin. Well, that was it. The three of us in one bed, trying to get some sleep. Mid-morning, I gave up and went to the pub. I stayed out for a couple of hours and showered when I came home and then rallied the troops. When we left, she nearly went without her false teeth. Not the sort of girl that you would take home to Mummy.

Now, I know that the boy in this story seems like a catch, but the truth is actually very different. I learnt at a fairly young age that, if you hang around drinking establishments enough, something happens occasionally. Very occasionally in the main.

Anyway, this was the second and, to date, the last time that I had sex with a woman while in my 30s. I never came close to shooting my bolt either time and, to be honest, I'm not entirely sure that I ever have come through sex. I certainly can't remember a time, and it is a fairly short history. It also occurs to me that the combined ages of my two lovers would now be well in excess of one hundred years old!

My mate and I managed to shake off our tail and decided to go for a couple of pints. I emailed my boss and said that I would work over the weekend to make up for today, but he said not to worry, there was no time pressure at the moment and next week would be fine.

After a couple of hours in the pub, I made my excuses and shook off my tail. It was time to get a load of Charlie and redress the balance from last night myself! I eventually got my head down sometime on Sunday morning and got myself ready for work on Monday. Fucking got away with it again!

Work had become a bit more consistent at this time, and on the whole, I was more reliable. I was still drinking far more than I should and taking every opportunity to have a sniff whenever I could. I needed this. My mental health was absolutely destroyed. I hadn't even tried to address any of the issues that led me to this. If I stopped using and lived in the real world, I wouldn't be able to cope. I knew this.

One week, I didn't make it in on a Wednesday. I can't remember what the circumstances were, no doubt drink and drugs played a part, couple this with debilitating anxiety, and you have a bad combination.

That evening, my boss actually knocked at my door. He was so patient and kind to me. He would be along in the morning to pick me up and we would travel to the job together, and he would spend the day helping me. It was only a few bits of snagging, nothing that I couldn't handle. I got my head down early, feeling good, in preparation for the next day. I couldn't believe how fortunate I was.

I woke up long before my alarm, avoiding my first real banana skin. I lay there waiting for my alarm to go. I was in pretty good spirits. But my alarm didn't ring. Had I fucked up? I was too anxious to check the time. I couldn't believe that I had done this again! I took the battery out of my phone. There would be no alarm this morning. Now just to wait.

It was a long time until I heard his car pull up outside, and I just had to lie there, waiting. It felt as though my heart was trying to batter its way out of my ribcage. I was sweating buckets and shaking uncontrollably. I had no control over my breathing and I am sure that if he got out of his car, he would have heard me. The game would be up. I wanted to be anywhere but here. I wanted to be dead!

Eventually, the car drove away. I had survived. Survived what? What was there to be afraid of? I was sure that I had burnt this bridge once and for all. For what? Because I couldn't summon the courage to check the time? It clearly wasn't late. Why couldn't I just have got out of bed, had a shower and a cuppa, waiting for him to turn up? I was never going to find another job where people were going to be so patient and understanding with me. What hope was there for me now?

Chapter 24

You Can't Help a Terminal Case

My sister very patiently read me the riot act. I couldn't keep doing this. It's time to get help, or had I just given up? With her persuasion, I registered with a doctor and made an appointment. A fortnight's wait.

They welcomed me around to theirs as often as I want. I was in limbo. I wasn't sure whether I wanted to get better or not. I was certainly not sure that I could get better. I split my time between them and my own private cage. Captivity might be a better option than a free life. Left to my own devices, I only seemed to spread discord and hurt.

It came time to go to the doctor and my sister came to meet me and walked with me there. She came into the consulting room and gently nudged me to disclose everything. I managed to keep my drug use a secret still. There was no referral that he could offer me, but he gave me the name of a charitable organisation that might be able to help, Working for Wellbeing. It was a self-referral service, so I would need to do this myself. I refused anti-depressants for what seemed like the hundredth time. *I'm not fucking weak!*

My sister, unaware of the volume that I was drinking, took me for a pint and a chat afterwards. It's only a couple to help me gather my thoughts, and I was back to theirs for dinner. I felt the slightest bit better. There might just be a way out of this. I was far from convinced, but there might be.

I registered with Working for Wellbeing online and awaited a response. Within a week, I received a letter giving me the date and time for a telephone assessment. If this didn't suit me, then I should let them know because I could be fined £99 if I missed the appointment. That helped me put my anxiety to one side!

I spend the night before my appointment at my sister's. This was a much more relaxed place for me, and I was actually up at a decent time, ready to take my call. I spoke to a nice lady who wanted to know all about my history and how I was feeling currently. At one point, she said, "Are you your own biggest critic?"

"I fucking well hope so!" I replied.

"Why?"

"Because, if I'm not, then there is someone out there who really doesn't think very much of me!" They said I would receive a letter shortly with details of a six-week course of group Cognitive Behavioural Therapy, due to start in the new year. I was to reply in order to enrol on the course, and once I had been accepted, I had to attend all six weeks. Failure to do so could result in a £99 fine. Well, that put me at ease. I could feel my heart rate dropping. Fuck me!

Christmas was spent with my parents in Swansea, trying to remain positive about the new year. Due to my excesses of the previous year, I hadn't paid December's rent. This should be another worry, but all my anxiety seemed to come from the shit that I created in my head. The real things didn't seem to affect me. My shields were up, and nothing of any real consequence could harm me. I didn't have any time for true concerns. My reality, however destructive to my mental health, needed to remain what I invented. If I allowed any actual problems to fester, then I had no chance.

Shortly before I left, my father asked if I needed help with my rent and any more money on top. I said that that would be useful, and I left to catch my train, knowing that I would have a decent amount of money in my account when I got to London. It didn't take much of my journey for me to convince myself that, as I was already a month in arrears, there was no way out. I knew very quickly that when I got home, I would be getting very drunk, and then very high, very quickly.

Sure enough, I had a couple of pints at Victoria Station. I was now not responsible for the way that the evening was going to pan out. I had no control whatsoever over events yet to unfold. I rushed home to drop my bag off and was out of the door even quicker. Straight to the pub. Solo drinking, my favourite.

I ended up talking to a couple of the boys, but for once, I managed to make my excuses and left. Where I was going tonight, there was no room for any passengers. A load of beer and a load of chop. I was winning at life, that was for sure.

Forty-eight hours later, and I was still going. The nights had been filled with Charlie and wanking, still no luck with my online pursuits, the days with drinking. Just me and a magazine. Staying away from the town centre, drinking in small local pubs to avoid detection. I didn't need company. I only stopped because I had my first CBT session the next day.

I woke up late in the morning, and straight away, the anxiety spiked. They were going to know what I had been doing. They were going to say that it was all my fault. I was going to be held to account, publicly, for the way that I had chosen to handle life. *I know, I won't go. They'll fucking fine me. What the fuck do I do?* I thought. I knew that a pint would solve everything. It would calm me down and allow me to make a wise, considered decision. I resisted, walking past several regular haunts to get to the venue.

Inside, I started sweating profusely. We were asked to fill out registration forms. I could hardly hold the clipboard or pen. This was pure anxiety. Trust me, I know the difference between terror and DTs. The meeting passed in a blur. I was not particularly receptive to anything that I heard, and I left, feeling no better, or worse, than when I walked in. I needed a fucking pint. I headed to the sports bar, hid away with a pint, and so on and so forth. You know the score.

I continued to attend the sessions, paying only perfunctory attention, and none to any of the homework tasks that were set. However, some of it did sink in. Scheduling is something that I have used many times since. No matter how small a task, I always try to have something in the diary just so that I have a reason to keep going. Something to look forward to. I think that this actually saved my life earlier this year. I attended the first four sessions but missed the fifth, I can't remember exactly why. I daren't go back for the last one, just in case they fine me!

My birthday was coming up at the end of the month, and my brother was going to take me to watch Charlton play Blackburn Rovers. Unfortunately, this had started to become outside of my comfort zone. I knew that the hard part was getting out and on the train. Once I was on that train, I was unlikely to bump into anybody that I knew, and once I was up at Victoria Station, I would have a drink and be on my way. To get over the initial anxiety, I did have a four-pack on the train. I met my brother, and we were on our fucking way.

We got to Charlton early doors, and I was feeling great. We met up with my best mate, and he had sorted out tickets to one of the lounges. We had a fairly civilised ten pints or so before the game, and the atmosphere was lively with some bite to it.

There were protests going on about the cunt that owned the club. We got a point and congregated outside the West Stand as part of a huge crowd for a protest. There was real anger. Our club was being torn apart by this prick and his fucking useless puppets. It was not a nice thing to have to do, but the sense of togetherness with the fans was amazing. "We want our Charlton back!" rang out. I was alive again. I had my Charlton back. Somehow, I needed to find a way to do this more often.

After the protest started to die down, we headed off to one of the local pubs and really got down to business. We got talking to a bunch of German Charlton fans who travelled regularly from Gelsenkirchen, where they supported Schalke. The rest of the night is a bit of a blur.

At some point, we parted ways with my mate, and we went back to my brother's neck of the woods to sort out some Charlie. I have no recognition of being in his local, but apparently, I was. I had visited there a few times, so I knew some people. Once he had sorted out the evening's entertainment, he ordered a cab to take us back to mine, picking up beer on the way. Fuck knows what that cost him. We didn't live just around the corner from each other.

Back at mine, we got stuck into the drink and drugs. His phone was switched off so that his missus couldn't make contact. Of course, she tried my phone. I surreptitiously sent her a text just to let her know that he was at mine and safe. Well, that was it. All sorts of shit was coming through my phone, so I turned it off. My brother had said that he had a free pass and, having got to know her a bit, I believed him above her.

My brother left around Sunday lunchtime. He left me with a little money and headed off to face his fate. Including the money he had left me and the bullseye that I had left from the football; I had a decent little nest egg now. I had a good couple of lines of credit, so I didn't have to worry about drug money.

A quick shower, and I was out for the afternoon. Just me and a succession of pints. I knew as soon as I fancied it, I could tick some of the lovely old nosebag and carry on at home. Not having to pay for my drugs, I was able to make this money work for me. I sorted myself out a nice little two dayer. I wouldn't have to worry about what I owed for Charlie for a couple of weeks.

My father called while I was in bed one day. We had a good catch up. I told him all about the football but little else, and he offered to send me money for my rent again. Thank you very much. No sooner had it hit my account, and I was out for a couple of pints.

I sorted out my debts, rent excluded, and I was back to the business of getting fucked. I had two modes when I was at home now. Complete and utter fucking nervous wreck or mash-head who didn't give a fuck. I know which one worked better for me. When I wasn't high as a fucking kite, I was curled up in bed for days on end with my hand on a Stanley knife that I had started keeping under my pillow. I would never use it on anybody, but if there was a knock on my door, I was sure as hell going to butcher something. My wrists or my throat? Dealer's choice!

After this money ran out, I took on the life of a rock. I just lay for indeterminate periods of time on my bed. My only food over one week was the remains of a tub of Flora. Eventually, it got too much, and I was back at Cash Generators with my TV and a couple of other bits. I didn't even bother with a buyback this time. I was never coming back for them. Straight from there to the pub, via a newsagent for some fags.

I stayed put all day and only moved when my money ran out. I jumped on a bus home, but for some reason got off halfway. I had a pound in my pocket and bought a scratch card. This was it. All or nothing. Nothing as it turned out.

I walked aimlessly in the dark, and before long, I found myself at a familiar place. I was back at one of the railway bridges I used to visit when I was younger. Twenty-five odd years on, and nothing had changed. Actually, everything had changed. I had exhausted all of my options. I saw the lights on a train approaching and thought about it. Not today, but soon.

I moved off and walked the three or four miles home. I knew it would have to happen sometime. I didn't know when, and I had no idea how, but I knew that it had to happen. Not just for my sake but for everybody else's! I was toxic, a cancer that had to be destroyed before it destroyed everything else.

Incredibly, the phone would still ring occasionally with the offer of work. One morning, I had a job to do by myself. I had visited this company plenty of times and the work was really simple, so there should be no trepidation. I woke up early and decided to get out of bed, shower and have a cup of tea rather than waiting in bed for my alarm to go off. That hadn't worked for me previously. I nicked myself while shaving, but it wasn't a big deal.

I had plenty of time to spare, and it would be hardly noticeable once it had stopped bleeding. But it wouldn't stop bleeding. I began to panic. I couldn't go in looking like this. I was a fucking mess! I was going to let everybody down, again! I started to hyperventilate and sat on the edge of my bed with my head between my legs for what seemed like a long time. I might just have been waiting for the time to pass until I was late and had an excuse not to go to work.

I started to calm down and managed to compose myself and eventually looked at the time. *I can still make my train with time to spare. I can't travel in this state*, I thought. From somewhere, I summoned up some perpetually absent strength and managed to gather my tools and walk out of the door.

Once outside, it seemed as if a weight had been lifted. I was out of the confines of my room, my own private jail, and I knew that I had made an important decision. I was going to work. I was going to fight. Such a simple thing to do. Why had I never been able to do this before?

Work went well, and I would go back to finish up on Monday. This started a period of settled work. It may have been a few days; it may have been more than a couple of weeks. This cycle repeated itself with such frequency that I struggle to remember how long each lasted, but I do remember that this was the start of a more positive period. Inevitably, it would come to an end.

Again, I can't remember how, but it was either my anxiety that caused me to miss work, followed by a fucking massive binge, or it was a binge that led to anxiety and despondency, crippling me and therefore missing work. It was always one of these two. Eventually, the offers of work ceased.

Without work, I had no respite. I spent my days curled up in a ball, battling with my thoughts or, when I had some money, getting drunk and then high. I had earned my rent money for a couple of months, although I never paid it. I knew that I was going to be evicted at some point, so what was the fucking point? Beer and cocaine were much more useful to me. I started receiving letters that I knew were about rent arrears and court proceedings to have me evicted. These remained unopened.

One Sunday, I was lying motionless in bed when my phone rang. It was my brother. He had had a row with his missus and was staying in a hotel that night. He asked if I wanted to join him for a couple of pints. He put some money into my account, and I said that I would call him when I was on my way to where he was.

Getting ready shouldn't have been a problem, but everything is tricky when you are trying to conceal your very existence from everybody. I hadn't shaved for days, so, in order not to be detected, I plugged my clippers in and 'shaved' by touch under my duvet. I jumped through the shower in no time flat and was out of the door.

The buses to my brother's location an only once an hour on a Sunday, and I decided to let one go so that I could have a drink on my own. How selfish was that? My brother needed me to be there with him. He was going to treat me to everything, and yet, I still felt the need to spend some of the money he had given me on myself.

I eventually met up with him and he had already picked up some drugs. We went up to his hotel room, had a big boot, and went and found a pub to drink in. We had a good chat and didn't drink too much. After closing, we went back to his room and got right on it. The following day, reality hit him a bit.

After checking out, we wanted to find somewhere to drink, but we were in a small village and nowhere was open yet. We wandered around a bit, and he was despairing about what he should do. I couldn't offer any advice. I couldn't look after myself. I put up mock protestations about going to the pub when it opened, knowing that it was going to happen anyway, and that I was on a free ride.

We spent the whole day in the pub. From eleven in the morning until the football had finished at about ten. We actually had a really good day out, with lots of laughter, helping each other to cope with our various problems. Not to cope really but to avoid the consequences and reality of our actions. Our predicaments could wait for now.

He hadn't had any luck scoring Charlie, so I made a couple of calls and arranged to have some delivered to my house. We jumped in a cab, picked up a crate of lager and hot-footed it to mine. We didn't want the main course to get cold. We arrived home, and after ten minutes, we had everything that we needed. He had kept in contact with his partner, and she just seemed to want to argue, no matter how much he asked for a bit of space and time. The phones went off and we numbed ourselves the best way that we knew how.

This was Monday night, and he stayed at my place until Wednesday lunchtime. Neither of us ate the whole time that we were together and basically spent the time from early Tuesday morning until he left topping and tailing in my bed. Not the most comfortable. He left me with a couple of quid and went on his way to try and salvage his relationship. I was due at my sister's for some reason, and I travelled there, stopping in a pub for a couple of hours to empty my pockets.

I started to avoid home. I would go into town and drink or, if skint, sit in the library. Once the library closed, I would walk aimlessly until the barriers at the railway stations were opened, and then I would sit on various trains, just heading nowhere.

Wherever the last train that I got on was going, that was where I ended up.

Sometimes, I would have to walk for hours to get home. This suited me; home was no refuge anymore.

I was invited to spend the weekend at my sister's on the weekend of my brother-in-law's birthday. I can't remember what we did on Saturday, but I know that we had a nice civilised drink in the evening. They went to bed, and straight away, my mind turned to chang.

I got in touch with someone, and he could sort me out, but I would have to travel. No tick tonight, so I stole money out of both my sister and her husbands' wallets, hopped the side gate and jumped on a bus. It was about half an hour each way, but I got back in the wee small hours undetected and with my precious cargo.

On Sunday, his parents were coming around for a roast dinner after church. I was to walk my sister's dog while they were out at church. I only finished sniffing about an hour before they were due back. I chucked myself through the shower and took Daisy, the dog, for a short walk.

When they got back, I was sure that they had very quickly sussed that I had stolen money and was on edge the whole time. His parents turned up, and I became aware that my jaw was swinging. Did they notice? Did they know why even if they did notice? I couldn't wait until I got home.

His parents dropped me off on their way home, and I locked my bedroom door. I stripped to the waist and retrieved my Stanley knife from under my pillow. I looked at myself in the mirror and was disgusted at everything that I saw.

I was emaciated, I was weak, I was totally without any sense of decency or loyalty. I held the blade up to my throat. I looked into my own eyes. Nothing, totally fucking dead and unfeeling. *Fucking do it, Cunt!* I screamed at myself in my head. Over and over until I dropped my hand, knowing that I didn't care enough to kill myself anymore. For good measure, I stabbed myself in the stomach once, barely a flesh wound, more a token gesture against my own cowardice, and retired to bed. I honestly thought that I had gone over 12 years without self-harming. I had forgotten this isolated incident.

One week, my sister and her husband went away. I still had a key for their house and let myself in for the week. It was one of my new friend's birthdays on Wednesday, and as luck would have it, it was just after my father had sent me through money for my rent. Yeah, we were back to that again. I agreed to meet a couple of the boys and we had a couple of pints, on me, of course. I invited them back to my sister's house, and we got on it big style.

They were still there at lunchtime the next day when I managed to get them to leave. I was going to my brother's for a couple of days, and I arranged for him to pick me up from my sister's house. I decided to get another gram in for the afternoon, and not long after it had arrived, I heard the front door open. *Who the fuck is this?*

It was my sister's mother-in-law. She had come round to check the house and sort out the post. Word got back to my sister, and she was not happy that I had used their house without asking, rightly so. My brother picked me up and we no doubt had a good weekend of drinking and sniffing. I can't remember, everything became so mundane to me at this time.

One day, I had popped out for a couple of quiet pints and stumbled upon some of the boys. I was most probably hiding in plain sight, subconsciously seeking them out. We ended up back at the flat, and the next day, a few of us went out for a drink somewhere different.

After an afternoon on the beer and the Charlie, we decided to head back to mine to carry on. More Charlie was ordered, and I agreed to share half of the burden on some that we ticked. I had no intention of paying for it. I had spent shitloads on those twats, and the dealer we owed didn't know who I was. Besides, they all owed me money.

They stayed all night, and I got rid of them on the first train. We had been up all night drinking and sniffing and smoking in my room. This was something that was not allowed. Shortly after they left, my South African housemate got up and, although he didn't confront me directly, made it very clear that I had pissed him off. He would move out shortly after.

I would spend the day foetal, with my heart racing, hyperventilating with my hand on the Stanley knife that was still under my pillow, drawing the blade in and out, trying to pluck up the courage to do something to myself. I never did, and I ended up staying in exactly the same position for about 14 hours, before dragging myself out of bed and running straight for a bus to escape to my sister's, where I stayed the night.

I would bump into the boy who I owed money to a couple of weeks later, and he threatened to batter me. I didn't give a fuck. I had absolutely no sense of self-preservation by now, plus I had a huge amount of internalised anger. I didn't know what would happen when or if that all came out. I gave him some bullshit, told him that he wouldn't be getting any money out of me as he still owed me more and just walked away.

A couple of weeks later, he turned up at a flat I was having a sniff in. He said that he admired the bottle I had, we shook hands, wiped our mouths and carried on as if nothing had happened.

On the bank holiday at the beginning of May, the three of us, my sister, brother-in-law and I, went to watch Bromley play Forest Green Rovers. I was always on edge at this stage, and here was no different. I was out of my room at least, but I knew that I would have to return after the game, as my brother was picking me up to stay with him for a couple of days. My sister gave me money to go and get some refreshments, and I pocketed the change without asking her.

I hated being around my house during daylight hours. Being anywhere near it filled me with such dread that I would try and find all sorts of roundabout ways to get there without being seen. One time, I even tried to hop the fences of several back gardens to end up in my back garden, getting startled in the first one that I came to, turning tail and scarpering. I don't know who I was avoiding, the only person that was chasing me for money was my landlord and, deep down, I knew that he would use the appropriate channels. Don't get me wrong, I owed money all over the place, but only to good people at this point.

After the match, I went home, chucked a couple of bits into a bag and was out of the door in probably under two minutes. I went to a pub slightly out of the way and did my usual trick of trying to blend in with the wallpaper. I didn't need to seek anybody out today; my brother would provide me with Charlie.

My money ran out and my brother was still going to be about an hour. It was pissing down, and rather than go home, I walked the streets for a while, and then, I waited on the platform of a local railway station. Eventually, my brother came and the usual ensued.

My sister and her husband were to go away again towards the end of the football season, and they gave me permission to watch Charlton's last match at their house, as it was being shown on Sky the day that they departed. I let myself in and had a couple of quid for some beer and cigarettes.

After the Charlton game ended, I knew that I needed some cocaine, so I called up one of my dealers, and he was happy to tick me a couple of grams on the never-never. I stocked up on supplies of beer and fags and settled in for the day/night.

I decided to stay for the week. I kept in touch with my sister and knew the days on which her in-laws were due to come around. On those days, I would get out of bed when I woke and just lie under it until they had been and gone. Hours confined to a space in which I could hardly move, and in which I was extremely uncomfortable. My world was closing in on me, and it wouldn't be long now. I couldn't even relax here now. I had no safe haven anywhere. Certainly, not anywhere alive.

On Saturday, I kept in touch with my sister to see how their journey was going and left when they were still over an hour away. I left them with an empty freezer, and I raided their change jar in order to get ten fags. I had some money on my Oyster card, so I jumped on a bus and stayed on until it terminated. I stepped off in Lewisham with no money and no idea where I was going or how I was going to get there. I walked around the shops and started the long walk back towards mine.

After a couple of hours, it had started to get dark, and I found myself approaching 'home'. It was still early and I didn't like being in before one in the morning, just in case anyone was still up. I sat on a railway bridge near my house. *Plenty of trains, is this the time?*

I actively filled my heads with negative thoughts. *You fucking waste of space! You parasite! Nobody has benefited from knowing you! Everybody's lives will be better once you're gone!* As hard as I tried, I couldn't get to that point. *Nope, not today, but soon.*

I snuck into a local park and curled up by one of the pavilions, trying to get to sleep. I knew that it would be one day soon, maybe tomorrow. I just needed to get through to that day. It sounds so fucked up typing that. I needed to survive until the day when I could end my life.

After a couple of hours, the side that I had been lying on was in severe pain. Partly numb and partly frozen. This was May. How could I be so cold? I got up and made my way home, sneaking back into my room.

I couldn't move from that room now. I stayed in there with the door locked and a screwdriver jammed under it. I would only leave my room once a day, sometime in the early hours, to empty my bin that I had taken to pissing in so I didn't have to run the gauntlet of bumping into anybody. I would also see what food had been left in the kitchen.

The bloke who had replaced the Spanish girl was a scruffy bastard, yeah, I know, and left shit all over the work surfaces. He had some cheese that was going off, and I would cut a little bit off each day. There were a couple of mouldy crusts for a treat for the first couple of days; after that, I was left with any crumbs or spillage.

I can't remember whether it was the following week or the one after, but one day, a Wednesday, I found out later, I heard voices outside my window. Time had ceased to be a concept I was aware of. My only perception of it was that it was passing around me, and that my time was dwindling. Every day that passed was one nearer the grave.

Another day nearer the peace that I craved with every fibre of my being.

Soon the inevitable knock at the door came. I had been waiting so long for this. I was being evicted. I was allowed to pack some essentials and I was out with a note for the Housing Department. Was this my rock bottom? Was this finally going to shock me into action? Nope.

As I walked into Bromley, bag over my shoulder, I tried to gather my thoughts.

I had none. I felt the sum total of fuck all. I got to the gardens by the library and called my father. He was out, I was told, and wouldn't be around until lunchtime. I decided to sit in the library.

After reading a book about something or other, the morning had passed and I left and got on the phone to my father. I said that my phone bill had bounced, something to do with bank charges again, and asked if he could put £100 in my account to cover that and allow me to get some food.

Good as his word, the money was there lickety-split, and I picked up some cigarettes and headed to the pub. A different pub than any of the multitude that I usually frequented. I needed to be alone with my thoughts. I knew that after a few pints, I would come up with a solution. It may seem weird, but this felt like the most positive that I had been for months. I was homeless, but I had escaped my prison.

I was due round my sister's on Sunday for dinner. My brother and his partner were going to be there. I just had to make it until Sunday. I know that I could have called either my brother or sister and sorted out a bed, but this was something I had to do myself. This was my penance.

I formulated a plan. My sister and her husband were out at a house group on a Wednesday, so I just had to wait until they were out before going there and stashing my bag. I would work it out from there. I stayed in the pub until about seven and jumped on a bus. I turned up, and their car wasn't in the drive. I had timed this well.

As I put my key in the lock, I heard my sister from behind me. They had seen me as they were leaving, and they wanted to know what I was doing there with a big bag. I said that my washing machine was broken and I needed to use theirs. They didn't buy it, but they left me to it.

I went in and had a quick shower.

What to do? What to do?

Logically, the answer was to stay put and explain what had happened when they got home. When does logic ever come into decision making? I spied my brother-in-law's wallet. There was a nice bit of money in there and his bank card. I emptied it and popped across the road to the offy with his card. Unfortunately, they didn't have contactless technology, so I had to dip into my precious reserves. I jumped on a train and went to visit a place I knew well. A place where I could go to forget.

I had dressed in my work clothes to try and portray that I was still an upstanding member of society. Things couldn't have been further from the truth. The only person who was there was the boy whose flat it was. We had fallen out about money earlier in the year, but we genuinely got on well together when it was just the two of us. I gave him the money that I had and just asked what we could get for that? It was never mentioned, but I knew that heroin was an option. I really thought about broaching the subject. Something stopped me, so we got a load of Charlie and some crack. This was to be my only experience of smoking crack, and, to be honest, I wasn't overly impressed. It wasn't that I felt it was below my station, look at the way I was living, but I just preferred a sniff.

I stayed there for about 24 hours. We chilled for most of Thursday, and one of his mates came around and we shared a couple of spliffs. Very pleasant. I started to get itchy feet during the evening and made some excuse about work in the morning and got on one of the last trains.

I could have stayed there as long as I liked, I don't know why I decided to leave, but I did. I ended up back close to where I had lived until recently. I had no idea where I was going. I ended up back in the park and settled on a bench. This was slightly more comfortable, and at least, I was off the freezing concrete.

I must have fallen asleep for a little while, but my jumper and T-shirt had become untucked, and I was awoken by an icy blast up my back in the breaking dawn light. This was May, and I was fucking freezing. How anybody can survive on the streets during winter, I will never know. My heart goes out to them. Nobody would do it by choice.

I sat there huddled up for a while, and then I heard the park gates being unlocked. People started to pass me. Early morning joggers and dog walkers. Having a dog, I understand, but jogging? For fun? Nah! I headed into Bromley; it was still several hours until the library opened.

I checked my bank account. There were a few pence in there. I popped to a supermarket, and I managed to buy a packet of custard creams and one of bourbons. *This will be my sustenance for the next two and a half days. Don't eat them all at once, you wouldn't want to make yourself uncomfortable!* I thought.

I sat on various different park benches, waiting for the library to open. I was torn between sitting still, trying to stave off the cold, and walking around to keep warm, using up what little energy I had, struggling to pick up my feet properly after short distances. Eventually, the library opened and I picked up several books, fuck knows what on, and found a chair tucked in the corner to take the weight off.

I spent the whole day in the warm, reading. I studied every word of the text, taking nothing in, but averting my mind from what was to come. I left at closing time with no plans. It had warmed up now and my big parka was not necessary. I just picked a direction and started heading that way. Walking for a while, finding a bench to sit on for a while and to savour a biscuit or two. Where am I going to sleep tonight? Looking back on my adventures over these three days, I walked fucking miles.

Once it got dark, I settled on a park not far from my sister's where there were a couple of benches in the middle of a large open space. I followed the path to these benches and was pleasantly surprised how remote it seemed. It was close to pitch dark, and I was fairly sure that I wouldn't be found. I settled down with everything tucked in and tried to get some sleep.

I was absolutely exhausted and must have fallen asleep quite soon. I say that because I woke up at some point to the sound of voices. People were making their way home from the pubs. *Shit, please don't come any closer.* As long as they stayed on the periphery of the park, I would be OK. Then I heard voices approaching. My heart started to race. The voices passed right by me and slowly receded into the distance. I couldn't get back on top of my anxiety and lay there motionless for hours, waiting for the sun to come up, being intermittently disturbed by distant voices.

Once daylight came, I got myself together and headed towards Bromley Town Centre and the library. My phone battery had died, so I didn't have any clue of the time. I popped into Bromley South Station. It was 6:30. I had three hours until the library opened. I made my way to the gardens by the library and found a pagoda to curl up in after finishing my last couple of biscuits. This was obviously used by kids to congregate and smoke drugs, and I checked all of the empty cigarette boxes. There was one with three fags and a lighter in. Result! Today was going to be a good day! I just had to get to today.

Eventually, I decided that enough time must have elapsed, and I made the short walk to the library. The doors still weren't open, so I sat on one of the benches outside to wait. I smoked my last cigarette, and then, it dawned on me that these were the last things that I had to live for. My whole existence, after my biscuits were gone was those three cigarettes that I had found. Now they were gone and I had nothing.

I spent the day in the library, getting funny looks and wrinkled noses from anybody who ventured too close. I must have fucking reeked. With a few days' growth on my face, grubby clothes and stinking to high heaven, I was a fucking tramp. How had it come to this? What had caused this once bright, young lad to plumb such depths? The answer was clear. I had. Everything that I had become was the result of decisions that I had made. I had chosen this path, and I was the only person to blame. I had lost all sense of pride and shame. *Today? Maybe.*

After the library, it was back to that long, endless road to nowhere. Walking for a bit, watching the ground in front of my feet, looking for cigarette butts of a half-decent length. Anything that might partly fill my lungs. *You're halfway there. Just one more night, and you can start to put things right.* How many times had I told myself this? Even I didn't believe it anymore.

After a few miles, I came across a picnic bench in a secluded spot. I sat, folded my arms on the table and rested my head, finding some semblance of comfort. I thought that this would be a wonderful way to drift away. The world would carry on spinning, and I could just cease to exist within it. This was never going to be the case.

I don't know how long I sat there drifting in and out of sleep.

I lifted my head at some point and it had got dark around me. Should I just stay here all night? I put my head back down and waited for the sun to rise. It wasn't long before voices began sounding around me. I just stayed there in my defenceless position, trying to remain invisible. I felt a tap on the shoulder. "Are you OK?"

"Yeah, cheers, mate," I replied. I knew now that I had to move on.

It dawned on me that I wasn't very far from my childhood haunts. My railway bridges. I made my way to the most remote one and stood there for a while. I had no idea of the time, but I knew that there wouldn't be many more trains that night. *Stop fucking pussyfooting around and get down there before you bottle it again.*

I walked along the footpath beside the railway lines for a bit and then hopped the fence. I made my way down the embankment, making sure of my footing with every step. Bonkers, I know. I was going to jump under a train, but I didn't want to twist my ankle!

I found a place in the bushes where I was hidden from view. It was a nice long stretch, so I would see any train coming from a long way away. There were four lines here. I wouldn't have to wait long. My resolve never wavered. I just needed to hear that buzz of the rails or see a distant light approaching. I had no concept of time now, but I knew that, if I just waited, sooner or later, my train would arrive and deliver me to my final destination. That train never came. I had bought my ticket, but I never got to my final destination.

After a while, it became clear that I was out of luck. I made my way back up the embankment to the fence, dragged myself over and made my way back to where I had come from. Not today!

I found a bench hidden in a little fenced-off area in Petts Wood and tried to get my head down. I knew now that I was going to continue to live for a little while longer. I just had to make it through the night again. Very recently, I had been totally committed to killing myself, and yet now I was concerned with surviving for the next few hours.

I lay there for a little while and then got restless, so I set off towards tomorrow lunchtime. Using a large, circuitous route, I ended up in the park where I had spent the previous night and went and settled on the same bench as I had called home only one long day ago. It didn't feel like long before the sun came up. I needed to see what the time was. I set off, and there was a church not far away with a clock tower. I had about four and a half hours to wait until my sister went out to church and I could let myself in.

I walked around the block a couple of times and made my way back to my bench for some rest. I repeated this exercise, partly to pass the time, partly to keep track of the time. Eventually, it was time, and I set off on the short walk to my sister's and salvation.

I opened the door and was welcomed enthusiastically by Daisy. The first thing I needed was a drink. One, two, three pints of beautiful cool water. When had I last had a drink? I had no idea. Over 48 hours probably. After spending a little time with Daisy, I was up for a shower, shave and to get dressed, making myself as presentable as possible.

I took Daisy for a walk and we ended back at my hotel for the last couple of days. It was much more inviting in the daylight. I got back to my sister's and waited for them to arrive back from church. When they did, we sat down with a cup of tea and had a chat. I explained about my eviction, they had guessed as much, and they said that I was welcome to stay with them for a little while. I had to call my Dad to let him know what had happened. That call went better than I had imagined.

We had a lovely afternoon with my brother and his partner, enjoying a barbecue and some nice cool beers in the sunshine, and then relaxing indoors after the heat of the day went. I was safe for the time being. Or I would be once I had picked my stuff up from my old place the following evening. As exhausted as I was, I got very little sleep that night, worrying about returning to get my belongings. I was very tempted to just fuck them all off. I had very little of any worth. Everything with value had been sold.

My sister drove me round on that Monday evening to collect my worldly possessions, and I was in and out as quickly as possible. Absolutely petrified the whole time. Who was I frightened of? The only person who might do me any harm was my landlord, a big Hungarian fella, but he was just sitting in his Range Rover, waiting for us to finish. As we pulled away, I felt the panic subside. This was a bad chapter of my life that I was leaving behind. Another bad chapter!

We got home, and I unloaded my things, making their house very cluttered. I would sort that out in the morning. We all sat down and relaxed, and I went to bed quite early. I had the best night's sleep that I could remember. The sleep of the righteous, although I was very, very far from righteous. I was, however, safe for now. I had got away with it again. I knew that this could never happen again. I was out of chances.

Chapter 25

A Change of Scenery, Again

I settled in at my sister's quickly. They are a remarkable couple. So caring and compassionate. I had fucked them about something chronic, personally and professionally, and yet here they were, opening their home to me, again. They even went to the trouble of finding me little jobs to do around the house, paying me even after all of the money that I owed them and that I had stolen. They were only interested in repairing my sense of self-worth, and by allowing me to be able to buy my own cigarettes and the odd beer, they did just that.

I was willing to try anything, and they visited a church where they held events called the Prayer Rooms. Basically, you went there and people prayed for whatever ailed you. I didn't believe, but I went with an open mind.

When we got there, we were greeted by someone and were told to take a seat. Soon a man and a woman came over to us. I explained what I was feeling and my sister said that I desperately wanted the release that crying would bring, but that I was unable to. They both prayed over me, and then the woman asked, "Do you feel like crying yet?"

What the actual fuck?

I said, "I can't cry." Full stop. I certainly was not going to be able to do it in a fucking alien setting to order. I shook my head. More prayers.

"Do you feel like crying?"

No, I fucking don't! Prayer.

"Do you feel like crying?"

I feel like dying! I had said that I was suffering with anxiety, and yet I felt that an incredible pressure was being put on me. This went on and on.

"Do you feel like crying?"

I want to jump through that big, fuck off window!

"Do you feel like crying?"

I just want to fuck off, to anywhere, anywhere but here!

"Do you feel like crying?"

Fuck off! Fuck off! FUCK OFF! LET ME FUCKING GO HOME! I honestly began to think that I wouldn't be able to leave without crying. I knew that I wouldn't be able to cry, so I would be stuck here forever. Eventually, they relented and I was free to go.

I know that my sister and her husband have derived great comfort from that place, and I wasn't receptive, but I do feel that the people misjudged the situation and lacked understanding. I don't expect anybody to be able to understand how my mind works. It remains a mystery to me, and I don't blame anyone for not knowing how I feel, but the mention of anxiety should be a cue to relieve stress from a situation. People who are fulfilling pastoral roles should be aware of this. Asking someone with anxiety to do something that they themselves have said that they find difficult, or in my case, impossible, just exacerbates any feeling of unease. I was able to put this behind me, and the summer passed fairly uneventfully.

I arranged to visit my parents in early August, but first, I was to spend a week with my brother, dog-sitting for his partner while he worked. To earn a couple of quid, I was to do some interior painting in his partner's house. This sounded like the perfect idea.

Earn a couple of sovs to take to Swansea with me. By the time that I had got there, my remit was to paint the entirety of the house. No small feat in a fully furnished house with a highly strung, OCD bulldog. His partner didn't want to pay me for painting the bedrooms that were extra, but my brother managed to get me some concessions. It was still an absolute steal of a price.

My brother picked me up from my sister's on Friday night, and we headed off to his. The first night, just the boys, so the usual. These were nights that I treasured.

My brother and I really enjoyed each other's company now, and we would have a few pints then head back to his, picking up some cocaine, the proper stuff as well, and just chill indoors with Juddy, the British Bulldog. We both knew that we could handle our drink and drugs, and there was absolutely no tension between us anymore.

On that first Saturday, my brother got up and went to work while I got up to feed the dog and then went back to sleep on the sofa. I woke up at lunchtime and thought that I should get on with something. Time was of the essence. When my brother got back from work, we had a quick tidy up and then back out to the pub for a couple of pints. We left the pub at about five in the morning. Whoops.

We got back to my brother's and still had a nice bit of Charlie on us, and a relaxed Sunday came and went. A few beers while we came down, and then a roast dinner.

On Monday, he went to work as usual and I got on with the painting. A couple of beers after work and the same on the menu for tomorrow.

On Tuesday morning, I made the mistake of looking around the house at how much I had still to do. I became overwhelmed. I had my coach booked for Saturday, and I was never going to make it. I couldn't hold a brush, I had forgotten how to, and I just curled up on the floor of the bedroom that I was working in, shaking. I got a phone call from my brother saying that he was on his way home, having been rained off. I told him what had happened, and he told me to leave the painting and just sit down in front of the TV until he got home.

He returned and I was starting to get on top. He was brilliant to me. We popped out for a couple of pints, and then went back, and he helped me smash out a couple of rooms. Things are so much easier double-handed. After that, we went back out for a couple of more pints, and then it was coke o'clock.

The rest of the week went quite well. It was a big ask, and I changed my coach ticket to Sunday, as Saturday was going to be a long day in order to be finished. His partner wasn't happy; she was getting home early Sunday morning and said that she didn't want me there. I painted her house for next to nothing while looking after her dog, and this was the gratitude that I got. *You are more than fucking welcome!* I thought.

We got finished about seven o'clock Saturday evening and just chilled in the house with a couple of beers. Nothing major, my brother had to pick his partner up from Gatwick Airport at silly o'clock. I got up in the morning, and she had gone out. I packed, had a bite to eat, and then my brother ran me to the station. My train was due in a couple of minutes when she pulled up. She flung her arms around me.

"Steve, it looks great!"

Fuck off, you two-faced cunt!

I relaxed on my journey to Swansea, fitting in a couple of pints at Paddington. I was definitely on the mend. There was no pressure for this trip. It was fairly open-ended, and I hadn't made a decision to move to Swansea or to stay in Bromley. Limbo, my favourite place. Similar to the purgatory that my life becomes on a regular basis, but without the pressure of trying to achieve while swimming against the tide. Just, meh!

I had a few days reacquainting myself with my parents, Klint and the area. Klint and I would enjoy some lovely long walks along the beach and in the surrounding area. God, I loved that dog. During that first week, my neighbour, a sparky, found out that I was back and he needed a helping hand on a big job that he was doing. Fuck me! Back in work without trying. Lucky or what?

I worked with him for the next month and on and off for a while afterwards. He introduced me to a builder friend of his who was looking for a labourer for regular work. He was working on the same job as us, and he seemed like a good bloke. Easy going and full of praise with a wicked sense of humour. I felt good about this.

During this time, I started drinking locally again. The pub closest to my parents has always had a big draw for me, and I soon slipped back into old ways. After a few large sessions there, I came to the conclusion that I was going to fall into the same trap as before, so I made the decision to drink in town on my way home from work once I started my new job.

Chapter 26

Better Off Alone?

First, I was popping back to my brother's for a week to dog-sit and do a couple more jobs. This was a good time. My brother and I really enjoyed ourselves, chilling out in the evenings with a few beers and a few stripes. His partner had her flight cancelled due to strikes in Greece and so couldn't make it home in time for me to get back to Swansea to start my new job.

I called my boss-to-be and asked if I could start on Thursday rather than Monday. He was fine about this, and I booked a new ticket home. I felt good about the future. What was this weird feeling? Maybe not quite hope, but definitely optimism.

I soon settled into work with my new boss, and we found that we worked quite well together. There was always a good atmosphere on site, and he was always concerned that I was OK. Good to my word, I started having an hour in a pub in town and then going straight home.

After about a month with him, he was taking a couple of days off before the weekend, so I was to have a few days off myself as well. I went for my usual couple of pints in town and then decided on a couple more. Then a couple more. Then I fancied some powder.

It wasn't busy in the pub, but I got talking to a fella in the smoking area. We got on well, both being big football fans. It truly is the universal language. We decided to watch the football together, and at some point, I turned the conversation to drugs. He didn't know anyone who sold Charlie, but he could get some MDMA.

Fuck it! Let's go then! I thought.

We went back to his, and he got in touch with his dealer. She picked us up and took us to the offy. While he went inside, I got talking to her and it turned out that she did sell the old nosebag, at a reasonable price too. I bought one to sample another day and tucked it away, as I had done with the Mandy. When we got back to his, I couldn't find the Mandy, only the coke. He called up and she said she would drop one around. We had probably dropped it in the car anyway. I took her number for future reference.

I remember playing Trivial Pursuit with him and one of his housemates. It turns out that I had been calling him the wrong name for most of the evening. We were up all night, and the poor bastard had work in the morning. So we headed into town for nine, him for work, me to go home to sleep for a bit.

I didn't go home though. A couple of pints to straighten myself out first. God Bless Wetherspoon's! I bought a magazine and settled into a booth for an hour or so. Well, I came to life pretty quickly after that and knew that I would be meeting my new purveyor of all things good.

At some point, I was sitting there, going through all 17 pockets in my work trousers, and I came across a little bag of wonderful happy dust. One of the employees walked past my booth as I had it in my hand. "I wondered where that had got to," I said. He just laughed and carried on. I thought about having a boot but knew that I had to be on Charlie in public. I didn't gurn so much on that shit.

Anyway, I stayed in the pub until about 12:30 and then sent a text. Ten minutes later, I was sat in a car, buying some cocaine. I gave her back her bag of MDMA. "That's very honest," she said.

"We're all just trying to earn a crust," I said. Who said that all drug users are dishonest? Yeah, I know.

Freshly stocked, it was straight to the toilets in the shopping centre. To be honest, I was flagging a bit, not being as young as I used to be. I probably should have gone home, but that would have been admitting defeat. *Oooh, lovely drop, that!* Re-energised, I went to tackle a couple more pubs. I was in town for another three hours or so, and then I headed home to beat the traffic.

Once off the bus, I started to walk home when I bumped into a mate that I hadn't seen since I moved back up to Bromley. Well, the polite thing to do was to arrange a drink sometime. Preferably in the next hour. Sorted. I got home, had a few short words with my parents and then jumped through the shower. Got dressed, one big hooner, fuck your nose, up it goes, and I was off.

I can't remember how long I was out, but I think I got close to the finish line, and I got home with over a gram waiting for me. *Nice! Bosh it in and settle down for the wank of your life!*

I was in the dog house for the next couple of days. What was their fucking problem? I was 35 years old. I had been living away for over two years. I could look after myself. In all fairness, I was quite good at keeping my head down no matter how fucked up I got. I should probably have taken a few hidings over the years but have always got away with it. They probably looked at my face and thought that someone had beaten them to it! Besides, nobody could inflict more harm or injury on me than I was prepared to myself.

We worked pretty constantly up until Christmas and got to know each other quite well. I slipped into a nice routine of having a couple of hours in a pub in town on the way home from work and then picking up a bit of chop for a Friday night party for one. The weekends consisted of little more than a long walk with Klint, each day topped off with a quiet couple of pints. Literally just a couple.

Saturday afternoons were spent watching the football scores come in with my father. These were really special times. We are both big football fans and, though Charlton first and foremost, we follow all football. Equally at home talking about Yeovil versus Accrington Stanley as we are about the Merseyside Derby, probably more so.

At work, we were in the middle of a big job, so we were up and running straight away in the new year. My boss was encouraging me to try different things at work and was prepared to be patient with me. One day, we got talking about mental health and I said that I had had my battles. He was very interested and wanted to understand something that he had no grounding in. I was getting regular work and the money was always there. He definitely had my best interests at heart, and he appreciated that I would do a good day's work for him. I was on to a good thing. At some point, I would need to start earning more money, but for now, I could do this and learn the skills that I would need in a safe environment.

My sister's birthday is a week after mine, and this year was to be her fortieth. Her husband wanted to take her away beforehand, so my parents took Klint with them to go and look after their pets. I was to follow them up a week later for the celebrations. This would mean that I would be home alone for my birthday. Perfectly OK by me.

The Friday before, they were due to leave on Saturday, I kept to my usual routine of a couple of pints in town and then a takeaway of class As. Once I was ready, I called my order in, but she was out.

"I've got some MKAT."

"Lovely, I'll have a big bag of that!"

I wasn't going to touch it that night. This was for the weekend after they had gone.

I caught the bus home and became very aware of the smell coming from my pocket. *Hello para's, I haven't seen you for a while.* I jumped off the bus a couple of miles from home to walk along the prom. I picked up some cans and thought that I might have a little sample while I walked. *Fuck me, this is going to be a good weekend!* I thought.

They left around ten the following morning, and I was very quickly down the shop. A shitload of beer and plenty of fags. I got home, locked the door, pulled the blinds and tucked in. I was flying straight away. I knew that once I started, I was to be stuck inside.

I sat downstairs for a while, sniffing away until I was staring at the TV through one eye. Then my cock started to tingle. *Already?* I thought. Oh well, I retired to my bedroom to see what would happen.

I finished the gear about four or five the following morning, and I hadn't put my dick down much in that time. I wasn't sure if I was going to rip the fucker off or rub a hole in the little bastard. As it happened, it survived, and so did I! I didn't get much sleep until Sunday evening, but with a few beers in the house and plenty of food, I avoided any sort of comedown and felt great on Monday morning.

After work on Monday, I had a couple of pints in town and then went home, showered, cooked and just chilled. Tuesday was a regular day at work, and it was my birthday the next day. I decided to stock the cupboards the night before so, after a customary couple of pints, I made a call. Everything was back in stock. Quality. I had the foresight to know that I would most likely have a little aperitif tonight, leaving the main course for tomorrow.

I got home, boot! A quick shower, boot! We're on our way now, boy. Boot!

Boot! Boot! Hooner! All of a sudden, it was two in the morning, and I was wired. *Fuck me! You're up for work in a bit!* I wasn't going to sleep, so I had no option but to try and wank through it and straighten up for the morning. *It's alright. You can grow up tomorrow; you're still only 35 years young.*

I went to work, feeling a little tired, but other than that, OK. The day passed well, and I had a couple of pints on the way home. Once home, I ordered a big, fat kebab and went for a shower. I had just finished my kebab and was drinking a couple of cans in the house when there was a knock at the door. It was my neighbour, the sparky. He insisted that I join him for a few pints for my birthday. Well, who was I to argue?

It was a decent night down the pub. Being pool night, there were a few people there, many of whom I knew. I stayed until closing and got home with half a dozen beers in the fridge. Well, it's only your birthday once a year. They would have to go.

I finished them and went to bed, ready for work in the morning.

The next couple of days went OK, and I got to Friday in one piece. A couple of pints and a couple of grams of Charlie, and then a fairly relaxed weekend before travelling up to my sister's on the Monday for the festivities.

I was up there from Monday until Friday and had a really enjoyable time. They were pleased to see that I was doing better, and I was pleased to be able to perpetuate that illusion. We all went out for a meal at their favourite Italian restaurant on her birthday, and it was a really chilled evening. The rest of the time, we just enjoyed each other's company.

Back to Swansea and back to reality. Work was good, a regular five days. Hard work but not in the slightest bit pressured. Good laughs and the days flew by, productively. A few weeks of this, and I was off for a weekend to visit my brother for my birthday trip down The Valley.

I travelled up on Friday and waited in a pub near my brother's for an hour or so until he finished work. He picked me up, and we headed to his local for a few. Six weeks late, but technically this was my birthday celebration, so we were on it. After a while, it was home to his, stopping at a couple of shops. One overt, one covert. His missus was away, so we had the place to ourselves. Perfect.

We got up on Saturday morning and just had a chilled morning around the house. Our first pick, Charlton Athletic versus Milton Keynes Dons, had been called off, due to international call-ups; would you believe it? We were off to Hayes Lane to see the mighty Bromley take on Chester. I used to go to watch Bromley a lot when I was younger, and I was too young to travel to Charlton on my own. It was good to be back there, and our sister joined us.

It had been years since the three of us had done anything, just as the three of us, and we had a great afternoon. Bromley were to lose one-nil to a late goal, but we had a good time. After the football, we made our way back to my brother's, stocking up on essentials on the way. We had a lovely, chilled evening, playing the now obligatory couple of games of Scrabble, while we could still see straight.

Sunday was spent around the house, eating and drinking, mainly drinking. On Monday, he went out to work, I fed and walked Juddy and then made my way to the station and then Swansea.

Life carried on in the same vein for the next couple of months. I started allowing myself a cheeky gram on a Tuesday as a reward for fuck all. Fridays would be a few pints in town, pick up, home for a swift espresso and then out to the local with a score in my pocket. I found that I could behave myself if I limited the amount of money that I took out with me. Genius, hey! Half a dozen pints, very civilised. The six in town beforehand didn't count.

Saturdays and Sundays were still all about Klint, and we started drinking in the club next to my local. It was a nice big room where Klint was free to roam, and there was a lovely lady who ran it, a genuinely warm person. She loved the boy, and over time, I think that she grew a little fond of me. She would always have treats for Klint and lager for me. She was also just damn good company. Always there for chats about a plethora of topics, from the mundane to the existential. Sometimes afterwards, Klint and I would pop into my local next door where I was starting to get to know the bar staff and re-engage with some people I had known before. I was slowly getting drawn back into the Mumbles. Well, if you are going to drink heavily, you might as well have some company doing it!

Chapter 27
Reasons to Socialise

One day in the spring, I was working on a flat roof. It was a beautifully sunny day, the sun beating down on our backs with the banter flying around and the radio blaring. I honestly can't think of a better place to be working on days like this. You are up above the world, tucked away to some extent, and the sunshine just seems to improve everybody's mood.

The two of us made the decision to work on and break the back of the job. We finished approaching eight, and he decided to drop me home so that I didn't have to catch two buses. No lager in town for me tonight.

When he dropped me off, I made the decision to pop into my local. Well, I had done a good day's work, so I deserved a beer. There was a beautiful girl who worked there, and to top it off, she had the naughtiest little Irish accent.

I walked through the door and the place was deserted, the pool team playing away. They were out of Carling, so I ordered a Grolsch. We made eye contact, and I was like 'Fucking hell!', internally, of course. I managed to maintain my cool, sophisticated persona on the outside.

We got talking, and I realised that I might be starting to fancy her. I hadn't allowed myself to become attracted to anyone since the barmaid all those years ago back in Bromley, I definitely have a type! Time to go on the charm offensive! "Oi! Oi! I'm Steve, and I work really, really hard. Do you want to talk about my mental health issues?" Or words to that effect. I know what women like!

Anyway, one thing led to another, and I had worked up quite a thirst and proceeded to smash the pints in leaving at closing time a little the worse for wear. I was aware, though, that she seemed to take an interest in everything that I said, and we spoke quite freely. The cynical side of me kept telling me that it was just her job.

She wouldn't give you the time of day in the wild.

I woke up the next morning and reflected on the way to work. I knew that I had absolutely nothing to offer her. I was never going to have anything to offer anyone, but I had missed the feeling of having a crush, so it made sense to let it run for a while. After all, I could spend time with her whenever I liked, and she was duty-bound by her job. *Yeah, OK, I fucking know, alright?*

I was back to drinking in Mumbles on the nights that she worked, and I also found myself reconnecting with people that I had known previously. Work was going well, pretty consistent, and waking up each morning without any trepidation, looking forward to every day. My boss had even started sorting me out with some Saturday work, even though he didn't work weekends. He was showing that he trusted me to do an honest day's work, even when he wasn't around. This made me feel really good.

It was one of the bank holiday weekends in May, I forget which, and the Sunday was the birthday of someone that I knew from the pub, a friend somebody else might say. I decided to have a night out at the weekend for once. I only had £30 left after celebrating the bank holiday in my own unique way on Friday. That was fine; that would buy me nine pints. Just about enough; besides, I wasn't really there to see him. I was hoping to catch a glimpse of somebody else!

As it turned out she wasn't working and I didn't see her at all that night, but I did have a good drink with the birthday boy. My money ran out, and I wasn't ready to stop. I asked my companion for the night if I could borrow a score; he handed me forty pounds. Game on!

We stayed until close, and I went with him to the cab office to keep him company while he waited for a taxi. There was a large queue outside, so I told him to phone one from mine. As we walked back to my house, we passed a cash point. Spotting an opportunity, I asked if he could lend me another bullseye so that I could get some Charlie. He went along with it, and I made my own phone call. My drugs arrived before his ride home. I was due to have a day out with Mum, Dad and Klint the next day. I didn't get out of bed until fiveish.

He was quite a secretive bloke and very guarded over who had his phone number. I had no way of contacting him, and it was several weeks until I saw him again. I had heard from someone else that he had been asking after me, but every time that I was in the pub, I never bumped into him. I tried to arrange the time and place through somebody, but we never managed to rendezvous.

This went on for a couple of months and, predictably, the one time we did meet, I didn't have his money. He was fine about it, and the next time we met, I was able to repay him in full. He said something about being shocked by my drug use. Now I had been stood beside him at the bar once when he tried to play the big boy, telling someone else that he could get hold of the best cocaine in Swansea. He clearly wasn't a user, and I let it slide. This whole thing about having a problem with drugs pissed me off though. I fucking hate a hypocrite. Yeah, I KNOW!

In June, my parents had a two-weeks holiday booked in Slovenia. They were travelling up to my sister's for a couple of days beforehand, as Klint was to stay with them while they were away. I had nearly three weeks to myself.

They left on a Tuesday morning, and I didn't have work. Straight away, I was at a loose end.

What to do? What to do?

I decided the pub was calling, and I had to line my stomach first. I made a round of cheese sandwiches and had about two bites out of the centre of each half, leaving rather generous crusts.

It was shortly after ten when I left the house. My local wasn't open on Tuesdays and wouldn't have been open until later anyway. I headed to a big pub in the village. I bought a Daily Star and a scratch card with a box of fags. Tuesday was also a cheap day at this place, and a pint of Carling was just £1.90. The sun was shining; it was hot outside, cheap beer. This was going to be a good day. I found a quiet, dark corner and settled in for a couple of hours to read my paper and watch Sky Sports News. It's not as if I was just in the pub drinking alone, I was catching up on current affairs!

I decided that it was time to move on to town, as I needed some lunch. I fancied something Bolivian. I was waiting at the bus stop when the girls from the pub and the club came along. We got chatting, and I filled them in that I had no work but couldn't understand why. They seemed to show genuine concern and they carried on their way, wishing me all the best. Fuck me, maybe they did give a shit about me after all.

The buses were all up the wall, so a change of tack was needed. I knew that I could get the delivery if I bought enough, so I made a call and started the bidding high. My first offer was accepted, and I was homeward bound, picking up beer and fags on the way.

I had a really pleasant afternoon and evening at home on my own, behind closed blinds. I think. The time passed anyway and, to be honest, I got everything that I expected and wanted out of the experience. I received a call to say that I had work the next day, and I had a short commute, literally just the other side of the alleyway out the back. Perfect, time for four more Red Stripe.

Working so close to home, I started to realise how many people I knew in the area. A lot of these were good people who I genuinely got on with. I started to feel good about my situation, as if I had finally found a place where I might fit in. I continued to drink heavily, mainly indoors, but I was in danger of being happy. Unsettling!

That Saturday night, I decided to pop out to the pub for a couple. I was enjoying my evening and knew that I would be there until I was non-forcibly removed. There was a brief scuffle, but I was unmoved, sitting at the bar, grabbing precious moments with you-know-how. I started to get that itch and felt like a twat for not sorting this out before I came out. I had had all day. As luck would have it, I got a text message, and my dealer was heading in my direction, asking me if I would like anything. Yes, please. I disappeared home, after picking up some cans, to take delivery, a quick boot and back out, leaving my drugs indoors for the darkness.

Later that evening, a woman that I knew years ago came in smashed. I knew the couple with her, loosely. I got chatting to the bloke while his wife went out the back with my old friend to have a cigarette. They sat out there, and he took them a drink. He came back in with a message for me. Basically, it was there on a plate for me if I so wished. This girl used to be a fairly good friend; a few years ago, I might well have gone for it with her, but I didn't know her anymore, and I certainly wasn't going to use her just for a bunk-up.

I continued to drink with the bloke, and towards the end of the night, they called a cab. The four of us headed back to theirs. Even though I was suitably lubricated by now, I still knew that nothing was going to happen. She was less sure. We picked up beer along the way. I just wanted to put off getting fucked on my lonesome for a while. This reminds me of when I would go to a nightclub purely for a late licence. I was just trying to extend the party. Prolong the time until it was just me, without any drink or drugs.

After a little while, my friend and the husband had gone to bed, separately, and I had a nice chat with the wife. I decided that I had overstayed my welcome and made my excuses, taking my last couple of cans for the walk. I stepped outside and was not too sure where I was. Luckily, I could see the sea far below, and I just headed for that. Once I hit the prom, I knew I didn't have long to wait. I started anticipating that first line, for the second time that night. I had a fair bit, so I did not need to worry about running out for now. I went up to bed about eight that morning.

One night, England's Under-21s were playing Germany's in a semi-final. I finished work and walked straight past my house to the shop to get provisions. I went home and watched the football while speaking to my brother through one form of media or another. England predictably lost on penalties, but I had never felt closer to my brother.

The following weekend, it was the Swansea Air Fair, and you could see the aerial displays from my front garden. I had stocked the fridge early on Sunday, as it was a beautiful sunny day and I needed to get the blinds closed and the door locked. My sister and I were in contact throughout the day, and I realised that I was extremely close with all of my immediate family, coupled with the fact that there was an outside chance that I might actually be making friends, life seemed pretty sweet.

My parents were due back in Swansea on a Friday. On Thursday beforehand, I finished work around the corner pretty early and was paid up for the week as the job was finished and we wouldn't be starting anything on a Friday, so it was a day off for me. I knew what was going to happen. End of the holiday blowout!

I went out for a couple of pints and got chatting to a couple of young lads that lived locally. We had a laugh, and I said that I had to sort something out, but they were welcome around mine later.

I sorted out what I had to, no prizes for guessing, and settled in for a night in. I wasn't too concerned whether they turned up or not. As it was, they did, and I would have company for the night. We had a good laugh, and I found out that the younger generation was much more easily offended than people of my age, and I didn't have to get to my sickest jokes to get a reaction. It didn't feel like sport at all. I still told them my worst jokes, though.

They left as the sun was starting to rise and would continue to speak to me when we saw each other, despite my abhorrent sense of humour. I settled down to attempt sleep on the sofa. I wouldn't get any and would just about get the house back in shape for my parents' return.

Sometime in July, my boss's daughter went on a school trip, and he wanted to decorate her room as a surprise while she was away. I had a full weekend's work with him, and we were going to have a laugh doing it. We worked fairly long days but kept the atmosphere good. I popped to the pub every evening; well, I had worked, so I deserved a pint or eight.

I walked into my local on Saturday evening and was pleased to see that my crush was behind the bar. It wasn't overly busy, but just enough people to have a bit of life. My evening was spent in the company of a couple of blokes that I knew, and it was a thoroughly enjoyable time. I was outside having a cigarette and I was checking to see how much cash I had on me. How many pints did I have left now? This had become my currency.

During the course of the day, one of the pockets in my shorts had ripped, so I was keeping everything in the other pocket, and I had to empty my pockets to count my change. After discovering that I had enough for a couple more pints, I finished my cigarette and went to drain the vein before returning to the bar. As I left the toilets, I absent-mindedly wiped my nose on the collar of my T-shirt. As I got to the bar, I was sure that the girl I liked gave me a stern look, shaking her head. I started to worry about this. I didn't want to do anything to upset her.

My mind went into overdrive. I formed a story in my mind. The pub had been having some trouble with some of its punters at weekends, so they had recently installed CCTV covering, among other places, outside the front door and the passageway from the toilets. I became convinced that she had seen me rummaging in my pocket for something outside, head to the toilet, wiping my nose as I left. I had been open about my drug use to her but had insisted that I never carried drugs when I was out in the pub. I was sure that she would now believe that I was lying to her. I wasn't, apart from a couple of times when I first moved back; I never had drugs on me in that pub. The trust was gone, through no fault of mine. With no trust, there is nothing to base a relationship on!

I carried on as before, popping in on the weekdays when she was working, and one night, I got pissed and, to my recollection, I kept trying to get her attention and monopolise her time. Recalling this on the way to work the following day, I had a good, stern word with myself. I told myself that I was making a fool of myself and there would never be anything between us. I had absolutely nothing that she could possibly want or need. It was time to move on. I resolved to just enjoy her company. Oh, and to visit the pub on days that she wasn't working to prove that I was just a regular customer, you know.

Throughout that summer, I was working Saturdays, so Sundays became my day with Klint. We would be out the door around ten and have a good long walk for a couple of hours before heading to the club. Klint would be as keen to get in there as I was. He would get a fuss made of him plus plenty of treats, and I would get my treats, beer, and plenty of it. When we would go out for a cigarette, Klint would settle on the steps, keeping guard. After a couple in the club, the pub would be open, and we would pop in there on the way home. More treats for the pair of us.

One day, as I smoked with the lady who ran the club, Klint made his own way into the pub. Straight away, he was given a biscuit. I had to explain that we wouldn't be in yet, as I had a pint in the club, but I would be in after. I was duty-bound now.

I soon cottoned on that, if I took Klint outside either place with me when I went for a salmon, he would make his way into the other. He was immediately rewarded and I would have to visit, or re-visit, each place after. This could go on all day until his dinner was ready. I am convinced that he genuinely enjoyed those days, I certainly did. It wasn't my fault that we were in drinking establishments all day. I got to spend the weekends drinking with my best friend and my two favourite girls, not including family, of course. Wink emoji! My dog had become an enabler and it was fucking awesome!

I had been invited to a wedding back in Bromley one weekend. Work was getting a little frustrating as we were being scuppered by the weather on a large concreting job. I used this as an excuse to stay back in Swansea. I had to make myself available even though my boss said that we wouldn't be working under any circumstances. I had engineered the chance for another solitary session.

I spent the money that I had on Thursday night and woke up basically skint. That afternoon, I really wanted a drink and a sniff, so I called my brother-in-law with some cock-and-bull story that has been lost to posterity now.

Soon enough, one hundred pounds arrived in my bank account. I got a load of Charlie delivered, bought some fags and cans and left myself a bit of money for a couple of pints in the pub. So fucking unnecessary, and yet, it had to be done.

On the August Bank Holiday, Monday, I had a private job on. I was laying some AstroTurf for friends of my parents. The anxiety had been rising in anticipation of this. As the day approached, I felt my bottle go more and more. There wasn't much to the job, all in the preparation, but they didn't want to spend the money prepping the ground as recommended. I thought about dropping out, but I didn't.

On the day, everything went well. My father stayed there with me, drinking tea with his friends, and I got the job done to a good standard at my leisure. They asked me how much I wanted, and they gave me extra on top, saying that it was worth much more than I said.

Feeling good; it's only right that I have the couple of pints that my labours deserved. With the pub closed. I went to the club and was not there too long. I didn't want to take the shine off the day. I knew what would be nice, spend all of the money that I had just earned on something that would keep me up all night.

Sure enough, I made a call to my own personal Deliveroo, and a couple of hours later, I was provided with the finest dessert. I stayed awake all night, finishing sniffing in the wee, small hours. I had two hours until I was up for work and I was buzzing. Only one thing for it: try and powerwank through it.

I felt like a right cunt on the bus to work the following day. I knew by now that nobody who we meet in the cafe had been able to detect my drug use before, so that wasn't much of a concern. I felt like a cunt because I ended up losing money on the previous day's ventures. I missed another night's sleep, and any feel-good factor from what was a good personal achievement had been totally destroyed. *I'll get rid of my numbers*, I thought to myself. Later.

Waiting outside the bus station, smoking a cigarette, I started to scroll through some of my text messages, assigning monetary values to all conversations. I didn't have to go very far before I reached a seriously considerable number. *No, now.* I deleted all of my numbers, text conversations and tried to eradicate any trace of a dealer from my phone. I didn't honestly think that this would be the end of it. I knew that I could easily find cocaine if I wanted to. It was a token gesture, but maybe it would become a turning point. Since that day, I have only taken cocaine once more, I shared a couple of stripes with my brother that Christmas and, as I type this, I have not touched it since.

Chapter 28

The Day My World Ended

Monday 30th October 2017. Just like any normal day at work. I got a slightly early finish. I left thinking about a couple of pints in the closest pub and then a bus into town and an hour or two in a watering hole there before getting my bus home and maybe stopping off at a pub in the village. My local wasn't open, but that didn't matter. I could have a decent drink with an early getaway.

As I was walking to the pub, I received a text from my mother. She said could I come straight home from work, as they needed to speak to me about Klint. For once, I did the right thing and headed straight home without a drink. Klint wasn't there to greet me when I got there, and my mind started to race.

I sat down with a cuppa and my father started to explain things. He went about this in a very long-winded way, and he and Mum started having a side discussion about whether something had happened at ten past or ten to some hour. *Just tell me why my fucking dog isn't at home!* I screamed silently. It turns out that Klint had had a couple of seizures and had been taken to the vet, where he would stay overnight.

Well, at least he was alive, and he was in the best possible place.

The next day, we went to the vet's and we were told that Klint's seizures would have been caused by a brain tumour or a bleed on the brain. The only way to ascertain this would be to do an MRI scan. He was heavily sedated and we were given some epilepsy medicine for him. We were told that he could go on for another six years, but it could happen in the next six months, even the next six weeks. We must just enjoy the time that we have left. That was exactly what we planned to do.

Klint came home with us, and he was very wobbly but unmistakeably, the same dog. Two days earlier, he had still been running around like a two-year-old puppy, now he acted his age, nearly ten. He had got old overnight, but he was still the same old Klint, and we had been told that he should improve once all of the sedation had worn off. I looked into his eyes, and he was clearly the same dog. The spark was still there.

I was back in work the following day and resolved to come straight home from work to be with my friend. My best friend. I did make it home fairly quickly, only stopping off for a quick couple, nothing major. I got through the door and Klint came to greet me. I didn't get the exuberant welcome that I was used to, but he sauntered up to me, wagging his tail.

I struggled to deal with this and made my excuses to pop for a pint. He needed to rest, and he wouldn't settle with me around. I would continue to use this excuse for the rest of his life. When my best mate, who had never forsaken me, really needed me, I made my excuses to dampen my own pain rather than just sit there with him and try to ease his.

Over the next week, he made some improvement, as he was clear of all of the sedation, and started to adjust to the epilepsy medicine. He was well enough to take out on walks, and at the weekend, I took him to our favourite haunts, and he got plenty of attention and fuss. He was slower than a week previously and noticeably less stable on his feet, but everybody agreed that he was still the same boy. I also learnt that weekend that my local pub was closing at the end of January. Anything else?

I noticed that his eyesight wasn't as good as it had been, although he could still chase a ball if I threw it straight past his nose at a low level. He continued to make slow, steady progress throughout the second week, and we started to accept that this was the Klint we had from now on. He was obviously older now, but he was still the same dog.

That weekend, my mother and father were going away to Llandudno for a week. I stayed behind needing to work. Or maybe needing to be left alone to pulverise my feelings and emotions.

On Tuesday, I travelled in for work, but we were rained off, so I was straight into Wetherspoon's for a while. It was Tuesday, cheap day in the big pub in the village, so rude not to. I left there mid-afternoon and returned home with a few pre-drinks before showering and heading out for the evening. I left the club just in time to make it back to the offy to pick up a nightcap or eight.

I worked the next day after very little sleep. There was to be no work for Thursday but might be something on Friday. I knew now that Thursday was going to be a tough day. I knew that I was going to spend the day drinking alone, behind the blinds, trying to fill the endless hours until I could go to bed. Even though I could see this, I knew that there was nothing that I could do to change my fate. I just needed to find a way to get through it with as little erosion to my mental health as possible.

As expected, I woke up before six as my current routine demanded. I stayed in bed, dozing for a little while and then got up to make myself a cup of tea. After that, I had a quick shower, and I went to the shop for the first time that day. Beer and fags, or the usual as it had become. I was on my way by nine o'clock.

I couldn't settle on the sofa in front of the TV, so I went up to my room to have a look for something to do. I came back down with some of my nineties' CDs. Oasis, Manic Street Preachers, Lightning Seeds, Blur and Ocean Colour Scene. Those were my glory days. I started listening, and great memories flooded back. I was never alone back then. Not like now.

I needed something to do, something to occupy myself. Without realising, I started kicking one of Klint's balls around the living room. After a while, I picked it up and started bowling off-breaks, trying to get it into the kitchen sink. I did this for the next few hours. It had broken the monotony. I was getting through the day. The only damage to anything was a clock that I had knocked off the wall. Some positive lyrics were resonating with me.

I needed to keep some money back for the weekend, as I wasn't working on Friday, so I didn't go and get any more cans. I started to hunt around the house for any hidden alcohol. I found a couple of bottles of wine, and they took up a bit of my time.

It was now around two. Time for bed. Bollocks to that.

They say any port in a storm. We didn't have any port, but we had some sherry. Now, sherry is supposed to be an acquired taste; I was not a fan. It turns out that it is a taste than can be acquired pretty damned quickly when you are chasing oblivion. I started by pouring a little drop into a small glass. Once that had gone, I ended up sitting down with a pint glass full to the brim of sherry. I genuinely enjoyed that sickly sweet sort of shit. Three o'clock, and it was time for bed. Or to pass out on the sofa at any rate. Friday would be spent in bed if I ever got there.

I totally missed Friday and can't remember too many details of Saturday other than the fact that I must have drunk shitloads. I had some jet-washing to do for a friend of my parents on Sunday morning. I felt rough as all fuck and managed to struggle through it. When I got home, I tidied the house and was straight down the pub. I couldn't remember the last time that I had eaten. I must have had something on Friday, I reckoned.

I hadn't been in the pub that long when I had a message off Mum. Both Klint and Dad were struggling, and they were coming home a day early. *Why can't they just enjoy their holiday and leave me in fucking peace?* I thought. I stayed in the pub all afternoon and remained there for an hour after they were home. I wasn't going to jump to it just because they had changed their fucking plans!

When I eventually got through the door, the sight that greeted me brought me to my knees. Klint was so thin, having refused almost all food over the last few days. He came up to me; he could hardly walk, and I was convinced that he was now blind. This wasn't the same dog.

I sat on the floor, and he nestled into me. My eyes were welling up, yet I still couldn't cry. My Dad's voice was breaking as we spoke, all three of us choking back tears. I thought about staying downstairs that night, but Klint needed his rest that night. He was going back to the vet's in the morning.

As I was working on that Monday, I was the first one up. I went into the kitchen where Klint slept, and he was in one hell of a state. I went through my usual routine after sitting with him for a while. I went to sit beside him once I was all ready for work, but he kept trying to get up, with little success. I decided that it would be better if I left him to lie there, conserving his energy.

I made my way into the living room and sat on the floor, leaning against the sofa. I knew that things didn't look good. I turned to see that Klint had managed to get up and was making his way, as best he could, towards me. I got up and went to where he was and sat down. He tried to sit next to me, but now that he was standing, he couldn't get back down. He finally did and he lay across my legs, and I started to cry. Properly cry. For the first time in fifteen and a half years, the tears flowed, but they offered no release. When it came time to leave, I was beside myself. I was convinced that this might be the last time that I would see him. I couldn't stay, but I didn't want to go.

I gathered myself to get on the bus but was aware that for both journeys, I was fighting tears all the way. In the café, I didn't join in any conversation, there in body only. My boss and I left to go to work, but the weather closed in, and we were to be rained off. As we jumped back into the van, I received a message from my mum.

Klint was due back at the vet in 45 minutes, and they would keep me posted.

My boss insisted on giving me a lift, and we sat just around the corner, waiting for Dad's car to come past. We spoke and he asked me what I honestly thought. "I don't think that he's coming out," was all that I could muster.

Soon my parents came past, and I met them in the car park. I lifted Klint out of the boot, and he seemed like he may have had a bit more energy than first thing that morning. He always loved going to the vet and would bound into the waiting room, saying hello to everybody of every species on the way. He was known by everyone at the practice, and they loved him.

We settled down in the waiting room, and Klint lay flat. As the receptionist came towards him with a couple of gravy bones, he lifted his head and started to wag his tail. He tried to get up but didn't have the energy. He wolfed down his gravy bones. This WAS the same dog!

We were called, and Klint managed to get to his feet and get into the examination room ahead of us, tail wagging as usual. The vets that we use have always been fantastic. She didn't put him through an invasive inspection, and we quickly made the decision to send him for an MRI. "We're not going to give up on him!" Those are the only words that I remember being said from the whole consultation.

Klint would stay in the surgery overnight where they could manage his pain and keep him as comfortable as possible. We would pick him up in the morning and take him to Weston-Super-Mare for his scan. We said our goodbyes, and he was taken out the back. We all left feeling a bit more positive. They wouldn't be sending him for the scan if it was a done deal. There was still a chance. A good chance, I thought.

I can't remember anything about that afternoon other than the fact that Dad went out and bought loads of treats for Klint for his day out. I don't remember how I filled my time. I know that I didn't have a drink. I didn't feel like having a drink. I knew that it wasn't any good to me in this situation. I didn't want to shield myself. I needed to feel whatever it was that I was going to feel.

We were sat down watching the television after dinner when the phone rang. It was the vet. We all readied ourselves for the worst. It was a false alarm. They were just giving us an update. He was comfortable and they would call in the morning to arrange for us to pick him up.

I think that we all relaxed a little bit. It wasn't more than an hour until the phone went again. Instinctively, I put the TV on mute. We all knew what this was about. We just fucking knew. Mum answered, and we got the gist of the conversation listening to her side alone.

Mum put down the phone. Klint had had chest x-rays taken earlier in the day.

They showed that his lungs were riddled with tumours. We had a decision to make. We all knew what we had to do, so Mum rang back and said that we would be in shortly. I went out for a cigarette and texted my boss, explaining what was about to happen, and that I would be in no fit condition for work tomorrow.

We made the journey in silence. None of us wanted to admit to what we were about to do. What were we about to do? He had been such a wonderful, loyal companion to all of us, and we were about to bring an end to his life. At that point, I would gladly have given my own life to save his.

We were let in and shown through to an examination room. Soon Klint came through the door, his back legs being supported by a member of staff using a towel. The deterioration in him over just a few hours was clear to see. He wasn't going to last much longer anyway. This was definitely the right thing to do. He smiled and wagged his tail when he saw us. This was the same old Klint.

They settled him down on the floor, he could no longer stand, and gave us some time alone with him. His tail continued to wag intermittently as we each had our own private moments with him and then knelt around him together, stroking him. This was horrible, but I never wanted it to end. What was to come was going to be infinitely worse.

After a while, the vet came back in. It was time. They would be giving him an overdose of anaesthesia and he would slip away peacefully. She injected the first syringe into the line that was already in his leg. He slumped on to his side and the tip of his tongue slipped out of his mouth, just as it sometimes did when he fell asleep as a puppy. One syringe wasn't enough; he had some fight in him! A second syringe was dispensed, and he slipped away in front of us. I helped the vet wrap him in a blanket, just his head exposed. I couldn't believe how heavy he felt. As I looked at him there, he was so peaceful. This was the first time I had seen him free of pain for three weeks. That was the same dog. That was MY dog. That was Klint.

We said our 'thank yous' and made our way back to the car. My Dad was the only one who spoke. "What a horrible thing to have to do." There was nothing else to say. We were all in tears, and the rest of the journey home was conducted in silence.

When we got home, I popped to the shop to get some cigarettes. I didn't expect to be going to bed very early while my father boiled the kettle. We sat up for a couple of hours, drinking tea, reminiscing about all of the good times that dog had given us. We could have spoken for weeks. He had helped all of us so much, and now he was gone. There was such a big hole in our lives now. We just didn't know how big.

My parents went to bed and I sat up for a while on my own, trying to get my head around everything that had happened over the last three weeks. It was only a day over three weeks previously that I had been out all day with a wonderful dog in the best of health. He must have been suffering long beforehand, but he never let us know. He didn't want to bother us. Dogs have such resilience; they live in the moment, trying to make the most of their time. We could learn so much from them. Three fucking weeks? At least, he didn't have to suffer more than absolutely necessary, but it was fucking brutal for those of us left behind.

Eventually, I went to bed, and I just lay, face down on my pillow, and bawled my eyes out. This was Klint's final gift to me. He had restored my ability to cry. Something that I had longed for. It didn't have the desired effect. There was a release, but not enough.

I woke early the next morning. Everything seemed OK with the world. My brain told me to cling to that. I knew that it wasn't the case and was soon to be shattered by something; I just didn't know what at the time. This could only have been for a split second, but it felt longer. Then it hit me. Klint's gone! Klint's fucking gone! It was probably a fortnight or so later before I woke up in the morning without having to learn that I had lost my beloved dog. My best mate. My soulmate? It was certainly the most intimate relationship I had had in my life up to this point, and I had to wake up each and every morning and tell myself, for what seemed like the first time, that I would never be with him again.

I went downstairs and had a cigarette while the kettle boiled. Mum and Dad came downstairs soon enough. "Happy Birthday, Mum," I said, knowing how hollow those words were. We all tried to support each other while still trying to process our own feelings. After a couple of hours indoors, I needed a change of scenery. Too many memories in that house.

As I walked aimlessly, I became aware that there was no respite outside. I would have to travel miles to come across a path that we hadn't trod together. I slowly ambled around and decided to make my way up to the castle. Klint loved it up there. I would let him loose and he would run around the grounds. He liked nothing better than rolling in the grass there; it usually had a bit of length to it, and he was always happy to lie there if nothing else. During periods of wet weather, a large, muddy puddle appeared at one end that Klint loved to lie in. Sometimes, it was so deep that only his head was above the surface, like the most adorable periscope from the world's friendliest submarine. He also liked to drop his ball in there, I don't know how many he lost, and try and retrieve it, making his face all muddy in the process. That was never a problem; Klint never needed a second invitation to go in the sea for a wash. I was lost in my memories. They were great memories, but they were now bittersweet.

I was at the Castle for quite a while, misty-eyed, in my own world. Suddenly, a much smaller world. Eventually, it was time to move on. Where the fuck should I go? Everywhere I would be reminded of him. I knew the big pub on the corner. They didn't allow dogs in there, so I had never been in there with Klint. I went in, ordered a pint, £1.90, it was a Tuesday after all, and found a table tucked away. I expected this first pint to fly down. I could see this becoming a drink to forget day. I barely finished it in an hour or so. Christ, when I drink routinely, I go at about three pints an hour. I had a good reason to sink them now, but I clearly wasn't in the mood. I had that one pint and headed home.

Now, this may sound incredibly selfish, but I was so aware of how this would impact on my own life. That dog understood me better than anyone I had ever met. I have an incredibly patient and supportive family who try to understand me and just accept me for who I am. I have a few amazing friends who, again, have accepted me with all my faults. The people in my life are so compassionate and sympathetic, some empathetic, to my needs, and know what to say and how to behave around me, but I have never felt that any human has been so in tune with my emotional needs as Klint was. He knew exactly what I needed when I needed it. He broke the ice for me; he expanded my world. I am convinced that he kept me going through some very difficult times, perhaps to the extent of saving my life, and I knew that he wasn't going to be around anymore. I was going to miss him terribly, and life was going to be so much harder without him.

We spent the afternoon letting those who had known Klint well know about our loss. Mum opened her cards and presents, and we tried to make it as happy a day as possible, but there was a huge, black cloud over our house. A black dog on our shoulder, if you will. Later that day, I posted on Facebook. Mum did the same, and the news was out. It was official.

The following day, I bumped into the lady that ran the club. She saw me and couldn't handle it. She had to walk away from me. That evening, when I was out, she came and gave me a big hug and apologised. I told her to forget about it and that I understood. I would see the girl in the pub the next day and would be surprised about how they had been affected by Klint's passing. I realised that there were so many people that loved that dog, whose lives he had touched in some way. It wasn't just the three of us that were grieving. He was such a special dog, and his loss would be felt far and wide.

My boss had been in touch to see how I was doing, and we had a job to do on Thursday and Friday of that week. The client had two chocolate Labradors. He asked if I would be OK with being around them? I said that I would be fine. Klint had loved to play with other dogs, and when I was out and about in the weeks after he went, I would make a point of saying hello to every dog that I bumped into. It was what he would have wanted, to coin a cliché.

It was the following week, I think, when the news broke that my local pub was actually going to close after New Year's Eve. My world was falling apart. I had convinced myself that I had got over my silly, little infatuation with the Irish girl behind the bar. I was probably kidding myself, but it suddenly became clear to me that I wasn't going to see her on a regular basis. I think that I projected some of the loss of Klint and the pub onto her. Fucked up, I know.

Work remained fairly steady up until Christmas. At least, I had one constant left in my life. The weekends became a massive void. As soon as I was out of work, I was in the closest pub, hammering down three pints as quickly as possible before heading into town for half a dozen more. Then it was home on the bus, drop my bag off and straight across to the pub. In there for a few hours, and back home, shower, food, bed.

I convinced my parents and myself that I had to go over to the club on Saturday and Sunday lunchtimes. This is where I would have been with Klint, and it was somehow part of my healing process. Basically what this really meant was that I only had to face the mornings without Klint. I could drink myself into oblivion after midday. My friend in the club was always there for a chat and understood my pain, having become very attached to Klint herself. Sometimes, I would pop into the pub afterwards, depending on who was working.

Christmas was fast approaching, and we actually had a works do. Just my boss, his mate, who I knew, and myself. We met at one in a pub and had a good drink. Plenty of laughs, just what the doctor ordered. We went our separate ways around six, and I headed back to Mumbles via Burger King. I was quite wobbly by then and only stayed out for a couple. Home to bed. Work was done for another year.

My sister and her husband came down shortly afterwards, with Daisy. It felt so good to have a dog in the house again. She seemed to notice that Klint wasn't around and refused to go in her bed when it was put in the place where his had been. She seemed to realise that we needed some TLC and made a big fuss of us all, even Dad, who she hadn't always seemed that close to.

My brother arrived on Christmas Eve, having just split up with his partner. This was a good thing; she was fucking toxic, and he had changed massively for the better over the years. He would be staying down until the New Year.

On Christmas Day, I took Daisy out for a walk in the morning while the others, minus my brother, were at church. I ended up at a little beach just beyond the pier. This was another of Klint's favourite places with rock pools and plenty of places to sniff around. I let Daisy off the lead and just watched her go about her business. I'll use the word bittersweet here again. I'm pretty sure that I sat there, watching with half a smile on my face and tears running down my cheeks. I'm not sure what people would have made of me if we hadn't been alone on that beach.

Christmas Day was much like any other Christmas Day. Grandma came around for the day, as she did on Boxing Day. We opened presents, ate a huge amount, and my brother and I drank a lot of Fosters, never quite getting pissed. It was a pleasant, immediately forgettable time. My sister and her husband returned to Bromley and their lives sometime before the New Year and my brother stayed on.

I popped out for a couple of drinks one night, and my brother followed me a little later. We started sinking them, and towards the end of the night, we did our usual thing. I had no contacts, but I knew who to ask. A couple of dead ends, and then some info from an unlikely source. We were sorted and took some beers back home to enjoy with our Charlie. I knew that this was going to happen at one point, so I wasn't too fussed. As far as I was concerned, I was still off the gear. I haven't had a toot since. I may actually be done with it. Even though it was good gear that night!

We only went out one more time before he travelled home. New Year's Eve. We started in the pub, went to the club, and then drank in the house into the early morning. We have a tremendous relationship now, we may not keep in touch very much, but when we are together, there is a very real bond.

My brother stayed all day on New Year's Day and left very early the following morning to be back in time for work that day. I knew that I wouldn't be back in work for a week until my boss's daughter was back at school. There was plenty in the pipeline, so I knew that we would hit the ground running. At least, I still had that constant in my life. Besides, my parents and I had a conversation to have.

We had agreed not to talk about getting another dog until the new year. We weren't thinking about replacing Klint. We knew that that could never happen, but we knew that the house had a massive void in it. It was a short conversation, and we agreed to look for a new dog, all agreeing on a rescue.

That Friday, we went to Many Tears Rescue Centre for a tour and to look at the possible candidates. The night before, I had found myself crying in the garden and thought that the best way to deal with this was to go and buy some beer. After a couple of cans, I tucked into the sherry alone, after my parents had retired for the night.

When the morning came, I said that I wasn't going. I was too hungover. "Either we're all going or none of us is," my father said. I dragged myself out of bed and we headed off. I felt rough as fuck.

There were so many dogs at the centre, and I would have loved to have taken them all home. They had had a consignment of street dogs from Romania, and they all carried scars of their experiences. None of them had let it affect their spirit, and we knew we had a job on our hands to narrow it down. There was a very excitable St Bernard called Grace Kelly that we all would have loved, but we agreed that she would most probably be a bit too much for us.

After leaving the centre, we went for lunch to discuss our options. There were certainly plenty of options that would suit our home. My paternal grandmother was originally from Loughor, and I asked if we could have a little detour, as it was on our way home. We had been through there many years ago on a holiday in South Wales, but I had been too young to remember. Dad drove around for a bit, and we managed to locate the house where my great-grandmother had spent her final years, long before I was born. Heritage is important, and this allowed me to fill in a little bit more of the picture that was me.

When we got home, we got the laptop out and connected it up to the television so that we could all see. We went through some of the dogs that we had noted and decided to register an interest in a Yellow Lab called Louise. We were soon given a response that they wanted her homed somewhere that already had resident dogs, and so, she wasn't for us. We applied for a dog believed to be her mother, Thelma, and met the same problem. We tried for one more dog from here, but it was already reserved. The search would have to go on.

The following week, I still wasn't back at work, and we had been looking at various websites and we decided to go for a look in a couple of places on Thursday. The night before, I went out for a couple of pints and snuck a few cans into my bedroom for later. When I went up, I soon despatched them and found myself drinking the best part of a bottle of white spirit. This wasn't a suicide attempt, and I'm not sure why I did this, all I know is that I was really struggling with the idea or process of finding another dog. I desperately wanted another dog, our home needed another dog, but something was really playing me up about the whole process.

Through the night and in the morning, I was sick, and I told my parents that I wouldn't be joining them. Thankfully, they decided to go. It was a day that would change our lives, very much for the better.

Their first stop was the Dogs' Trust in Bridgend where we had seen that they had a beautiful Golden Retriever called Honey. According to the website, she had been there for approaching two years, and she seemed perfect for us. When they enquired, it turned out that they had been working with a family for a couple of months and she was to be placed with them. They also met a German Shepherd called Jager but, again, he was too much of a handful. They continued their journey to Cardiff Dogs' Home.

I had seen a stunning Alsatian on the website, Charlie, if my memory serves me correctly. Yeah, I know. What the fuck attracted me to him? They were shown around the kennels and, just as they were finishing the tour, the volunteer asked them what they were looking for. They said that we had recently had to say goodbye to a Labrador Retriever. "Did you meet Toby?" she asked. They hadn't, so she took them back to his kennel.

Toby was hiding in the back of his kennel. When he was called, this heavily overweight Golden Labrador waddled out, smiling and wagging his tail. They asked if they could take him for a walk and were permitted. He didn't walk far or fast but seemed to be very relaxed with them.

They were told that he had been with an elderly person who had had to be admitted to hospital and then kept in residential care. He was 58 kg when he had come into the centre and was down to 52. Still, a lot to do. He would need to lose about a third of his body weight. They were still waiting on adoption papers, but that wouldn't be long now, and they were looking to re-home as soon as possible, as he had been in kennels for two months.

When Mum and Dad got home, I was feeling much better. They told me about Toby, showing me some photos, and I encouraged them to make regular phone calls to check on the progress of his adoption by the centre. They had been told that there had been some interest from other people.

The following Tuesday, Mum phoned up in the morning to see how he was and was told that he now belonged to the dogs' home. Later that afternoon, they received a call. They asked my parents if they would like to come to the centre on Thursday and take Toby? My father thought that they meant for a walk, but no, they meant permanently.

Toby came home on Thursday, 18 January 2018, and our home was complete again. I actually worked that week, and on Thursday, I was going to go straight home to meet my new dog. I stopped twice on the way home. Two pubs, two pints in each. What was wrong with me? Knowing that there was a dog waiting for me at home and I couldn't leave the beer alone. I wasn't in the pubs for more than an hour, so no real harm was done.

I walked through the door and was immediately pounced on by this big barrel of a dog. I couldn't believe the energy that he had, given his size. He was also extremely libidinous for a dog that was supposed to have been 'fixed'. He seemed relaxed and at home straight away. We certainly felt at home with him there.

Three half-hour walks a day was the prescribed exercise regime. Coupled with reduced rations, the weight started to fall off him. Within six months, he was down to a healthy weight and had more energy than ever!

Toby had only been with us for a week when it was my birthday. I wasn't working and so spent the day with Toby, enjoying our short walks. He wanted to walk further, and I certainly wanted to be out for longer too, but we had been told that too much exercise, while he was carrying the excess weight, would put a strain on his joints.

My sister had sent me some Minions slippers, with big, protruding eyes. I was 37, would you believe. I suppose it was a step in the right direction from the previous year and my Minions duvet set. I had put them on the sofa, and they must have been looking at Toby funny. He took one down and ripped its eye off.

I just had to laugh. We had a bit of a hooligan on our hands, and I couldn't be happier!

Chapter 29

Reunion with an Old Friend

I was expecting to have a good start to the year on the work front. I knew I would be off for that first week but was assured that I would be up and running from the next week onwards. The phone didn't go that week at all, but I worked the whole of the following week. I was on my way, or so I thought. I would only work for one week in January.

The Friday of the week that I worked, with a bit of money in my pocket, I went monstrously on the piss. Even though I had a dog waiting at home for me, there was still a massive emptiness that could only be filled one way. I took Toby out with me at the weekend, to show him off, and he seemed quite happy to accompany me to the club.

I was around for the rest of the month, and Toby would join me for a pint on our evening walk. I really needed him at that time. Since Klint had gone, work had got sporadic to say the least. Without a dog, the days were endless. Toby gave me a reason to get out of bed in the morning. After about a week, Toby stopped wanting to go to the club. I had a problem on my hands. He wasn't going to be an excuse to be drinking for hours. I would have to find a new tactic.

This didn't prove to be a problem. I would just drop Toby at home after our walks and pop back out, saying that I would be back 'in a bit'. My drinking was really beginning to get out of hand. February was a pretty solid month for work, and this facilitated my self-destructive drinking. Once I started, I couldn't stop. It had been a long time since I had ever had any real control over the drink, but now I had totally misplaced the off switch.

I got Toby back into the club by allowing him a couple of treats. The weight had been flying off him, so I concluded that he deserved a bit of a fuss. We enjoyed this routine at the weekends, and one Saturday, during the Six Nations, we were out all afternoon. We visited four different watering holes, and Toby got treats in them all. So he was happy.

Toby would get bored quite quickly, so I made sure that when I 'noticed', I still had part of a pint left. I could drop him off at home and return to get wankered. Saturdays became a blur. I would drink to blackout and beyond, go home, straight to bed, get up on Sunday and do pretty much the same thing all over again.

One Sunday, it was the day before the birthday of the girl who used to work in the pub. Remember her? I hadn't really seen her since the pub had closed, so I decided that the best option was to hang around in the club until she came in, in the evening. I had been told that they were starting over at the Rugby Club, so I just had to sit tight.

Starting at twelve might not have been the best idea, but I could handle my drink, and I only really needed a little 'hello' with a smile, and I would be all set. I drank all afternoon, chatting with anybody who came in. I borrowed money from a couple of people that I knew when funds were beginning to get low. I don't know what time it was, but sooner or later, it got the better off me. I was sick on the floor at the bar where I sat. Happy Birthday, Treacle! I'm still waiting for my 'Thank You' card. I never did see her that day.

I woke up about five the following morning and had that horrible feeling of dread that I had done something well beyond the pale. Finally, it came to me. *Fucking seriously, Steve?* I messaged the lady that ran the club, forgetting that it was about five in the morning, to apologise. She told me not to worry. I waited for my alarm to go off and got up for work. That Monday was the only day that I worked that week.

I eventually plucked up the courage to go and apologise in person on Thursday. I was close to tears as I said sorry, and she gave me a big hug and told me to forget it. She asked if I wanted a drink. I said that I was going to have a bit of time off the ale and walked out. Straight into the pub next door that had re-opened under a holding company. I had no self-control left.

One weekend, I was in the club and a bloke I know came in. We greeted each other, and he told me that he was very close to knocking me out the last time that we saw each other. I couldn't remember seeing him that time, but apparently, being ridiculously drunk, I had got to the stage that I often get to where I try to say the most outrageous thing I could think of, trying to get a laugh. I told him that I had fucked his mother! His mother had died 11 years ago. He should have knocked me the fuck out. I couldn't stop apologising, but he told me not to worry, I had been drunk, after all, and these things happen. What the fuck had I become? I did have a big mouth at times after a skinful, but to say something like this was too much.

Work was all but dead, and I had started doing some decorating at my parents' church to earn some beer tokens. They knew that work was good for my soul and tried to help any way that they could. This kindness was counter-productive unfortunately. I could drink. That was all that money was to me now, beer.

When I had got back on the Charlie, I had regularly dipped into my Mum's purse to fund my habit. When you are looking to have a drink and then pick up cocaine, the equation is a fairly easy one. Pints + cigarettes + cocaine + cans + bus fare = X. You know exactly how much money you need, and you take any shortfall. Drinking to oblivion is a more difficult calculation. It is infinite, and so you take whatever you can lay your hands on. Beg, borrow or fucking steal. Where the drink was concerned, I had no morals.

I had the occasional bit of work, and one Tuesday, I was left with the key for the job to open up and start the next morning. I popped for the obligatory unquantified amount of lager and went home. I was soon in bed with some cans that I had brought home. I had become curious about self-harm again. I had had a razor blade prepared for a couple of weeks, and I decided to feel the relief of blood-letting again.

I drew it across my right thigh, easily hidden, and was surprised that this was accompanied by a little scratching pain. I didn't remember that from all those years ago. Then the slow appearance of blood. There it was. The sight of blood, the warm wet feel as it ran down my thigh. That's what I was after. I distractedly cut myself another couple of times and went to sleep, unconcerned. I was in complete control, and I wouldn't do that again.

The following morning, I was hit by terrible anxiety, undoubtedly brought on by the previous night's events. I couldn't bring myself to put my feet on the floor, and so I resorted to type, switching my phone off and curling up into a ball under my duvet.

Later that day, I turned my phone on and had a couple of messages from my boss. He wasn't happy, but he was worried as he knew that it was unlike me. We were going to the same funeral the following day, and we would talk then. He was so understanding and considerate, he always had been, and said that he would be in touch regarding work. I had got away with it again. I felt a little better.

News about work didn't arrive for a little while, and I was able to fit a couple of small, private jobs in. I could keep drinking, and that was all that mattered. It was arranged that I would return to work on a Monday, and I was looking forward to this. We always had fun at work. On Sunday, I messaged him just to double-check, and got a message back later saying that it was off but would be coming soon.

I got up that Monday morning and took Toby out. As he had lost a lot of weight, he could now have longer walks. We hit the beach and headed straight for a garage about a mile away. I walked in with him and bought a dozen cans of Red Stripe. We spent the morning on the beach. Toby making the most of his time, sniffing around and enjoying the sand. Me, also making the most of my time, drinking and laying the foundations for my demise.

How the fuck had it come to this? How had I ended up here again? I knew what was coming now. There was only one destination, and I was going to go for it hammer and tongs. I would go through the motions of fighting it, but I knew that there was only one way that this was going now. I googled The Samaritans' number and saved it to my phone. I never used it. I never really had any intention of using it; I just had to make it look like I was trying. There was a new, dangerous thought in my mind. I couldn't do this for another 40 years!

I listened to Rachel Platten's excellent *Fight Song* over and over again, hoping that I could take something from it. I couldn't kid myself any longer. I had no more fight left in me. It was best for all concerned that I didn't hang around any longer. I didn't know when, but I knew that I was inevitably going to take my own life. I just had to get to that place, and there was only one direction to travel in, down.

Toby and I were out for about three hours. We got in, I sorted him out some freshwater and he went to sleep. I had the house to myself for a little longer, and I went and bought another dozen Red Stripe. When I saw my parents' car pull up across the road, I escaped upstairs. I wasn't interested in anything uplifting now. I started to listen to dark music. I needed to find that place; the sooner the better. For everyone.

My Mum came up, and I said that I was just having a nap and would be down soon. I spent the afternoon drinking in my pit and then went to sleep.

One Monday, I had work, and this went well. I left feeling good. Maybe things were turning around. Workwise, I was told that the outlook was promising. I had a drink on the way home, sneaking some indoors for later, as was customary now. That night, I drank myself into despair and the razor blades came out again, this time across my forearms. The point of no return. I stubbed a cigarette out on my leg. This didn't have the desired effect. It didn't hurt at all. I was impervious to pain.

I didn't sleep much and was late getting up for work. I made the excuse that I had spoken to my boss and was meeting up with him at the job rather than the café. I packed some razor blades and a knife into my bag and walked out of my house for what I thought would be the last time.

I made my way to an off-licence and filled my rucksack with Red Stripe. I fucking loved Red Stripe, lovely drop. Just because I was going out didn't mean that I couldn't enjoy the journey. I needed somewhere to sit where I wouldn't be interrupted. I headed for the castle. There were public toilets there, and I locked myself in one of the cubicles. I took my jacket and hoodie off and opened up a wound on each of my biceps. I couldn't stay there, I would be disturbed; besides, I wasn't going to waste the beer that I had bought.

I moved to a bench on the top of a grassy hill and sat there for a couple of hours. I listened to some music for a while and then let my thoughts take over. I honestly can't really remember what was going through my mind that day. I didn't feel in any turmoil and was extremely calm. I was drinking quickly and would occasionally cut my arms under my clothes. I was no longer in any rush to end my life. I knew that I was on auto-pilot. I just had to let nature take its course.

I became aware that the castle grounds were getting busier. Mainly dog walkers, but I had to move on. There were no railway tracks around here, but we had plenty of coastline and the tide was in. I headed off to the coast path to look for a plot. I found a bench just past one of the beaches. I was visible from the path, but I knew that I wouldn't be noticed by anyone. The sky had clouded over while I walked; thick with symbolism, I thought.

Only feet away, the waves were lapping against the rocks. I am not a strong swimmer, and it was quite choppy. I knew that I would be in serious trouble very quickly. I just had to wait. I sat there for hours, drinking, staring at the sea. I was totally unmolested by anyone passing. The urge in me grew as I waited for that moment. I wasn't trying now. I was so certain that I would just get there. My bottle started to ebb away with the tide. I felt deflated as I realised that I would live today. I got up and headed home with the remainder of my lager. Soon, not today, but soon.

I got home and went straight up to bed; this was where I was going to spend most of my remaining time. I would just lie there and stew. I knew that I had it within myself to get to where I needed to be. I clung to my new favourite thought. *I can't do this for another 40 years!* If I can't get better, I am better off dead. I knew that I couldn't get better, so the sooner I died the better. For all concerned.

One Sunday night shortly afterwards, I lay in bed, unable to sleep. I had a massive internal conflict going on in my head. I was fighting the urge to cut myself again. I desperately needed something to live for, and in two days' time, I would be going to Shrewsbury to watch the mighty Charlton in action. I just had to make it. We had had the tickets since October as the game had been postponed twice.

I was restless the whole night. I honestly didn't know what side of the fence I wanted to land on. Did I want to resist the temptation to cut myself? Was I fighting the desire to self-harm? Or, did I want to continue down this path? Was I trying to defeat the last vestiges of self-preservation in me? I never did resolve it that night, but I made it through, and when I got out of bed in the morning, I made myself an appointment with the doctor.

I walked up to the doctor's that afternoon. It was only a five-minute walk away, and I had the slightest slither of positivity about me. This was a really good decision, for once, maybe there was a chance.

I had a great consultation, and the doctor didn't lay it on too thick about the drinking, as others have done. She gave me a couple of numbers that might be of some use to me, referred me to the in-house mental health support team at the surgery and asked me if I wanted to be prescribed anti-depressants. I jumped at the chance, for the first time in my life. I was desperate, and I would try anything. "Would you like 14 or 28 days' prescription? I'll give you 14 and see how we go." Neither of us knew then, but she had just saved my life.

My walk home should have been one of hope and cautious optimism. My mind, however, had other ideas. As I walked, I was feeling some genuine positivity. I might just get better. Get on the anti-depressants, and I should have a bounce. I was going to find some tangible support as well. I was going to get better. I would never feel like that again. I would never want to kill myself again. I would never want to cut myself again. I would never want to cut myself again.

I would never want to cut myself again. One last time wouldn't do any harm then, would it? For old times' sake.

By the time that I got home, I knew what was going to happen. I also knew that I hadn't been able to bring myself to slice myself the previous night, and I knew what I had to do to make sure that that didn't happen again. I borrowed a tenner off my parents. "I won't be able to drink once I'm on the pills," I said. With the change in my pocket, I could have three pints and take some cans home. Everything was in place.

I had my hour in the club and then stashed some cans in my room. I ate dinner with my parents and made my excuses to have an early night. I hadn't slept at all last night, and I was excited about tomorrow. I went up, opened a can and put some mood music on. I drank and got myself into the right frame of mind as I prepped a couple of razors. I pulled the first one across my left forearm. *Christ, that feels good!* I continued drinking and descending, making occasional incisions. This felt so good. How could I live in the knowledge that I would never do this again? Life without self-harm wouldn't be worth living. I carried on cutting and had a half-hearted go at my wrists. I knew that this wasn't the way that I was going to go, so I didn't really attack them.

The next day, I predictably didn't get up and we didn't get to Shrewsbury. Everything that I had done slowly dawned on me. I had fucked it all up again. *How the fuck can I take something as positive as Monday and use it against myself? Too many people are getting caught in my wake. Time to go.*

I spent a bit more of Wednesday downstairs. Mum and Dad said that they were out all of the next day and asked if I would be alright. "Yeah, no problem," I said.

"Toby is booked into doggy crèche; would you like to have him here?"

"No, he'll have a good day there." I spied, with my little eye, something beginning with O. Opportunity!

That evening, I took my first anti-depressant, I felt so serene. I went to bed and had a wonderful night's sleep. I knew what the next day had in store for me, and it was what I had always craved. Peace. I just had to wait.

I woke up at a decent hour on that Thursday. I knew that Mum and Dad were going out at ten that morning, so I waited in bed until I heard the front door shutting. I was straight out of bed and went downstairs. I had a cigarette while the kettle boiled. I took my first tablets with that cuppa and proceeded to make a cup of tea every 20 to 30 minutes, taking pills with each, until they were all gone. I was definitely feeling the effects of something. One last cigarette and to bed.

I was all over the place, feeling sick and very light-headed. I felt as if I was coming up after triple-dropping some cracking disco biscuits. Just no euphoria. I think that it was already occurring to me that this might not be going the way that I wanted. I was certainly in a pretty poor state, but I wasn't falling asleep, I had no feeling that I was about to lose consciousness. I just lay in bed, waiting for it to happen. It never would.

Mum was dropped off by Dad who went to collect Toby. Shortly, she came up to my room. She had realised quite quickly that I had taken all of my antidepressants and was soon on the phone to the doctor. Going by the weight they had for me on record, they said that the quantity could prove to be a toxic dose and they were to get me to Accident & Emergency as quickly as possible. I refused at first. I didn't want anything to interfere with the outside chance that this might be it.

My father returned home with Toby and immediately came up to see me. By this time, I had realised that my number wasn't up, and so, I agreed to go to the hospital with him. I didn't know what else to do. Maybe they would be able to help. We arrived and I booked myself in at reception, and we went through to the waiting area.

We were sat there for hours overall, but it wasn't too long before I was seen for the first time. A quick interview, and then basic tests in Triage. An ECG was done and a blood sample was taken. I was sat on the bed with my top off. I was fucking pale with raw slash marks down both arms. I wasn't feeling sorry for myself. I was disgusted at myself. I had done it again. The pain and hurt that I was prepared to inflict on those close to me knew no bounds. There was no element of relief to my emotions this time.

I was called in for various tests and consultations throughout the evening while the rest of the time, I was sat with my Dad, making small talk, trying to pass the time while trying to avoid the whacking great elephant in the room. I would pop out for the occasional cigarette and my father would watch the entrance area to make sure that I didn't abscond. I couldn't fucking blame him! My lighter stopped working, so I had to start asking for a light. People gave me some really funny looks, and then it occurred to me. I must look completely off my box. I certainly felt that way.

172

Nobody was ever going to believe that this was a genuine suicide attempt. Did I still believe this? Was I just an attention-seeking cunt?

After midnight, we were called in again and I had a chat with a doctor. She was great and asked me the circumstances leading up to the overdose. Upon being asked, I told her that this was premeditated, and she asked me if I wanted to get better.

Without thinking about it, a firm "Yes!" escaped from my lips. Did I want to live?

She referred me to the Crisis Team, and we were to come back in the morning.

Dad and I made our way home and filled Mum in with the details. We had kept in touch by text message throughout the evening. I stayed in a different room that night, too many bad memories in the other one. I wouldn't sleep there again. I dug out the blanket that I had had as a child and curled up in my new bed. I didn't sleep a wink. I was still flying high from the drugs. I had no idea how I was feeling about anything. No relief that I had failed, but I couldn't work out if I was happy to have survived or not.

I stayed in bed as long as possible the following morning, despite sleep being impossible. Once I knew it was time, I was straight up and through the shower. A quick cuppa and to the hospital.

I met with a lovely lady who put me at ease straight away. We spoke for a while about my history of mental ill-health amongst other things. I told her a potted history of suicide attempts and self-harm. About my feelings of worthlessness and the fact that I had come to believe that my existence was to the detriment of everybody else's. About my drinking and my drug use. About my under-achieving and the fact that the fear of failure always beat any remaining desire to succeed that I had. "What's the worst that could happen?" she asked when talking about putting myself out there in various situations. She was right. When I was better, I knew what I was going to do.

We spoke about medication, and I mentioned that I was aware of the stigma around taking anti-depressants and that they were perceived as a sign of weakness. "Is a diabetic weak for taking insulin?" she asked.

"No, not at all."

"Well, a diabetic doesn't produce enough insulin; your body doesn't produce enough serotonin. There is no difference." The penny dropped, and ever since that moment, I haven't looked upon the Sertraline that I take as medication. It's a supplement. Pure and simple. As natural as taking Vitamin C or Cod Liver Oil.

She referred me for a psychiatric assessment. This would be in 10 to 12 weeks, so she suggested that I get in touch with my GP for guidance in the meantime. She wished me all the best, and we went our separate ways. Although I didn't necessarily feel any better, I thought that there was a chance that I might get there.

The last thing that she asked me was, "How likely are you to attempt suicide again?"

"Seventy-five per cent," I said, thinking 'one hundred per cent'.

"That's quite high." We settled on fifty.

I hid myself away for that first week. I heard from my friend who ran the club on Tuesday. She was checking in to see if I was OK as I hadn't been around for a couple of weeks. I said that I was just sorting a couple of things out. She, with a heavy heart, had to let me know that a friend of ours had died suddenly the day before. I had known him for a number of years, from my previous time in Swansea, but we had really connected since I had been back. We had gone to football once, and he ended up living across the road from me. We saw a lot of each other and got on really well. He was a gentleman. Always greeted me with a smile and never had a bad word to say against anyone.

Six weeks previously, there had been three of us who would regularly be in the club at lunchtimes on the weekends. I was the last one left, and I was clinging on. The third was a woman who drank there at the weekend. Not everybody's cup of tea, but she had a good heart. You could have a really good conversation with her and a bit of a laugh and a wind-up. News had broken a few weeks earlier that she had hanged herself. Her husband has just been sent down for her murder.

I struggled to take all of this in. I could have added to all of this. I felt incredibly selfish. There was so much going on, and I could only have added to it. I felt selfish for thinking about the impact that my death might have had on everybody.

I was nobody special, yet I was incredibly self-obsessed.

I squirrelled myself away for most of the next week too. I was back on the anti-depressants again. Sticking to the recommended dose this time. My mum was keeping hold of them for safe-keeping and dispensing them to me daily. I was starting to feel brighter and had definitely turned a corner. This might just be the start of something good. It was now time to start putting myself out there.

I messaged my friend from the pub. I asked if she wanted to walk Toby with me on Saturday. I planned to see if she wanted to make it a regular thing. I was playing my trump card in the first hand. She loved the dogs, and I knew that Toby was my ace in the pack. It didn't occur to me at the time, but I had recreated my little fantasy from the previous year. Her, me and the dog, taking long walks in the sunshine. The only difference was that the dog would have a golden coat rather than a black one.

We met up on Saturday and started walking. We chatted freely, and she seemed genuinely concerned about how I was doing. This couldn't fail. We walked for a while and decided to stop at a picnic table for a cigarette. Was this the time? We carried on talking, and she mentioned that some prick had been causing trouble between her and someone that she had started seeing. That's right. She was seeing someone, and as soon as she mentioned it, I remembered that he had told me. I was just too pissed to recall it. Now that memory was crystal clear to me. I felt like a cunt in the first degree.

We ended up having a lovely long walk and a really good chat. It was time to get over her, not just try and convince myself that I had, and I did, pretty quickly. I was aware that what I needed was to have friends around me. She has been an incredible friend to me and remains a good friend of mine to this day. We headed to the club for a couple of drinks, well for me, she was working later. I took Toby back home, and I came back out.

It was the last game of the football season, and Sky, in their infinite wisdom, had decided to broadcast Charlton's final match away at Rochdale. Dad and I had agreed to watch it indoors; this meant ordering it on the NOW TV box. Something that Dad couldn't do. My friend behind the bar in the club practically had to force me out of the door. It was my own silly fault. I had told her my plans, and she wasn't about to let me let my Dad down. I got home and we got the football on just in time for kick-off. Charlton lost one-nil, but we qualified for the play-offs.

The next day, I walked Toby and we ended up at the club. I don't know why, but I had woken up that day knowing that I was going to get absolutely fucking shitfaced. I did nothing to fight that urge and the day was a complete blur to me. It seriously was time to stop drinking.

That Monday was a Bank Holiday, and I went out with my parents and Toby to Craig-y-Nos, a country park somewhere. We had a lovely time out, and Toby had fun exploring a new environment. I felt rough all day and went straight back to bed for a little while once we got home. I didn't sleep, but I curled up under the covers with the book that I was reading. I was really starting to get into reading again. It had once been such a joy for me, but I had lost any real motivation to pick up a book. Since my overdose, I had started reading a bit. It gave me respite from my thoughts, in a less destructive way than drink or drugs ever had.

My mate's funeral was two and a half weeks later. I decided that I wouldn't have a drink until then. I had gone back to work and, though sporadic, a day or two here and there was probably what I needed then. A couple of times, I snuck in an hour in a pub far from home. I knew that this wasn't sticking to my plan, but nobody knew about these drinks, so they didn't count.

The day of the funeral arrived, and it was a big occasion. After the service, I went back home. I walked Toby and had a bite to eat. I then went food shopping with my parents before I headed over to the club. I wasn't going to have a lot to drink, just a quiet half a dozen, so it seemed stupid to go too early. I had had a couple of weeks off the booze, I was in control of it now. Dickhead.

I headed across and tasted that first pint of Carling. Lovely drop. I probably drank three pints before I said a word to anyone who didn't work there, but I did start chatting to people when they approached me. I well overstayed my welcome and left after fuck knows how many pints.

I woke up in the morning and found that I had been sick in my bin and on my bed. *You've done it again, you fucking prick. No time to clean it up now, off to work.* I can't remember much about the next couple of weeks, but I know that I didn't drink and that work dried up completely.

I would find out late at night that there was no work for the following day, and this would leave me unable to book any private work in. This had been the pattern for the year so far. I know that it was a difficult situation for my boss. I had become a little unreliable, and he wasn't busy. I think that he found it difficult to inform me of the lack of work, as he felt a sense of loyalty to me, as I did to him. He knew that I was struggling emotionally, and this just compounded these feelings. I needed to be busy, though. Spare time was still my greatest enemy, and I got increasingly frustrated about being at home for endless days, especially as there was work that I could be doing. Eventually, I stopped getting replies to my text messages regarding work, and waking up in the morning, not knowing whether to leave for work or not drove me back into the clutches of anxiety, and I would just stay in bed, unable to figure it out for myself.

At the end of May, my parents went away for a long weekend over the Bank Holiday weekend. I would have a couple of pints a night. I had done well over the last month. I deserved it.

I made myself some dinner on Friday night and went across to the club. It was absolutely dead, which suited me, and I was able to have a quite few, nothing too much. I left with a few take-outs and went home.

I got up sometime on Saturday morning and got showered, had a quick bite to eat and was at the club soon after it opened at 12:00. I stayed there all afternoon and intended to stay on, but the lady who ran it persuaded me to go home and have something to eat before coming back out for the Champions League Final, later that evening.

I went home; the quickest thing for dinner that I could figure out was a packet of 12 Turkey Drummers. I followed this up with a whole mint Vienetta, and I was all set. I most probably wasn't away for much more than an hour, but at least, I had eaten. I stayed in the club for the rest of the night and took some drinks back for myself.

On Sunday, I felt rough, and so I stayed in bed until mid-afternoon. I got some beer from the shop and had something to eat. I would go out for karaoke. I wasn't drinking alone anymore, although I did cut a solitary figure most of the time. I was going out for social occasions. Again, I had far too much to drink and, again, I took some drinks home.

Monday mainly consisted of feeling sorry for myself. My parents got home late afternoon, and I took Toby straight out for a walk. When I got in, I said that I was just going to pop over to the club for a couple of orange juice and lemonades, my tipple when I wasn't drinking. I got a sarcastic comment from somewhere, and I had my excuse to get absolutely trollied. This would be the last time that I would drink in public.

The end of that night became a bit of a blur. I ended up drinking with someone that I had known for quite a while. I was well away and agreed to go back to his. I expected to carry on drinking. He had something entirely different planned. As soon as we were through his door, his cock was out and his tongue was in my mouth. I had seriously misread the situation. I got out of there as fast as I could. I had no idea that he was gay, and I certainly don't remember where the fuck he lives. I vaguely remember stumbling all over the place on the way home and falling over somewhere.

I woke up in the morning to a text message from the night before, saying that work was cancelled, most probably for the best. I also woke up with bruises all down one side and without my glasses. I wouldn't go back to work again, and I would only get out of bed over the next 48 hours to piss and shit.

My parents were going away in June, back to Slovenia for a week. Toby would be staying with my sister, and I was welcome to visit for the duration. I had told my parents that every time that they made a sly comment about the drink, it made me really fancy one. Just like a fucking disobedient teenager, I know, but I was struggling with the urges, and I told them what I needed them to do. Dad took this on board, but there was a comment every single day from Mum.

The other bone of contention was about me staying in Swansea. I can understand their reticence about leaving me, but again, I told them not to pressure me, I would make my own decision. I had started to come around to the idea, but I was still getting some comments from Mum.

The day before they left, I got in touch with my boss, asking for assurances about work for the coming week. I was told that there would be work. I would be staying in Swansea, and I would have two weeks to myself. Looking back, I think that I would have stayed regardless. I still had this self-destructive instinct and I would have engineered something or other in order to stay. Besides, I had something that I needed to do. I had unfinished business. One way or another, my life would never be the same again.

Chapter 30

The End

Mum and Dad departed on a Tuesday morning. No work for me, and straight away, I was at a loose end.

What to do? What to do?

Ordinarily, I would have been straight in the pub, but I knew that there would be plenty of time for drinking later.

I looked around the house for something to do. It was their anniversary shortly after they were due to return, so I thought that I could surprise them with something when they came back. I decided to freshen up the garden a bit. There was a block wall that I would paint and some timber work that I would paint white. For today, I would prep everything. First things first, jet washing.

I washed everything down and moved all of the plant pots and garden furniture to a place where they would be out of the way, and then I dismantled as much of the timberwork as I needed to and cleaned that. I was feeling good about my time alone.

After finishing all of the prep work, I had a bath to dry off and came downstairs. I fancied a beer, but I had a funny idea of how this would end up and made myself a cup of tea. I stayed on the soft drinks that evening; look at the willpower in me! I had something to eat and spent a bit of time looking at masonry paint colours. I settled on a nice light blue. I would go across to B & Q tomorrow to pick it up. I had everything else that I needed. I was in bed at a reasonable hour.

I woke up the next morning and was full of positivity. I had sent a message the previous day, enquiring about work and had heard nothing back. I had a mate who had been offering me work since August. I knew that this would be a consistent five or six days a week. I decided that my loyalty had extended as far as it should, and I messaged him. He got straight back, and I was to have a trial day on Friday.

This friend was the boy my brother and I had worked with a few years ago. I knew that Friday was just a formality. I would be on the same money, but he could guarantee me consistent work. This was such a positive decision that I had made. It also left me enough time to finish the work in the garden.

Within two hours, my current boss texted me, asking me to travel to return his electric plane that I had borrowed. We would talk about work when we met. What the fuck had I done? How could I ever explain this to him? I panicked and said that I would be in for the next couple of hours but was leaving to travel up to Bromley then.

Quick as fuck, the doors were locked, and I was upstairs on my bedroom floor in the foetal position, a quivering wreck. I stayed there for nearly four hours, never in total control of my breathing. What was wrong with me? I had made a really positive decision for my benefit for what seemed like the first time in my life, yet I couldn't stand by it. He was a good bloke, and he would understand. It wasn't really working for either of us. I had no idea how to handle this situation. I undid my original decision and decided to see how it would play out.

I made my way to my bed for a couple of hours, but I was restless. There was no peace under my duvet. *Shit, how can I get back on top?* I needed some inspiration. If I could just sit down for a while, control my breathing and my heart rate, I would know what to do. I put the television on but could not settle. I tried reading, but the few words that I was taking in made no sense and the text wasn't holding my attention. I knew what would help.

I gathered myself and walked to the shop. I only needed one can of lager and that would calm me down, allowing me to think clearly. They only sold them in four-packs, so that would have to do. I picked up some cigarettes too. You could never have enough.

Once I got home, I put three cans in the fridge and opened the fourth. I took a large gulp and, ah, serenity. A couple more sizeable quaffs, and I realised that I had already drunk half a can. I would need more; even with three in the fridge, I knew that I would be out within the hour. After a quick-fire three cans, I popped back to the shop, leaving the last one chilling. A dozen cans this time. That should do it.

The fridge was abundantly stocked. I had plenty of cigarettes, so I should have been all set. I wasn't; I still couldn't relax. For some reason, I decided to go up to the loft. I had some old things up there, including some mementoes from my days in the band. I needed good memories now. I sat up there for a while and the thought occurred to me that I could just close myself away up there until my parents came home. I found a bag full of cassettes and decided to take those down with me when I left.

I found a tape player and took it up to my room. I never listened to anything on those cassettes, but I did return to my CD collection. It was beginning to get dark, so I decided that another trip to the offy was in order. I just needed enough to get through the night. Tomorrow was a new day, and I would be able to make clear my intentions to one and all. I would sleep sometime, but it was important that I didn't run out of lager before I fell to my slumber. Another dozen should do it.

I never did have the peace of sleep that night. I can't tell you how I passed the time, but it passed anyway. The sun was coming up, and I was feeling great! I looked around my room and the walls were bare. I needed to make this new space my home. I hung a couple of pictures that I had and thought about what else I could do. I had a project.

When I used to travel to away games with my father, I used to buy a pennant from each new ground that we visited. I would start putting these up on the wall. I had plenty of screws and plugs, but I decided it would be easier to use cable clips. Once they were all hanging, there was still plenty of space. I had two Welsh flags, and they went up, but I didn't have any crosses of St George. That's alright; I had some red paint. I masked a couple of crosses either side of the window and painted two red crosses on the white walls.

I was drinking the entire time and, to be honest, I still think that I did an OK job. I topped it off with a couple of scarves and some of my football shirts. I had no use for anything short-sleeved now. It was a work in progress, but it was undoubtedly my room now.

I had been manic, like a whirling dervish. Surely now, it was time to put my feet up and relax. I had used up a lot of energy and had accomplished something. I needed to get ready for my new job tomorrow, having definitely burnt my bridges with my other option. I hadn't made a decision. I was incapable of that, but my actions had seen to it that there was only one avenue left for me.

Calm would not come, and I found myself taking another trip to the off-licence. I had already been there twice that day. I carried on drinking, hiding away in my room, from nobody at all. Sunlight started to come through the curtains, but this meant nothing to me. I had nothing scheduled.

I looked at the time, and it was 7:20. Then it hit me. I was due across town in ten minutes' time. Norfolk Enchants! I sent a message, saying that I had to meet up with my old boss, just to sever ties, and I would be in on Monday. He wasn't happy and asked for assurances about Monday. I was never to answer him.

I finished the last few beers and retreated to my bed to hibernate until I could formulate a plan. I would stay there until the following Monday, getting up to have the occasional piss in the basin in my room and to replenish my glass of water. I didn't need to shit; I hadn't eaten for days.

The World Cup in Russia had started, and England had their first game against Tunisia that Monday night. It was gone six by the time I ventured downstairs. The blinds were still closed and, as it was light until late, I knew that nobody would notice the TV on from outside. I watched the entire match on mute but couldn't stop myself cheering England's late winner. I was pacing the whole time, but that was to be expected. It was a tense game.

I didn't know what to do. I was too paranoid to go outside and buy beer. There were too many people out there who wanted to surprise me. Too many people looking for me. I went back upstairs to my bedroom. I couldn't find any peace there, but I could find some solace in the knowledge that I wouldn't be detected. I would try again tomorrow.

Over this fortnight, I must have had a sprinkling of sleep, but I am conscious that it wasn't a lot. I made sure that I responded to any messages from family and friends. It was easier that they thought everything was hunky-dory. I kept the pretence of work up to people, and it became a decent excuse to borrow money from my sister and her husband.

I came down quite early that Tuesday. Probably around one. I still didn't have any appetite, but I thought that I would watch some football. The blinds would remain closed, and the door locked. I had been out of cigarettes for a few days now, but the fear of detection far outweighed the need for nicotine. I sat down to watch the afternoon match. I was pacing straight away. This was Poland versus Senegal for fuck's sake. I had no vested interest in the outcome of this game. Why couldn't I just relax? Oh well, back to bed. We'll try again tomorrow.

I stayed in bed as long as I could on that Wednesday. I knew that there was nothing good for me outside of my room. I went downstairs and boiled the kettle. In the time that it took the water to boil, I came to the conclusion that tea was not the answer. I had tried this for the last couple of days and it hadn't worked. I knew what would. I went back upstairs and had my first shower in a week. I couldn't go to the shop looking like a tramp, so I shaved as well.

Knowing what my mission was, I had no trouble whatsoever plucking up the necessary courage to go out into the wide world. Fortunately, I didn't bump into anybody that I knew, but I still convinced myself that I only needed a four-pack to take the edge off. I would be back out really quickly.

Two more trips, and I was sorted for the twilight hours. I was still going outside to smoke at this point, the alcohol having numbed the feeling of dread that even a short excursion into our small, high-walled backyard had been able to bring on. I eventually started using an empty can as an ashtray. Even in the stillness of the very early hours, there was too much risk to go out for a cigarette.

Soon the sunlight came again. I checked what time the shop opened. I had to be pro-active. I needed to get in and out without meeting anybody. The key was about going early. I still had a few cans left when the shop opened, but I knew that I could never have enough now. I was preparing for something, and I was pretty sure that I knew what it was. It was Thursday, the 21st of June. The longest day. I just had no idea how fucking long it would be.

I got back in and put my purchases in the fridge. I filled my basin full of cold water and put a four-pack in there to keep cool. The less time spent out of my room, the better. This was my world now. My prison and my sanctuary all at the same time. I knew what was coming, and I knew how to get there. I prepared my razors and pulled one across my arm. There was that release. Why hadn't I done this last week?

The fight hadn't totally deserted me, and I hadn't yet made the decision to take my life, but I knew that it was on its way. I started sending messages out to a couple of friends to try and book something in for the weekend. I hadn't completely given up. That was what I needed to tell myself at any rate. I carried on cutting myself, careful not to blunt the three razors that I had left.

I finished my last beer around, fuck knows. Time was not important now. All I knew was that mine was limited. I took out a pad of paper and just began to write. 'If there is a God, then he is a cruel cunt. This could all have been finished 25 years ago, but I have had to live in absolute torment for nothing more than his sick entertainment. I am fucking worm food! To everybody who has ever tried to help me, I am so sorry I never meant any harm.'

I left this on the chest of drawers by my bed and went to run a bath. I knew that I shouldn't, but I sent one last message, trying to get a reply from somebody. I messaged the recent object of my affections, not expecting to get a reply. She would be at work anyway. As I undressed, my phone buzzed and she had given me a 'maybe' for the weekend. *Would this be enough to save my life? Too little, too late, most probably.* I picked up my last two razors and made my way into the bath.

I woke up some indeterminable time later. I don't know if I had drifted off or if I had passed out. I was just very aware that I had woken up. The water was a pale orange, like a grubby Irn Bru colour. I'd fucked up again. I looked at my arms, several tiger stripes down the length of both. I checked my wrists, and there were some scratches. I'd left it too late again, and now, I had no plan to get over the line. Mum, Dad and Toby wouldn't be home until mid-afternoon the next day. I was somehow aware that I had several hours of daylight left today. I had a long way to go yet, and I couldn't do it alone.

I pulled the plug from the bath and sat there as the water drained away to reveal my pitiful form and two razor blades. I tried each one, both struggled to draw blood.

I put on some comfortable clothes, counted my money and headed to the shop.

Twenty-four cans and 40 cigarettes. I didn't even think about buying more razors. This oversight may just have saved my life. As I held my hand out for my change, my sleeve rode up and showed the angry scratches on my left wrist. I quickly pulled my hand away and looked at the lady who had served me. She looked at me and smiled. Had she seen them?

Isolation was the order of the day, and it had become too risky to keep popping down to the fridge. Somebody might be peering over the wall at the back of the house and see me. I took all of my shopping up to my room and closed myself away. The curtains were drawn; they always were. For good measure, I forced three screwdrivers under my door. I couldn't be found now. I just had to sit tight until my saviours arrived.

I sat or lay in bed as the light disappeared outside. Drinking. If I kept on drinking, I would be ok. I became conscious of my dwindling supplies. Twenty cans will never last. The more anxious I got about running out of beer and fags, the faster I drank and the quicker I smoked. Soon light started to come. Not long now. It was Friday, the 22 of June 2018, and this would be the longest day.

A couple of hours later, I opened my last can. I tried my hardest to make it last, curling up in between sips. I don't know how many cigarettes I smoked with this last can, but it seemed like a way to pass the time. I wasn't worried about the beer getting warm, it had been room temperature for hours. Eventually, it was empty, and I was left defenceless.

Just me, myself and I now. I needed more to drink, and a frantic search of the house ensued, but there was nothing to be had.

"I need a fucking drink!"

You can't have one, I told myself.

"Then I need a fucking razor!"

I bet that there is one in your old room. You never throw anything out, you scruffy cunt!

Sure enough, I was able to find one quite quickly, but only one. I started to take the individual blades out but couldn't be bothered, and so, I was left with a triple blade. It looked pretty clean; there was plenty of life left in them. More than I had, definitely.

I was in contact with a couple of friends and continued our conversations. I was trying to eat up the seconds. I knew that I had thousands to get through, and every single one of them counted. The more seconds I had to myself, the more chance that this would end badly for me. Or did it give me more chance of achieving what I truly desired? I just didn't know. I hadn't resolved that internal conflict, that choice between life and death. I knew that I wouldn't have to wait long for my decision. It was my decision, but it was totally out of my hands now. I had no way of influencing the outcome.

You shat yourself on the Snowdon Mountain Railway!

What?

Remember when you were at Boys' Brigade and you couldn't pluck up the bollocks to ask people who you knew where the toilets were?

I did.

You just sat there and pissed yourself, and you sat in your own piss until it was time to move. You pathetic little wanker!

I was just shy.

185

You weren't too shy to stick your tongue in your mate's ear in Year Seven! You thought that it would be funny. How did that work out for you? Fuck off! You were so desperate for approval that you told everybody at school that you had slept with your 'girlfriend'. Had you?

No, but...

Nobody believed you. Everybody saw you for what you were. A fucking bullshit cunt who couldn't be trusted.

No.

You have always been an object of ridicule! People only spend time with you because you make them feel better about themselves. "At least I'm not Steve," they all say. Why have you never excelled at anything? I'll tell you why, because you have never tried. Why haven't you tried? Because you are destined to fail! Everything you touch turns to shit! You have enhanced the life of absolutely nobody. If you hadn't been born, the world would be a better place right now.

Fuck off!

You fuck off!

You know that I'm right. How much money have you stolen from people trying to help you? You have used their completely misplaced affection for you to fleece them out of thousands.

I know.

You are nothing but a dirty fucking doormat. Something for people to trample with their shitty boots. You dropped a drumstick playing 'The Rock Garden'...twice! No wonder they wanted you out. That was your closest, oldest mate, and once he had no use for your money, you were gone! He knew you better than anyone, and he fucked you off first chance that he had! You still bought him drinks and drugs and watched them play. You fucking desperate muggy little cunt! It could've been so different. You've got a good brain, but you never ever stood up for yourself. Think about what you have done to yourself over the years. The violence that you have used against yourself could have been used for your defence.

But I'm not violent.

Look at your fucking arms! You are violent. You just don't have the bottle to use it against other people. How many times have you taken a good fucking kicking?

Never.

Exactly, you are so pathetic that people feel too sorry for you to kick the shit out of you.

I'm a good bloke.

Ha-ha-ha! You have continually taken liberties with people who have just wanted to help you. Is it any wonder that you have ended up alone? You fucking waste of spunk! You have been a constant disappointment to everyone that matters. It's time to give them a fucking break and let them get on with their lives.

But my family love me.

How the fuck can they fucking love you? All you do is take. Financially, emotionally, materialistically. They would be so much better off without you. There would be no grieving, a quick shock perhaps, but just relief. You would be one less thing to worry about. You fucking parasite. You drain everything from everybody's lives! All you care about is yourself.

That's not true.

Name one thing that you have done for the benefit of somebody else.

I worked hard for my brother.

You worked hard for your fucking drugs! He worked as hard as you and had all of the skill and ability, and you fucking ponced off him. You probably ruined his marriage, you complete and utter arsehole! You probably caused your sister to have a miscarriage the way you were carrying on, you cunt! Just fucking go! Do it! For the good of your family! Fucking kill yourself!

I drew my triple-blade across my left forearm. The deepest, widest gash that I had ever inflicted on myself opened up and filled with blood immediately. The blood started to run down my arm. The severity of the cut shocked me. I knew that I couldn't stop what I was doing. I had lost all control. I curled up again. *Please, Steve, stay alive today!* A voice in my head pleaded.

Fucking stay alive? How selfish can you get? Haven't you caused enough pain? What possible good can come from your continued existence? You are just an absolute fucking arsehole! The only emotion you bring out in people is pity. It took Dad 25 years to build up the business, and you fucked it up in 6 months! For what? Drink and drugs, and playing the fucking big boy. Where was the big boy at work? People used to laugh at you because you were so weak. You have always been the butt of the joke. People only drank with you because they knew you would do something stupid. You are nothing but a fucking prank monkey. Absolutely useless! Remember when you were sick and immediately stuck your tongue down that bird's throat? Watch out Casa-fucking-nova! That really was your most successful moment with the ladies. If you don't count the lies, of course! Cunt! You used to think that you were a good person.

I still am.

Ha-ha-ha! Fuck off! You are the lowest of the low! When was the last time anybody invited you anywhere?

My sister always invites me up.

She's fucking family; she has to. Everybody in your family would have done better if you weren't around. It's too late to make amends. You've had enough chances. Cunt! The only feeling of joy that you invoke in others is the gratitude that they aren't you. Everything else that you provide for people is negative. You have been spoon-fed everything, and you have fucked it all up. You unbelievably useless cunt! Why do you insist on diminishing people's lives? Haven't you done enough? Cunt! You were the big boy at football, weren't you? Yeah, in a fucking crowd. That old geezer put you in your place. One of your own fans putting you in a headlock because you got out of your seat from time to time. You shat yourself. Cunt! Why don't you have a wank then? That's what you would usually do? Everybody knows it. Steve, he has a line and can't wait to burp the fucking worm! That's all that you are ever going to do. No matter how much you look on the internet, not even the dirtiest slag will want to touch your rancid cock! Cunt! You couldn't even step up when Klint needed you.

I know.

Your supposed best mate, and you let him down. You never gave a shit for that dog. All you had to do was go home, but it was too fucking hard for you to see him like that. His best years were away from you. You selfish fucking cunt! Cut! You're such a cunt that the only motivation you have for staying alive is to spread more misery. Cunt! Your only function is to spoil people's enjoyment. You live to bring them down to your level! Cunt! If you can't be happy, then nobody else has the right to be! Selfish fucking Cunt! Do everybody a fucking favour! Cunt! Cut! That's it. You've got the idea now. Don't let me interrupt you. Cunt! Cut! Cunt! Cunt! Cunt! Cunt! Cut! Cunt! Cunt! Cut! Cut! Cunt! Cut! Cut! Cut! Cut! Cut! Cut!!!!

And breathe. I looked down at my arms. They were almost completely scarlet. Blood was dripping from them and off my fingers; a puddle had formed on my bed where I lay.

Look at the fucking state of you. You have got to go now. Your fucking wrists! Do your fucking wrists! Cut! Cut! Cut! Cut! Cut!

Just a few scratches appeared.
Have I bottled it?
No, you useless cunt. You've blunted your fucking blades! What now? You have got to go!
I checked my tool bag and I had nothing that would do any good. I got my nail clippers and pinched my upper left arm with them.
Ha-ha-ha! I thought that you were meant to be fucking intelligent! I guess we got that one wrong.
Now what?
I lay my head on my arms on my pillow. I felt like I should be crying, but nothing. Although I had all of the physical manifestations of still being alive, I was breathing and my heart still pumped blood around my body to spill out of my self-inflicted wounds; to all intents and purposes, I was a dead man.

I received a message from Mum. The traffic was terrible and they were going to be a little later than planned. *Please, no!* Time passed; I had no idea how much. I tried not to check the time. I knew that I just had to ride this out. Knowing how many hours to go was of no use to me. If I just lay there, hoping that I would make it. The silence was deafening. I needed fucking YouTube. 'This is my fight song.

You've never had any fight, you fucking bottle-job cunt! 'Take back my life' song, *Take your fucking life!* 'Prove I'm alright song', *You've never been all right and you never fucking will!*
'My powers turned on'.
You're fucking weak!
'Starting right now, I'll be strong'.
How many times have you said that?
'I'll play my fight song, and I don't really care if nobody else believes 'cause I've still got a lot of fight left in me!'

Ha-ha-ha! You don't even believe that! Nobody else believes in you. They've all got your number! Coward! Too weak to live, and you don't even have the bottle to do the decent thing. What will they think when they see you? Your dead body will be a better sight for them to come home to!

PILLS!

My sheet came with me as I tried to get up. I had to peel myself off my bedclothes. I caught myself in the mirror. The bulk of my upper body was different shades of red. My torso, arms and face were all covered in blood, different shades for different stages of drying and saturation. I looked into the eyes that looked back at me. Those cold, empty eyes. Did they really belong to me? There was nothing left inside of me. I was completely lifeless.

I went downstairs. I didn't bother to get dressed. Maybe I was hoping someone would see me and help me. I was incapable of helping myself now. I checked the kitchen cupboards for any painkillers or anything else. Nothing. Of course, nothing.

You are a 37-year-old man who can't be trusted around medication. You big, fucking baby!

I looked under the sink and spied a bottle of bleach. I raised it to my mouth but bottled it. *I would never be able to keep it down.* My stomach was in the tightest of knots, and I had had too much to drink. *How much?* I decided to count my empty cans; the kitchen worktop was covered. Between the kitchen, my room and the recycling in the shed, I counted 112 empties. In two sittings? I was probably only eleven stone dripping wet in my work boots.

Still don't think that you have a drinking problem?

I only did it because of my poor mental health.

I'm fucking done! I retorted to myself.

Back to my pit. I started looking through my tools. *A hacksaw?* I dragged it across my left arm.

That won't hack it. This is no time for fucking jokes. This is serious, cunt! Screwdrivers, spanners, scrapers and filling knives.

I know that I don't have any Stanley blades. I'm not allowed them anymore.

What about your fucking hammer?

My hammer is still out from decorating my room.

I picked it up and swang it full pelt at my head. My legs went from underneath me. My vision went like the static on an old television, and I fell to the ground. *Again!* I swang again, but my grip was weak, and I caught myself a glancing blow and the hammer flew away, landing on my bed.

A proper man would have made that count!
Fuck off, just fuck off!

I crawled back onto my bed. The respite of physical pain was all too brief. I thought about hitting myself again. I swung at my right knee. It hurt, but no damage was done. I wasn't even able to knock myself out. I lay back under my duvet and hoped among all hopes that I would soon be out of this hell, one way or another. My bed was tacky all over, and I was fairly sure that I had bled through all three of my pillows. I was not bleeding much now; most of my wounds had clogged, and so, it's not as if I would bleed out. I might just make it. I just needed to lie there.

I got another message. My parents were encountering traffic problems all the way along their route. *For fuck's sake.* I now knew that I was not meant to make it. It's my destiny to die today. I gave it my best shot. I knew that at some point, I would have to get up and finish the job that I started. I lay there for as long as I could, my thoughts torturing me the whole time. I knew that every moment was a moment closer to whatever conclusion that day would have.

Think.
What to do? What to do? Come on, you can actually be resourceful when you want to be.

My mind had changed tack, knowing when to encourage me.
Think. You must have plenty of ideas. Think about what someone else would do.
Hanging?
There's a good boy.
I got out of bed again, with renewed purpose. I didn't have anything to use.

Think.
I can't tie decent knots anyway.

Think. There must be another way.

Belts. I had not long bought two 'one size fits all' belts from Primark. I figured out a system using them both. I picked up my impact driver and four three-inch screws and went to the loft.

I set up the ladder we used and ascended to my final destiny. I screwed one of the belts into a rafter right above the loft hatch. I checked it, and it took my weight easily. I only needed to retrieve my other belt, and I would be out of pain. I went back to my room.

I was freezing. I had been shivering all day. The drink won't have helped. I had been wearing nothing but a pair of pants the whole time, and I had no idea how much blood I had lost. It was a fair bit. I just need to feel warm again. Just once. I got under the duvet and curled up, bringing the duvet up to my ears. This was approaching comfort.

Are you fucking bottling it again?
Yes, I think I am.

Chapter 31

Chapter 1

I lay there in my cocoon for what seemed like an eternity. I had succumbed to my fate. I would live. I was far from over the moon about this. It felt as though my fate had been taken out of my own hands again. Motionless for an unspecified amount of time, I worried about moving at all. I don't know why. I'd found a place where I had a modicum of security, and I didn't want to do anything to jeopardise that.

My phone vibrated. Another message from Mum. They were just passing Cardiff. About an hour then. *What to do? What to do?*

I couldn't let them find me like this. I got up and took myself into the bathroom. I ran the shower and just stood underneath it. I knew that I couldn't wash myself too vigorously; my arms were covered in congealed blood. Now that I was going to survive, I didn't want to make myself bleed too badly. I gently rubbed some shower gel over myself, and I saw the deep red hue slowly diminish. My hair was matted, a mixture of sweat and blood. I kept checking myself in the mirror to see that all of the blood was gone and then turned the shower off and dried myself, dabbing, not rubbing.

Once dressed, it was time to survey the damage. My bedroom looked like somebody had been brutally murdered in there. Not too far from the truth, another part of me had died in that room over the last 48 hours. I closed the door behind me and headed downstairs. I was still not sure what I was going to tell my parents. They were still blissfully unaware of the horror that awaited them on their return. Could I hide this all from them?

The kitchen didn't take too long to put straight. There were a few bloody smudges to wipe, and then it's just dozens of cans to crush and put in a recycling bag. As I put the recycling into the shed, I noticed the plant pots and everything else in the centre of the backyard. Christ, I was so full of hope and good intentions. This was only ten days ago, although it felt like another life.

Mum and Dad made it home. A journey that would usually take four hours or so had taken nine. As they crossed the road, I still wasn't sure what I was going to tell them, if anything. When they came into the living room, I just grabbed the first one, Mum I think, and said, "I've been stupid again." I don't think too much more was said, but Dad quickly went down to the shop and came back with some cigarettes for me.

We didn't talk too much. I asked them about their holiday but didn't really listen to their stories. Toby stayed close to me, licking the sleeves of my hoodie. I'm convinced that he was trying to soothe my wounds. The only time that they would cause me any discomfort was when the flesh started to knit back together. Mum took a look at my room. I said that we would tackle that tomorrow. I was asked if I wanted anything to eat, but I still had no appetite. When the fuck did I actually last eat? This week?

Last week? One of the two.

I slept in my soiled bed that night. Most of the blood had now dried, and so, the sheets had a crispy feel to them. When I say sleep, I may have drifted in and out for a while. I certainly didn't get my eight hours. Come to think of it, when was the last time that I actually slept? This week? Last week? I didn't know. All that I knew was that my body and my mind had been absolutely battered by the events of the last ten days.

Before I got up, I had to cancel my prospective plans for the day. I sent a message, saying that I couldn't make it, and had a ready-made excuse in place. I got a message back, asking if everything is OK. I responded in the affirmative, and I got the feeling that that was that. She got back asking again. I was going to tell her that I had a day's work. She was an incredibly perceptive person and somehow got me to open up. I didn't tell her the whole truth but a short precis. She knew just what to say and, although I was a long way from it, I felt a little better. She said that she would check on me during the week. It turned out that it was extremely unlikely that she would have had the time to meet me, but I guess she sensed something was up and gave me a 'maybe'. I honestly think that this might just have swung things my way. Without that, I might not be here writing this.

That Saturday was a day of nothingness. My Mum cleaned my room for me. I tried to help but kept going light-headed. I sat down and watched some of the

World Cup with Dad. We would watch part of every remaining game. It proved to be a great tonic and was a huge part of the healing process for me. England's relative success was great but incidental. We would watch any two teams slug it out and chat nonstop throughout. I really do enjoy watching football with my father.

Sunday came, and I realised that I hadn't resolved anything. I had never made the choice of whether to live or die, and this conflict was still very much alive in me. I knew that when it got to this stage, there was only one way that it would end. England's six-nil victory of Panama was enjoyable, but I was becoming very aware that I was still plotting my downfall.

I had a psychiatric evaluation booked for the Tuesday after next, and I just had to get there. I knew that one drink would put me on the way to eternal rest. I think that I was quite prepared to go that way. On Monday, my mother phoned our GP's surgery, and the earliest that I could get an appointment for my doctor was on Friday. Could I wait that long? Of course, I could. This left my options open.

My friend was as good as her word and messaged me when she finished work on Monday. She was glad to hear that I was feeling a little more myself, and she wondered if I fancied going for a walk. I wasn't there yet and said so. She said to let her know when I was. I knew that I had to get out of the house sometime, and that just the act of going for a walk would be beneficial for my state of mind. I messaged her back within half an hour, and we made preliminary plans for Wednesday evening.

Tuesday came and went, and I noticed that I was gagging for a drink. I knew what that would entail. It would facilitate the end of my life. As simple as that. I could have walked out of the house at any point and found a drink, but I needed an excuse. Nobody could blame me then. The fact that it had been only two months since my last breakdown, or whatever these episodes were, was extremely prevalent in my mind. I had been chemically assisted in my recovery this time as well. If antidepressants couldn't help me, then what chance did I have? *I can't do this for another 40 years!*

I got a message at lunchtime on Wednesday, just confirming arrangements for that evening. I met her at the bottom of the road, by the prom, after she had finished work. I was shaking like a leaf and chain-smoking. This was the first time that I had been out of the house in the last six days, since my final excursion to the off-licence.

We walked along the prom for a while and eventually found ourselves at the pier. She helped to put me at ease, as much as I could be, and helped me to talk through some issues, offering useful advice and words of encouragement. That girl just gets people. It was a beautiful, sunny evening, and we decided to stay at the pier for a cuppa, enjoying the weather.

We were out for about three hours, all told and talked freely the whole time, about any number of topics, even having the odd laugh. When we first found a table, she asked what the table number was. I laughed. It was 33. I knew she would have to say "Tirty-tree" at the counter. This backfired on me when I realised that I couldn't say thirty-three either.

"Firty-free please, mate." I got home feeling a lot better. This trip had given me a bit of a boost. I had no idea how important that would be.

The next day was a Thursday, and I had started getting up at a decent hour from Monday. I felt better that morning than I had for a long time. Next Tuesday didn't seem too far away now; I was starting to believe that I might actually make it. I was probably expecting too much from this appointment, but I was starting to think that I was being taken seriously. I was going to find out what was wrong with me. I was going to get better.

I spent the morning around the house, drinking copious amounts of tea and smoking every time that the kettle was on. I was able to sit down and watch crap TV, never fully relaxed but aware that every episode of *Judge Judy* was half an hour nearer my appointment.

Just before lunch, the postman came. I was the only one in and picked up the mail. There was a letter for me. I knew exactly what it was before I opened it. My appointment with the psychiatrist had been postponed for a week. It now felt further away than it ever had. I had my excuse. All I had to do was walk out of that door, for one last time, get a drink, and the rest would take care of itself. But I didn't.

Something held me back. I was really pissed off. I was despondent to the point that I knew that I didn't have a chance now. I couldn't fight it anymore. Everything was against me. Pointless fighting the universe, and it's destiny for me.

Go and have a drink and take what's coming to you, I thought. But I didn't.

I wasn't alone very long; Mum came in and then Dad shortly after. I was frantic for a good couple of hours. Drinking a cup of tea most probably every quarter of an hour, smoking every time that the kettle boiled, totally unable to settle. I couldn't stay seated in the living room, in the garden or in my bedroom. I just paced around, tea in hand. I finally settled for a bit when Dad put the afternoon football match on. I had no idea who played that day, but the anxiety started to recede.

The date was the 28 of June 2018, my parents' 43rd wedding anniversary, and I now believe that that was the day I chose to live.

I made it through that day and went to the doctor's the following morning. I feel so blessed to have found a doctor like her. She was so compassionate, and it was easy to believe that she was genuinely concerned for me. She doubled my dosage and gently reiterated her desire for me to contact an alcohol dependency agency. Even knowing the inevitable consequence of one more drink, I shied away from this. I wasn't an alcoholic. My problems were psychological, nothing else. Once they were sorted, I could continue to drink, socially of course. I wouldn't have to abstain for long. She gave my mum a number.

The weekend passed, and on Saturday, my father and I watched as England comfortably qualified for the World Cup semi-finals. I was feeling better, physically stronger, definitely, and some improvement in my mental health. I was holding out on contacting the dependency agency. Was I giving myself more time to fuck up? I don't know.

Sunday was my first time out on my own. This was the day that I had aimed for. Just me and Toby, and a nice, long walk. The anxious state that I was still in it was never going to be a long walk, and we ended up in the club after about half an hour. My friend in there, the lady who ran it, asked what I would like to drink. "Orange juice and lemonade, please." I don't think she would have served me a pint if I had begged her. I didn't stay long, but I had made it. I had made it without a drink as well.

That week, I carried on much as before—watching football, and I started to put my plans into action in the garden. Mum and Dad would have their anniversary present, even if they had to buy the paint themselves now. Oh, and the wall would be olive green rather than light blue, but we would get there. In the meantime, England lost their semi-final to Croatia, but they had had a great tournament, and I finally had an England team that I was proud to support again.

Thursday came and another letter. *You have got to be fucking kidding me!* My assessment with the Psychiatrist had been cancelled again, and I hadn't been given another date. Cue another frenetic couple of hours. Pacing, drinking scalding hot tea and chain-smoking.

Mum had given me the number for the alcohol dependency agency earlier in the week. Eventually, I picked up the phone. I needed some prospect to cling to. I had to get in touch with the assessment centre first. A quick call to them, and I was told that they had open hours on Monday and Tuesday mornings. I would go on Tuesday.

Sunday, and I was out with Toby again. I popped into the club and asked my friend, "Do you think that I'm an alcoholic?" What a question, I know. She didn't know, and I realise now that it was a terrible thing to put on her. I would ask my Irish friend the same question the following evening when we met for a cuppa. I went home and watched the World Cup Final with my old man.

Monday was a day just to get through. I finished the garden and was pretty pleased with the outcome. It definitely brightened the place up, and Dad put the pots back in such a way that the space felt bigger. That evening, I had a very pleasant time out at the pier again. My friend couldn't shed any light on my enquiry, and again, I realise now that I had no right to ask. I was starting to feel that I might just have turned a corner.

I woke up a little apprehensive about what was to come. Dad came with me and sat in the waiting room until I was taken in. He offered to wait, but I said that I would make my own way home. *Total honesty, Steve.* I was assessed and given two options. The agency that my doctor had suggested was about total abstinence and used the Alcoholics' Anonymous Twelve Step plan. The other choice was an agency called Barod, the Welsh word for Ready. They were about harm reduction and initial abstinence, possibly leading to pathways to controlled drinking. This was what I was after, and she sent a letter of referral off for me.

The way that I justified my choice was twofold. My problem was mental, not with alcohol or any other substance. Once I got help for my psychological issues, I would be able to go back to drinking. Secondly, I knew that I had to be one hundred per cent honest about everything. I couldn't stand up and say, "My name is Steve and I am an alcoholic." If I didn't believe it, and I didn't, regardless of whether it might open the path to some support. Yeah, I know. Whatever screwed up logic I used to come to my decision, I'm pretty sure that it has turned out to be one of the best decisions of my life.

Barod had a programme called SMART Recovery, and they had a meeting that day at 1:30. I wandered into town to see where they were and thought that I might attend my first group that afternoon. I still had some Primark vouchers from my birthday, so I went and bought a couple of jumpers. When I got out, I had about two and a half hours until the meeting.

What to do? What to do? I'll just do what I always do, get a paper and sit in a pub to pass the time.
Get on a fucking bus and fuck off home, you massive fucking bellend!

I did exactly that. SMART Recovery could wait for another day.

Chapter 32

Hope, from Somewhere, Hope

That Friday, I caught a bus into town to see what SMART Recovery was all about. I pondered whether I was an alcoholic or not. Alcohol was just something that I used to cope with my mental problems. This was something that I have convinced myself over and over again. I was attending with an open mind. I started wondering what would happen if I hear something that resonates with me and I had to admit to an addiction. I could never drink again. I thought about fucking it off and going to the pub. There's always another day.

Somehow, I made it to Barod where the group was held. It felt as if I had strained every sinew in my mind and body to avoid having a drink, but I made it through the door. Shortly, we were taken up to a room where we sat in comfortable chairs in a sort of circle. There were people from all walks of life there, of all different ages.

There was a short introduction explaining what SMART was all about. SMART stands for Self-Management And Recovery Training. They shy away from labels such as alcoholic and addict. Everybody was asked to check-in. Just a quick explanation of what you are each doing there and possibly how your week has been. I thought that I would just sit this first one out. As it came around to my turn, I found myself sharing a little about myself, explaining how my drinking was a direct result of my mental health issues.

After check-in, there was a group discussion and some work on a flip-chart, led by the facilitator, but not dictated by him. The work on the flip-chart demonstrated one of the many SMART tools. They were mainly Cognitive Behavioural Therapy or Rational Emotive Behavioural Therapy tools. It's not about trying to force you to admit powerlessness over your substance misuse, it's all about taking responsibility for it. You are the only thing that makes you use, and it is in your power to stop using and find another way. It ended with a checkout, just one thing that you had planned for the near future. Scheduling. Nice!

The meeting lasted an hour and a half. I walked out thinking that there was definitely something in it, to help with my psychological issues, of course. I was struck by the determination by the people in the room to become better versions of themselves. Everybody knew that they had behaved badly and hurt people around them, and the desire to make amends was immense. There was absolutely no judgement. I left knowing that I would be back.

Time for a pint. Dickhead! I jumped on the bus home.

I was trying to get a date for my psychiatric assessment. I called a couple of times, I was clearly feeling better but was told that the doctor I was to see was off with flu. This appointment was still critical for me, and I needed something tangible as soon as possible.

My best mate from back home had been in constant contact with me over the last few months. He had contacted Swansea Mind before my overdose to see if there was anything that they could do for me. They had told him that I needed to get in touch to arrange an assessment. He hadn't told me about this earlier because he didn't think that I would be receptive. He was right. Now, however, his timing was impeccable, and I called immediately to arrange a meeting.

Not knowing what to expect, I was a little nervous to go along. I had no idea how deep they wanted to delve. I walked through the front door and was met by over a dozen faces. I can't remember any of the faces from that day, besides the lady who interviewed me, but I am sure that some of those have become friends and people that I have come to care about very deeply.

The assessment was a very informal affair, and I was now able to attend their Anxiety and Depression peer support groups. I was also put on their waiting list for one-to-one counselling. I would become a regular soon enough.

The groups at Mind followed a slightly different format. Everybody got a chance to speak about what was happening with themselves and if they were struggling with anything. I was free to chip in with anything that I thought might be encouraging or helpful. Mutual aid is the term they use now, and it is exactly that.

I was put at ease very quickly and was surprised at how soon I was sharing some very deep, personal details. Through going to both Mind and SMART, I have come to realise that everybody's story can have some value to you. On the flip side, it has been quite empowering to discover that people can find some solace and encouragement from my words and experiences.

It was still incredibly important that I was keeping busy at this time, so I set about clearing out my old room. There was a huge amount of clutter and crap, and I was quite ruthless. My certificate for 'Most Likely to Die of Liver Failure' was finally thrown out. It was time to move on. I moved some of the furniture to my new room, and the rest was discarded. Any spare space on my walls was adorned with more scarves, shirts and pennants. My room looked like that of a ten-year-old boy, but it was mine and I was surrounded by great memories, if not necessarily successes, so who the fuck cares?

My old room was in dire need of decorating, and so, with my parents providing materials and a little financial incentive, I set about giving it a new lease of life.

Perfectionism is something that I have always suffered from in a work environment. The bedrooms in my parents' house had shitty Artex ceilings and walls poorly decorated with woodchip wallpaper. To get a sharp line between the white ceilings and the coloured walls was damn near impossible and was something that had driven me absolutely crazy in the past. It could look good from the top of the steps as you paint it, but from the ground, it looked shit. I now seemed able to appreciate that it was never going to be perfect and would accept what I had done. I did a few touch-ups, but I didn't let it cause me any insomnia. Was this personal growth?

No, you're just getting lazy!
Fuck off.

Over the summer, I redecorated the three spare bedrooms in the house. I was in my element, brush in hand, radio blaring. I could feel myself getting stronger. Since this time, I have been out of bed every morning at seven o'clock, eager for each coming day. I am in bed around nine most nights and read for anywhere between 30 minutes and 3 hours. Reading has become a huge passion of mine again. Almost exclusively non-fiction. I read a lot of biography and history, especially about the World Wars. True life stories of hardship and overcoming this by spirit and willpower alone are the most inspirational for me. My addictive behaviour began to manifest itself within this hobby. I found it increasingly difficult to walk past a charity shop without going inside and, more often than not, walking out with a bag full of books. This is now under control, and I am slowly working through my backlog, before the next inevitable splurge in the new year. This sort of relapse doesn't have too much of a downside.

I eventually got my psychiatric appointment 15 weeks after my initial referral. It was at nine o'clock in Swansea City Centre. I was excited by the fact that some progress might finally be made. I could go from there to Mind, and then on to SMART. If things went really well, I might be cured by this evening!

I was a little bit late being seen, but this was no problem; I had time. We chatted for a while, recounting my experiences for the umpteenth time. A lot of focus was put on my drink and drug use. "No wonder you're depressed," I was told. It didn't really seem as though she could get past this, and she seemed totally uninterested when I tried to tell her that I had had suicidal thoughts before I started using. It turns out that I didn't have a personality disorder, I had Mixed Anxiety and Depressive Disorder. I left with her final evaluation of me going through my head over and over again. "You're normal, you're normal. I don't know what you're doing here. You're normal." Had I chosen to live my life this way? Was that the path that I had decided to follow? Had I done this all to myself? I needed a fucking pint!

I didn't go to the pub. I went and got a cup of tea and sat down, trying to figure things out for myself. I let my family and a couple of friends know and was given some decent guidance. "At least they are narrowing it down," one friend mentioned. This helped to change my perspective. I had a referral to the Local Primary Mental Health Support Service, so it wasn't as if the door had totally slammed shut in my face. I was still very unsettled by the notion that I had sought out this existence for myself. Was I really that fucked up?

I got home in a much better frame of mind after my groups at Mind and Barod. Fortunately, that assessment didn't hold the absolute power over me that it had done a month previously. I had plenty of support, and I knew that I was heading in the right direction. I was finding a way myself, albeit with massive support and guidance.

About a month into my recovery, we received the sad news that a close family friend had lost the long-term battle with his health. This was upsetting, but not an absolute shock; he had been unwell for a very long time and had been in residential care since the beginning of the year.

I have never dealt very well with death, preferring to totally disregard it or shut it out with whatever was available at the time. I didn't feel an enormous amount of grief around this. I was well aware that I was experiencing proper emotions for the first time in however long, but I had no crushing sadness or feeling of loss. I started to worry that my supplement was numbing me to anything that might upset me. Was this what I wanted? I didn't want to substitute one unfeeling life for another, even if I was going to be happier in my new existence. Life without emotion is not any life at all. My answer would come soon.

Not long after this, we found a lump on Toby's right hind leg. It seemed to come up very quickly, almost overnight, and so, an appointment with the vet was made. We took him in. He loved going to the vet, just like Klint. After an examination, a tissue sample was taken and sent off to a lab. It could be either a fatty deposit, he had been a fat bastard after all, or it was some sort of tumour. He was weighed and only needed to drop one more kilo. We went home to await the news.

When the news came back, it was what we feared. He had a masked cell tumour, and it would need to be removed as soon as possible. This diagnosis opened up recent wounds and the rapidity of Klint's descent. He was booked in for surgery the next Tuesday but clearly couldn't wait to get to the vet's. For the second Sunday, in four, he managed to get at the fruit bowl. He ate a large bunch of grapes, very toxic, and nine doughnut peaches, stones and all. These could cause a blockage. He would stay in a doggy hospital until after his surgery and would actually have contact with the surgery for 9 of the next 13 days.

The surgery was a success and, after analysis, the tissue that they had removed was seen to be clear all around the tumour, they were confident that they had got all of the cancer, and now, Toby just had to convalesce and wait for his wound to heal before his stitches came out. Toby was resplendent in his cone but took far too long to figure out that he was a bit wider than he used to be. He was to be kept calm at all times, especially no jumping!

With the loss of weight, Toby also shed any lethargy that he may have had. It'd been wonderful to see him come out of his shell and exhibit his extra energy. He had certain puppyish qualities to his behaviour. This was cute, but it did mean that he popped a couple of his stitches, and his wound started to open up. He had to go back under the knife and be stitched up again. We were given Xanax for him this time, to try and keep him subdued. I don't think that it had the desired effect, but his wound healed nicely and, now that his fur has grown back, you have to know that it is there to see it.

For a double whammy, my sister was admitted to hospital around the time of Toby's diagnosis. She had been having stomach problems for a while and wasn't able to get any news from her doctor. Apparently, they couldn't find the time to read her results. She was to spend six days in the hospital and would never get a diagnosis.

She was put on a soft diet and things cleared themselves up.

My sister has always been there for me, with no exceptions, and I felt so helpless being over two hundred miles away. I knew that I was less of a burden to her now, but I wasn't able to offer any real help or reassurance. She knows what I think of her, and the better I get, the better brother I can be for her in the future. This is a huge motivator for me.

I met with my caseworker at Barod once a month. He had stated to me that I was his easiest client, as everything was going quite well for me. He gave me a great idea in one of our earlier meetings. I said that I needed to work for my self-esteem as much as anything, but I didn't know what I wanted to do. He suggested volunteering and gave me a couple of places to contact.

Part of my problem was that I had never had any idea of what I had wanted to do with my life. After a bad episode, I had always taken the first offer of work that had come along. Invariably, this had been a step backwards. After consulting with my parents, I decided that volunteering was a good idea. This could prove to be another one of the best decisions I have ever made.

I went to the local voluntary service and looked through the binder of opportunities that they had in their waiting room. One thing jumped out at me straight away. There was a role where you would go into a local mental health hospital and talk to some of the patients. This seemed like a good first tentative step for me to take. I asked for a copy of the details and the receptionist went one better, booking me an interview for that afternoon. I rushed home to change into one of my dress items of knitwear and was back out after something to eat.

The lady who would go through the application was friendly and contagiously enthusiastic. It was impossible not to get excited. I went through the formalities and had all of the documentation that I needed. I left to await dates for my training. I felt sky-high. I might yet be able to find a purpose in life.

The training was to take place on two consecutive Mondays. It was really interesting and informative. Lots of information launched at me. I always worry about retaining that much information in such a short space of time, but I left feeling that I was ready to do the role. There was also a further role that I was interested in, Peer Mentor.

Because I had personal experience of mental ill-health, I could do a further day's training at a later date and I would be placed with someone who suffers from mental health issues. My role would be to meet with them once a week and help them in general tasks or take them on short excursions. I put my name down immediately. I had found genuine direction without even having to look, just by taking a step back and relying on my instincts.

Next up was a post-training interview. All looked good, and I was getting quite excited now. During our chat, my options in the mental health facility were laid out in front of me. They had a drop-in centre for the patients where people would come to us for a chat. This seemed a perfect, pressure-free first step. There would be scope, later on, to go on to one of the wards, female, male, seniors or substance abuse. Without hesitation, before I had even thought about it, I said that the substance misuse ward really interested me. I just had my DBS check to do now, and I knew that that would come back clean. I was close now.

When the day of my DBS check came around, I was fully prepared. I had all of the paperwork that they would need and was ready for any eventuality. We went through the whole process, and just as I was about to send my details, the lady spotted that I was under Barod. "How long have you been going to Barod for?"

"About four months now," I replied.

"What's that for?"

"Drinking mainly, although I have used drugs a lot in the past." I was getting a little apprehensive now.

"When did you last have a drink?"

"22nd of June."

"Our policy insists on twelve months clean and sober for those in recovery." My heart sunk. I had done four months. I was pissed off; this should have come up in the initial interview. I had been one hundred per cent honest, and now the hope that I had built up was being dashed. There might be a way around it. I asked her to email me whatever they needed and left. Straight away, I walked the short distance to Barod to ask my caseworker for a reference and got in touch with a couple of other people. I was told that I would receive an email the next day. It would be nearly four weeks before I would hear anything back.

Soon after my application for the initial role, I also came across a 'Befriender' role with the Royal Air Force Association. I had a telephone interview, sorted out references for them, and the only sticking point with them was about proving my identity.

They didn't have a local office, so I had to have documents verified by the Post Office. They wouldn't photocopy a birth certificate, and so, I needed some other way to prove who I was other than my provisional driving licence and a bank statement. I kept in touch with them and kept having to chase them up for information. I scanned all of the documents that I had and emailed them across. The day after, I had my disappointing news from the other agency. I received another email from the RAF Association chasing up information, totally disregarding, or more accurately denying my previous correspondence. I had jumped through hoops for them, and they totally refused to acknowledge any effort that I had gone to. I decided that this didn't bode well for the future and informed them that I wouldn't be proceeding with my application. I was never to hear from them again, not even a cursory email of receipt.

I was really pissed off now. I thought that I was on the cusp of something. I was close to making what felt like it could be a major career decision, and two doors had slammed shut in my face in as many days. Looking back, the oversight in that first interview may have been a blessing in disguise. If my attempts to volunteer had failed at the first hurdle, then I may have lost hope and who knows what would have happened then. Fortunately, there was one other opportunity that had just come along.

In early September, some seriously fucked up news made its way to me. A mate from Bromley, who I had been a really close friend with throughout most of my time up there, had been charged with murdering his mother. What the fuck do you do with news like that?

I hadn't realised at the time how close friends we had been. We went to Boys' Brigade together, lived on the same road, did a paper round at the same shop, we were both drummers, and we had spent shitloads of time together. I had even spent two weeks in France with him and his parents at their farmhouse. He was one of only two mates who had told me that I needed to knock the Charlie on the head and get on top of the drinking.

I had no idea how to process this news, and it led to a definite dip in my mood. With advice from people at Mind and SMART, I was able to realise that

I didn't have the answers, no matter how hard I looked, and I was able to put it aside for now.

I was later to find out that he had had mental health issues of his own after his only brother moved to New Zealand and his parents retired to France. I felt that I had somehow let him down. He had tried to be there for me, and I was absent when he needed someone. It soon occurred to me that I was incapable of looking out for myself and would have been no good to him anyway.

He allegedly strangled his mother. This was something that shocked me. The boy that I had known just wasn't capable of such violence. He was very similar to me in terms of temperament, absolutely no aggression, outwardly, of course. What I became afraid of was that I could go the same way. I didn't have to look far to see that I was capable of severe acts of violence; my arms are testament to this. Could I be capable of doing this to someone else? I certainly have never had an outlet for my anger, being practically unable to lose my temper for most of my life. Could I?

On the fourth of September, I had an appointment with the NHS Primary Mental Health Team. I had a nice chat with a lady who asked me questions that it seemed I had answered dozens of times before. That didn't bother me. I would answer those same questions every fucking day if it meant that I got better. I was put on the waiting list for one-to-one CBT, and they would be in touch within two years.

Fucking great!

As I sit now, I have just been put on an eight-week Mental Health Management Course coming in the new year, which is something at least.

In September, I went away for a week with my parents and Toby to Denbighshire, North Wales. We stayed in a small village called Bodfari, with self-catering accommodation in a cottage adjoined to a farmhouse. The closest place on the map was a tiny hamlet called Sodom. Sounded like my kind of place. Yeah, right, chance would be a fine thing!

We spent our days going to various surrounding towns, Llandudno, Rhyl, Mold and even getting back into England with a visit to Chester. I would spend time going around the charity shops, returning to Swansea with 25 new used books and a couple of fine pieces of knitwear.

Our cottage was in a beautiful situation on a smallholding with chickens, goats and a resident dog, Barney. Toby made plenty of new friends, and it was one morning while I was outside smoking a cigarette and Toby was chatting to a goat that I had a bit of an epiphany. I was taking stock, and I realised that this was what I wanted from life. I wanted someone to go on holiday with. It felt so simple and, for the first time ever, attainable. I knew what I wanted, and it didn't seem too much to ask. It's up to me to make it a reality now.

We returned to Swansea, and I knew that I had some tests ahead of me. I would have two weekends to myself in Swansea with a trip up to my sister's in between. To say that time alone hadn't gone well for me in the past would be a bit of an understatement. Toby would spend the weekends with me, so I wouldn't be totally alone.

I foresaw that there would be temptation to drink, and I was able to bring it up in SMART. I knew that if the urge got really strong, I could pop across to the club to escape. I know that the idea of going to a licensed premises to escape the desire to have a drink must sound absolutely screwy to most people, but the club was a safe place there. My friend who ran it had my best interests at heart. I was totally convinced of it. She has been an absolute rock for me over the time that we have known each other and I truly treasure her friendship.

As it happened, the weekend went without any problems. Boredom had become less of a trigger for me. I could always sit down with a book, and I was now able to sit down and watch shit TV. *Judge Judy* always seemed to be on somewhere.

The following Wednesday, I was off to my sister's. I would catch the train after doing a first aid course at Barod. This did leave the potential that I might have almost an hour to wait between trains, usually time for a pint. In the past, I had even let trains go to have a pint. Not long-distance trains but local ones, definitely. In the event, I was able to walk to the station and straight on to a waiting train. I was excited to get up there.

My train arrived pretty much on time, and I stopped for a fag before jumping on the underground to Victoria. This would usually have meant a pint or two, but I was straight on a train to Bromley South. Once in Bromley, I was straight on a bus to my sister's. While sitting on the bus, my sister got in touch to see how my journey was going. I told her that I hadn't got to Paddington yet and would be a while yet. My idea was to surprise her, but it occurred to me that this was the sort of bullshit excuse I used to use to squeeze in a couple of pints at every juncture.

I had a great time with them. Thursday was spent around the house, and I popped to nearby Petts Wood to take in the charity shops. On Friday, there was a SMART meeting in Bromley that I wanted to attend, so I went in a couple of hours early to do some shopping. I must have been getting on top of my used book fetish now, as I only bought eight books over the two days. Oh, and a couple of smashing pieces of knitwear too, of course.

The SMART meeting was brilliant. Pretty well attended. I just love the brutal honesty of the people who attend SMART meetings. The strength and resolve in those rooms is something really special at times. People who are very aware that they have behaved poorly in the past but truly want to rectify things—this can be an irrepressible force.

That evening, a few of us had tickets to see Joe Pasquale at the Churchill Theatre. My sister, my brother-in-law, myself and some old friends had a cracking evening out. Cracking entertainment followed by a couple of drinks at the Wetherspoon's that used to be my local. I had Becks Blue. I'm not a big fan of the non-alcoholic lagers. I can't kid myself that I am having a drop of the good stuff, and I think that I am better off steering clear. Give me a St Clement's any day of the week.

Saturday was all about Charlton. I was meeting up with my best mate, and we were heading down to the legendary Valley. He had been in touch the previous day to say that he had sorted out lounge tickets for us. I responded with, "Quality, we are going to get fucking smashed!" It's funny, this boy knew my sense of humour so well but still didn't know how to take it, in the context of what I was trying to do. I totally understand it; it's a very difficult situation dealing with someone in recovery, but it really does feel as if people are walking on eggshells around you.

Once we met up, it was like it had always been. I stuck to my Becks Blue and we had a really good catch up and reminisce about our glory days, touring the country, when Charlton were a decent team. We used to drink shitloads! We both agreed that those days were long gone now.

It's always great to go to Charlton, but I always find it hard to see what that Cunt has done to the club that I love. While that club has fans, they will never give in. Some fans, long-standing fans as well, have taken the decision to boycott until the ownership has changed. I totally understand this action, whatever it takes to get this cancer out of our club.

Charlton lost two-one, conceding two goals in the last ten minutes to lose a game that they should have had won by half-time. If we didn't have a lift with my mate's Dad, I would have gone for a pint. I have no doubt about that. Luckily, that safety net was in place, through no fault of my own. By the time I was dropped off, outside the pub that I had called my local for so many years, the urge had gone and I went straight home to my sister's.

On Sunday, I got up and took Daisy for a walk. My sister made a lovely roast, and I was off back to sunny Swansea. I got to Paddington station in good time and had about 45 minutes until my train. I popped for a fag and checked the departure boards. My train had been cancelled, and I now had over an hour and a half to kill.

Without thinking, I made my way to the bar on the station where I had drunk many times before. I went up the escalator, through the doors, up to the bar and ordered. "Pot of tea, please." This was my default now. I was definitely changing.

I got into Swansea on time, and my father met me at the station. Gone were the days where I would insist on making my own way home, stopping off for numerous pints and quite often picking up a nice bit of nosebag on the way. Those days were gone.

The second weekend alone passed without event, and I could look back on this period for inspiration when I have time to myself in the future. I did it once; I can do it again.

We were fortunate enough in Swansea to have the national co-ordinator for Wales of SMART Recovery residents. She took a meeting on Thursday evenings at Barod. She was a wonderful lady, having had her own struggles and ten years in recovery for experience.

Around the time that all of my other voluntary options were falling by the wayside, she asked if anyone wanted to come with her on a couple of days into Powys to promote SMART. I immediately offered, and one Monday, she picked me up, early, and we made our way up to Welshpool, driven by her fiancé.

She did a presentation, and I was really there just to see how things were done and to do a bit of meet and greet if necessary. Only four people were to show up, unfortunately, but we had a fantastic buffet for 30. She took all of the surplus food back to Swansea to distribute to the homeless shelters. She had an incredibly generous spirit.

A couple of weeks later, we were to travel to Newtown for another SMART Awareness Day. It would be just the two of us in the car this time. Just the two of us for five to six hours. Would it be awkward silences all of the way? It turned out to be the exact opposite. We chatted non-stop for the entirety of both journeys; the conversation just seemed to flow.

The day wasn't the resounding success that the Welshpool trip had been, and ultimately, nobody turned up. We literally travelled there, picked up the world's biggest packed lunch and travelled home. The food was again distributed to the homeless shelters in Swansea, less our travel expenses and commission, of course.

For our next excursion, I accompanied her to Cardiff University where she does an annual talk about addiction, her experiences in particular, to a lecture theatre full of Pharmacology and Neuroscience students. I knew that she possibly wanted me to share something at a later date. I didn't say no immediately, but the thought of public speaking was terrifying to me.

She hadn't been talking long when I realised that our stories and backgrounds were polar opposites. She was great to listen to. So honest about her struggles and behaviours and so uplifting about her recovery. I started to think that I might need to do this. The students were hanging on her every word, as was I. Afterwards, the professor had a chat with me, and I said that my story was totally different and also encompassed self-harm and suicidal periods. She seemed quite keen.

On the way back to the car, we chatted about it, and I said that I thought that she was an inspiration, but I didn't think that I would be able to do that. "It's your story; you can't get it wrong." That was all that it took. If asked, I was going to accept the invitation. Had I stumbled upon a mentor?

The next week, we were to go to the residential rehab where she had been a decade before. She was delivering training on the SMART tools to the residents there, and I was to go and see how things were done. It was a cracking couple of days, and she made me feel included all the way. I'll say it again, but you just meet the best people in recovery. Everyone was so eager to learn and discover a way to a better life.

She had an appointment in Mold a little after and asked me if I wanted to go with her, for company as much as anything. It turns out that this was a meeting with the Substance Misuse Commissioner for North Wales with the Welsh Government. She was trying to secure some more funding for operations up there. I couldn't believe that she had wanted me present for this, but it made me feel like a part of things. She had always introduced me as her colleague. I had worked with people on the same pay grade as me who had never referred to me as their colleague. It's little things like this that make all the difference to me.

Another Tuesday, we went back to rehab in order to take a couple of sessions about addiction and recovery. In the morning, she led a group discussion about addiction and the choices that we make, not just in addiction, but in recovery as well. After lunch, I was to share a little of my story.

It was set up brilliantly by her. Really informal, everybody sat around in a circle, myself included. There was no big build-up; she just kind of led into it very naturally. "Steve is going to speak for, about 20 minutes?"

"Maybe," and I was off. It went really well. Beforehand, I was so aware of a big clock on the wall opposite me. Twenty minutes seemed like such a long time, and I knew that if I started clock-watching, it would seem even longer. I had a cheat sheet in my pocket that I didn't refer to in the end, and I managed to avoid looking at the clock too. I was aware that I was speaking well and following the thread that I wanted to, but I did jump back and forwards a little as more things came to mind.

Afterwards, I was on cloud nine. This was a serious personal achievement for me, and about the first time, that I have been able to recognise achievement in myself. I got lots of positive comments, and it's such a great feeling when people are interested in what you have to say. I really enjoyed the journey home, which was under an hour, but life was waiting there for me to fuck everything up.

I arrived home to the news that my father's best man, a really close family friend for my whole life, had had a massive stroke and wasn't in a good way at all. He was a wonderful, gentleman. Cracking sense of humour, full of encouragement and, seemingly, in good health. All of a sudden, bang, at 70, no age these days.

The previous Saturday, the 1st of December, I had taken myself up to Cardiff to sit an IQ test for Mensa. When I got home on Thursday lunchtime, my results were waiting for me. I had qualified and was invited to apply for membership. I sent in my application, to be honest, I just wanted a certificate that didn't have the words 'participant', 'attendee' or 'liver failure' on it.

Toby had been having a spot of bother with his right eye, and we had an appointment with the doggy optician that afternoon. Nothing seemed too untoward, but we were hit with the news that he had a tumour behind his iris. There was a fair chance that this could be benign, but the only way to ascertain this would be to take the eye out. Two tissue samples were taken from other suspect areas on his body. If one of these came back as cancer, then they would try treating it medically and see what effect that had on the tumour in his eye.

Why can't life just take a fucking day off once in a while and leave you to enjoy yourself? I know that I sound incredibly selfish. I'm not the one who has had a massive stroke, or might have cancer, or lose an eye, but any feel-good factor from what were two big personal achievements was stolen within hours. Having said that, I would expunge those achievements from history for the return to health for Toby and my 'uncle'.

That evening, I went to SMART and shared my feelings about how the first tangible success that I could appreciate had been taken away almost immediately without me having a chance to enjoy it. I shared that I knew that one of my favourite excuses to drink, "Nobody would blame me," was bound to rear its ugly head at some point. It felt good that I was starting to see possible dangers ahead.

As I walked to meet my father for a lift home, little over five minutes away, I analysed in my head how my thoughts could get me back to that place in June and put me in serious peril. Far from this being valuable insight, I now had a roadmap back to suicide indelibly forged in my brain. I could never forget this. It might leave my consciousness, but it was there, sitting dormant until I chose to use it. If I did. The fact that I put this there myself, cunningly disguised, as personal self-awareness just added another level to the way that I could fuck myself up. I had to be very careful.

It was the new year now; 2019. Toby had his right eye removed on Wednesday, 2 January. He was coping well, and the prognosis was good. Once he was out of his cone, I felt that we would be left with exactly the same dog. It didn't seem that it was going to affect him in any way.

Everything was winding down for Christmas now, and it was going to be a dry one for me for the first time in however many years. We never drink much in the house as a family, but the festivities leading up to the day and then before the new year have always been a good piss up. Recent events had meant that I was not sure whether or not I could join in the festivities.

Four weeks ago, there was a birthday party for my friend who ran the club. It was a surprise party at the Rugby Club. I had prepared myself that the urge to drink was going to come at some point, and I would make my excuses and leave. What I hadn't prepared myself for was social anxiety.

This was my first attempt at a night out since I gave up drinking, and I went across with absolutely no trepidation. There were dozens of people that I knew to varying degrees in that room, but as soon as I got there, I was desperate to leave. I nearly went before the birthday girl arrived. I couldn't properly hold a conversation with people that I knew, and I certainly wasn't able to instigate or join a conversation. I became so aware of my mannerisms and the way that I was standing. Everybody in that room knew someone else better, had more history with somebody. That old feeling of isolation was back.

I knew that getting a Jameson's slipped into my Coke would take the edge off, but it was never a serious option. This was a huge positive. The urge to drink just wasn't there at that moment, I knew that I was better off without it. The realisation that I have relied on alcohol in order to socialise and make connections, that is something that I have to figure out. I left after an hour and a half but worked myself into such a state that I was sick an hour or so after getting home. A massive wake-up call. I still have such a long way to go.

Chapter 33

Reflections of a Confused Little Boy

When I sat at my computer, nearly six weeks ago, the aim was to come up with something that would allow me to talk for about 30 to 45 minutes about my experiences. It has taken on a bit of a life of its own. This final chapter, my reflections, has now become the purpose. It's been a tough process. I have revisited some very dark times and have had to face up to my relationship with alcohol and drugs, as well as my behaviour associated with that.

The starkest realisation for me is that I no longer look on this as a series of isolated episodes. I always thought that I was stuck in a cycle where things were OK for a while, then my mental state slowly deteriorated to a rock bottom and, usually, an attempt on my life before being dragged back by those closest to me, just to pursue the same path all over again. I now see that this has been one long, concerted effort to end my life, spanning two decades or more.

Trial and error is all part of the scientific process. Each and every failed attempt has been analysed. I have made mental notes, collated information and formulated new plans to kill myself. Each time that I think that I have reached that rock bottom, I have managed to plunge deeper in despair. The violence of my thoughts and the actions perpetrated against myself have grown in ferocity. I no longer get any sense of relief from waking up after a failed suicide attempt. I nearly didn't stop until the job was done earlier this year. I honestly believe that I know too much now, I can never allow myself to go back to where I found myself six short months ago.

I am slowly coming to terms with the fact that this is a lifelong affliction. Recent thoughts that have started occurring to me show that I will always have to be on my guard. I have started having feelings of nostalgia towards that time back in June, romanticising it, if you will. Whether there is a part of me that is drawn to that picture of a tortured soul, do I think that that is something to aspire

216

to? My mind will constantly try to trip me up. Insight is important, but I am finding that anything that I learn about my thought processes is another stick that I can use to beat myself. By seeing what is coming, am I actually planting the seed? Even this revelation could be an act of self-sabotage designed to instigate my downfall.

I feel that I am in a mental game of chess with myself. It is a game that I can never win, I can't consciously learn something that I don't sub-consciously already know. Everything that I try and pre-empt can be used by me against me. All personal insight can be detrimental. How the fuck do you combat that? I can never get a move ahead, and so the best that I can hope for is a stalemate. I need to arm myself with a war chest. I need to be able to observe my thoughts and counter them. When this bastard rears its ugly face again, I need to be able to stare it straight in the eyes, kick it in the bollocks and say, "Go on, off you fuck!"

I have to be extremely vigilant and proactive from now on. I know that I have the necessary support around me. When I find that I am beginning to slip, I must reach out to somebody. There are people who want to know if I am starting to feel down. They, and I, know that the consequences of me bottling up my emotions and trying to fight this alone are infinitely worse than me coming to them for some encouragement. If I ever stop thinking that I owe it to myself, I have to remember that I owe it to them. My problem is that I am now acutely aware that I lose my own personal battle for life, long before the decision is made to take it.

I have daily reminders of my struggles. Every time that I take off my top, whether to wash or to go to bed, I only have to look down at my arms. For every emotional scar, there is a physical one. Over time, they will fade but, like the emotional scars, they will never totally disappear. They are as good a documentation of my story as these words.

I make no excuses or ask for no sympathy for the life I have led. Everything that I have done to myself and others is a consequence of a decision that I have made. I have made a royal fucking mess of the first half of my life and am extremely fortunate to have another chance.

I have ruined so much for myself. I have been afforded every opportunity, several times, and yet I have systematically sabotaged myself at every turn. I have had some very good career opportunities and I have sent them packing. I have fucked up friendships, alienating myself due to some fucked up desire for isolation. I can no longer enjoy a pint or a line, two things that I used to genuinely appreciate. Even Charlton has become a struggle at times. This, I am fairly sure, can be rectified. Some music has to be dead to me now. The Holy Bible by Manic Street Preachers is the most complete collection of music that I have ever heard. My favourite ever album by quite some way, but it accelerates any descent that I may find myself in. Along with several other albums, I am not sure that I can ever listen to it again, for fear that the association that I have previously had might prove to be right again.

The fact that I can find myself in a place where I am the only threat to myself, yet I am unable to stop myself from doing harm is terrifying. I can get to a point where I lose all control and am totally powerless to protect myself from myself. Is it better, therefore, to get to the point where I hate myself too much to kill myself? Feelings beyond suicide, is this actually a better state of mind to be in? It's a dark thought, the belief that living is a worse punishment, one that I have at times believed to be more worthy for me than actually taking my own life?

By rights, I should be a crocodile now, I have lived in denial for so long. I have tried to run from the fact that I have some mental health issues, blaming everything on some perceived weakness inside of me. Nobody is ever going to convince me that I couldn't have helped myself more. My refusal to take anti-depressants arose from the stigma attached to them. I'm convinced that this hesitance has had a terribly adverse effect on my life. My brain chemistry is slightly different from some. That is all. I am not a freak; it IS all in my head, but that is implied by the term 'mental health'.

The cruel thing about what I live with is that there are no outward symptoms. You can't put a plaster cast on your mind. I know that I am in no way special, or unique. This affects millions to varying degrees. I have been told that, clinically, I am normal. If this is normal, then we as a species are fucked. Things affect people to varying degrees, and sometimes, I wish that I was less feeling. I have tried that route and I found myself in a worse emotional state than ever. The absence of emotions leaves an all-consuming emptiness. For me, life without emotions is not life at all. It is existence but nothing else.

I truly believe that the secret to contentment and happiness is being true to yourself. If you can be as authentic and genuine as possible, then you will find the right people, and they will find you. If you are a flat-out arsehole, then be a flat-out arsehole, and you will end up surrounded by flat out arseholes. I have tried that and it didn't work for me.

I have been known as Walder, Charlton Steve, London Steve, Cockney Steve (just factually incorrect), English Steve, Geeky Steve, Pisshead Steve and many other prefixes. I have been likened to, and called, Where's Wally, Adrian Mole, Postman Pat (when I had my paper round), Penfold and Harry Potter. All of the derogatory terms that I have used in my story have undoubtedly been attributed to me by someone. Now it is time to find out who Steve is. Just Steve.

I am slowly learning about who I truly am. I have tried so hard to be accepted by some people, the wrong people, that I have totally lost sight of who I am. I became a stranger to myself. I am slowly becoming somebody that I can live with. Maybe one day I will become somebody that I can actually like. One thing that is for sure is that I can't go back to hating myself. If I do, things could come to a conclusion very quickly.

Depression I look on as the silent killer. My experiences of depression have been like those of an old friend. It is comfortable; it is familiar; I have been happy being depressed. Depression isn't always about being sad all of the time. It's about an emptiness, a nothingness, living in a void. It protects itself by cocooning you in a feeling of security from any outside influences. It is warm. It becomes natural to do and say what you need to in order to avoid awkward questions. Laughing and joking is the perfect disguise. By the time that you become aware that there is a problem, it is too late; it has got you.

Anxiety, on the other hand, is absolutely debilitating. The fear of everything and nothing together. Living in dread when you shouldn't have a care in the world. Sometimes the rational part of your brain kicks in and tries to assure you that there is nothing to be worried about, and you start to use this as a tool to exacerbate your anxiety. "I'm doing this to myself. Why?" I have almost enjoyed my time with depression, but the anxiety is nothing short of unmitigated terror and has been a catalyst to my later suicide attempts, definitely.

The rising panic, sometimes over weeks or months, strips you of your ability to do anything. You can function with depression, for a while, but anxiety is what has made me a total recluse at times. Curled up and motionless for hours, or even days, at a time. Unable to slow your heart, control your breathing or thoughts, totally paralysed by some perceived threat, often entirely of your own imagination.

Suicide is when mental ill-health becomes terminal. Plain and simple. When things go too far, and you start convincing yourself that there is no other way out. We have to get away from this idea that suicide is a selfish act. I think that categorising suicidal people as selfish is one of the cruellest and most harmful things that can ever be said to anyone. Somebody whose sense of self-worth has been so completely decimated that they see no other way out doesn't need to hear that they are selfish. They are well aware of this in their own heads, and pointing it out just adds to that feeling of being a burden and worthless.

I know that at times, the thought of the impact of my death has led to me postponing the inevitable. Suicide doesn't stop the pain; it just passes it on. Eventually, however, you will convince yourself that other people's lives will be better without you. Yes, there will be initial grief, but you won't be able to cause any more hurt after that. Those around you will thrive without your detrimental presence. Everyone will be better off if you are dead. These thoughts take away any selfishness in the act.

Let's get this fucking straight. Nobody wakes up one morning, spills the milk and decides that the only option is to kill themselves. Cancer patients are, rightly so, praised for their courage. You won't beat cancer just by medicine alone. It requires fortitude, fight, strong mental will too. This is also true of people with suicidal tendencies. People fight for weeks, months, even years to find something to keep them going. There is no permanent pain relief from your thoughts. Trust me. This perception in some parts of society that they are weak is all too prevalent when you are in that place. I have spent large parts of my life wanting to be dead. The majority of the rest of my time, I have been ambivalent to life, not really caring whether I live or die. Well, now, I choose to live.

I am so aware that there is still a part of my psyche that wants me dead. Thinking back to June, I have found myself thinking that, because I had my drills under my bed, I should have drilled myself through the heart, or the temple. I goad myself now for not spotting such an opportunity.

The admission that I know too much now and will not have another unsuccessful attempt has my mind urging me to prove it to myself. Some sick logic that I have never seen anything through to completion and that the only way to prove myself as a success is to take my own life. That is just so fucked up.

At the moment, I am not the slightest bit suicidal. I don't know why I kept my suicide note from June. It is gone forever now. When I looked at it, it was covered in blood. My handwriting has never been the best, but you could see the torment. It was as if I was stabbing or slashing at the paper with the pen.

As for the content, I am not angry at God. To be honest, I don't believe in God anymore. I envy people with faith, but I have to find solace elsewhere. The thought of an afterlife has no comfort for me. To live for eternity, the life that I have lived up until now is a horror best not contemplated. I have to concentrate on trying to find some peace and contentment on this plane of existence. It is the coming days, weeks and months that matter at the moment. I have toiled through life; physical pain doesn't hold any real fear for me, but to get back to the torture of that mental anguish again has me petrified. Pain so real that you want to scream out loud, that you try to supplant it with physical pain by doing the most unspeakable things to yourself. It is so difficult to explain, but it is oh so real.

I have been massively in denial about the hold that drink and drugs have had on my life and the enormous negative influence that they have been. I have been so delusional that it wasn't until I started this that I was able to admit to myself that I had a problem. Everything was down to my mental health. Getting fucked up was just a way to cope. I have been in recovery for nearly six months now, and for four of those, I didn't even realise.

The way that I have justified my using and behaviours associated with that are just plain crazy when held up in the sober light of day. I was dealing drugs for a couple of periods, and I managed to manipulate myself into thinking that I wasn't, purely because my currency was drugs and not pound sterling. Writing this, I have genuinely enjoyed reacquainting myself with some of the drug culture. It does have a very sordid side, but I had some great adventures taking and chasing drugs. Genuinely good times with some good friends. This isn't just rose-tinted nostalgia; we had a lot of fun. The difference is that they could leave it alone, I couldn't. The slang that is used I find genuinely witty and amusing, and there is a sadness that this is a world that I can never be a part of again.

I can see now, the destructive nature of my using and the catastrophic effect this has had on my mental health. It is not the root cause, but I have absolutely battered my state of mind through my habits. I don't think that I sought out anything to help me deal with life, but once I found that I could be more confident and feel part of something through drink and drugs; they took a massive hold.

The associations that I have made about alcohol and various parts of my condition are all very harmful. I found that a pint gave me confidence in social situations. I was able to make connections through alcohol. In order to remain confident and outgoing, I had to continue drinking. The result of how dependent

I have been on alcohol to socialise only hit home recently. I have no idea how to behave in those situations now, without alcohol.

Discovering that alcohol was a quick fix for anxiety is a link that I know many people have made. It works. No two ways about it, but then it becomes a crutch; you have no other way to deal with things. As your drinking becomes more self-destructive, you find yourself becoming more anxious, certainly when you get into the realms of being blackout drunk. *What the fuck did I do last night?* You are better off knowing that you kicked the shit out of somebody than not knowing what you actually did. The only way to deal with this blind panic is to drink. If you are looking for the most vicious of circles, this is it.

Finding out that, when I have been in that cosy, snug-as-a-bug-in-a-rug phase of depression, drink can accentuate that feeling, is just so fucked up. Drink makes me feel more depressed seems like a ridiculous reason to drink. Let's put it another way. A little money is good; a lot of money must be better. I have alluded to that safe, warm feeling of depression before. Well, being a little down in the dumps is quite nice, you will tell yourself. It would be great to feel this a bit more. Alcohol becomes your companion. You isolate yourself and want nothing better than to spend all of your time alone with your thoughts. Drink allows you to punish yourself more at the time and the following day. It gives you exactly what you want at that time.

Drink and drugs have definitely become weapons of self-harm to me. I have caused considerable harm to my mental health using them. It was only a matter of time before my physical health would suffer. Let's be honest; staying in a pub after breaking your elbow or wanting to go out for a pint when you are on the cusp of pneumonia show how much I valued drink above my physical wellbeing.

I would liken my relationship with drink and, as an extension of this, drugs to that of a Labrador to their food. I would take any opportunity to have a drink and there was never enough. I have had a drink because then I could justify ordering cocaine and, again, there was never enough. So, in a backwards kind of logic, rather than drinking leading to me using cocaine, the desire to use cocaine became my justification for having a drink. When it comes at you from both sides like that, you are in real trouble. I used cocaine because I had a drink, but adversely, I drank because I wanted to use cocaine.

There have been times that I have definitely used beer to get me over the line as far as physical mutilation is concerned. I have cut myself sober; I haven't always needed the drink for that. I have also held off the drink in various suicide attempts in order to give myself the maximum chance of success. Alcohol is a tool of self-destruction, and it cunningly disguises itself as a beneficial treatment.

It is clear in my mind now how, although inextricably linked with my mental health problems, alcohol and drugs became their own separate, serious issues. I know now that my improved state of mind depends on my abstinence from alcohol and narcotics. I also believe that my continued abstinence, to some extent, requires the maintenance of my improved mental health. I need to be very careful.

There have been several factors in my better state of mind. I am now taking my supplements daily. I have incredible support from family, friends and the people that I meet in my groups. It is all too evident to me that I could use this range of support as a way to allow myself to start drinking again. It would not take much for me to justify a drink by reassuring myself that everything else has contributed to my improvement. Besides, I've got the support now. I can handle my drink. I have to keep on top of irrational thoughts. If I can justify buying cocaine to save myself cooking, then I can plant banana skins every step of the way.

Labels like addict and alcohol are not useful to me. If I was to call myself an alcoholic, and that I could never drink again, I would have an incredible urge to have 'just one more drink'. I can also not go down the route of defining my substance use as an illness. If I do that, then I give myself the perfect excuse to relapse, over and over again. 'It's not my fault, I've got an illness.' I truly believe that at the moment, I am back where I was six months ago. One more drink could set off a series of events that could lead to me doing some serious harm to myself, or worse.

The provision for mental health seems to be virtually non-existent. I have had incredible support and guidance from a couple of GPs, but the individual has to be receptive and committed. Everything that I have found over the years has been self-referral. It is a massive task, for someone who is suffering, to come forward for help. To have to take several steps in order to receive some nominal help could prove nigh on impossible. I have been lucky. I have had people to encourage me.

The cancellation of my psychiatric evaluation was a definite watershed moment for me. If I had been alone, I have absolutely no doubt that I would have had a drink that day, and I honestly think that I would not be alive to write this now. If I had had that appointment when I should have, the realisation that I was 'normal' may have had the exact same effect.

I hear stories and personal testimony from people who have been right on the precipice between life and death. Reaching out only seems to get you the slightest sniff of something way off in the future. People are sent home even though they say that they are definitely going to attempt to take their own lives again. People are sent home even though they say that they are having dark thoughts and are a danger to others.

After a suicide attempt, if you get to see anyone in mental health, you are asked if you are likely to try again. I think that, if that will happen to me again, there is every chance that I would say no, then go home and try again. You have to do something particularly extreme in order to be sectioned or receive immediate attention. It's like telling someone who has just had a massive heart attack to go home and call an ambulance once their heart has stopped beating again.

The urgency of somebody getting treatment of some kind when they are suicidal is absolutely as critical as someone whose heart has stopped receiving CPR. There is no doubt in my mind that there is a need for some sort of mental health paramedic service. I know that we will always be told about lack of funding, but sort out the fucking waste then. Those moments are one hundred per cent critical. They can be the difference between life and death. I truly believe that.

I used to get frustrated by the emphasis put on my drinking and drug-taking by medical professionals. Dual diagnosis, as it is referred to, is a very common thing. I understand better now, my mental health has definitely improved since I have stopped drinking, but it doesn't alter the fact that my mental health issues were pre-existing. Drink and drugs did become their own, different issue, but they were also undisputedly linked. My use of alcohol and narcotics has been a weird juxtaposition of self-medication and self-harm. I know now that drink and drugs can never play a significant part in my life again, if any.

I have a family who have been incredibly supportive throughout. I feel so blessed. I have treated them abhorrently at times and yet they have always been there to pick me up when I have fallen. My parents have put up with my drinking for far too long, and my sister and her husband have always been a rock for me. My relationship with my brother has been slightly more complicated, but there is a huge sense of loyalty between us. It has always been there even when things have been problematic.

I have some fantastic friends. Some have been around for years, always there when I have needed them; some have only come into my life relatively recently, when I have desperately needed them. All have had a profoundly positive effect on my life over the years. They are the people who have not been afraid to say what I haven't wanted to hear. They have always had my best interests at heart, especially when I haven't myself. I have pushed them away to pursue my own self-destructive ways. I have taken advantage of their care and compassion to facilitate my own selfish, masochistic tendencies.

I have spent so much time, effort and money on the wrong people. Craving approval from people who don't give a fuck if I live or die. I have treated them better than truly significant people in my life. Why? I have never believed that these people liked me, but they allowed me to carry on doing what I was doing. In fact, they actively encouraged it.

The people who I need in my life have stayed around. They have taken all of the heartache and disappointment that I have given them, and they have kept coming back to fight my corner, picking me up from the horrendously worst places. I can never thank them enough.

Apologies mean nothing and will mend nothing. The word 'sorry' holds absolutely no weight when uttered from my mouth. I have said sorry so many times, without being sincere in the slightest, just for a quiet life and to continue as before. The only recompense that I can make is to lead a better life. The only way to assuage my guilt is to prove to them that I am reformed and just make sure that I treat them better in the future. I am incredibly fortunate that I haven't ended up on my own. I'm not sure that I could have had the patience that some of them have. When I start to lose motivation for myself, they must become my motivation.

I can never make amends to Klint. Everything that has happened to me has been, to some degree, my fault. That dog only ever deserved good things and kindness. He didn't deserve what happened to him. He was the most loyal creature, and he never deserted me when I needed him, yet I found it too hard to be there when he really needed me. He never asked for anything from me, and this is guilt that I will carry with me for the rest of my life. I can never have that time again.

Attending SMART Recovery meetings has become possibly the single most positive decision that I have ever made. It's a wonderful programme and has so much potential to be used in so many different circumstances. It has definitely changed my life. It is giving me life and has most probably saved my life too.

There are four points to SMART. One, building and maintaining motivation; two, coping with urges; three, managing thoughts, feelings and behaviours and four, living a balanced life. The fact that it is based in science appealed to me as well. CBT is something that, I have thought for a long time, should be taught, in some way, in schools. SMART is basically life skills, coping with what life will throw at you.

The meetings can be incredibly powerful. The desire of people in recovery to improve themselves, whether for themselves or those around them, is something to behold. It is a journey of discovery, empowerment and self-reflection. Self-reflection can be tough, especially when you have behaved in the manner that I have. Holding a mirror up to yourself and seeing things in yourself that you would despise in somebody else can be a very difficult thing to come to terms with. The trouble is that there is an excuse very prevalent in society. "Forget about it; you were drunk." You chose to get drunk, you are still responsible for your actions. End of!

Addiction, like mental ill health, does not discriminate. People from all walks of life are susceptible, and it would be a foolish person to think that they are above it. I have acted like a complete and utter cunt. A lot. I used to think that I was a nice, respectable person who struggled with certain aspects of life and took a couple of wrong turns along the way. This is so clearly not the truth. I have no hiding place now, and it is up to me to change.

I have found new outlets for my addictive behavioural traits. Instead of buying alcohol and narcotics on an almost daily basis, I now buy second-hand books and knitwear from time to time. I am in bed around nine every night and up at seven every morning. I have gone from the age of 18 to being a 75-year-old overnight.

Before anybody can change, they have to choose to want to change. SMART has a tagline: Discover the Power of Choice. It is all about taking responsibility for who you are and how you act. Nobody and nothing else makes you behave the way that you do. It is you, and you alone, who decides how you respond to situations.

It is all about finding the path that is right for you. In the interests of full disclosure, I am not one hundred per cent alcohol-free. From time to time, I will have a glass of Morrisons Bitter Shandy with a meal, less than 0.5% ABV. I know that I don't have a physical addiction to alcohol, and I can have a glass of this and leave it at that. It is a soft drink to me, and that is why I feel that I can say that I haven't had a drink since Friday, 22 June 2018, with every confidence and in all honesty. These are my rules, my boundaries, and I know that I am not cheating or deluding myself. Anybody who argues can do one. I chose to drink and take drugs, now I choose not to. I chose to dig myself into a pit of despair; now I choose to try and find a more positive way.

I don't believe in fate but I do believe in serendipity, definitely. Maybe, sometimes, somebody is put in your path just when you need them. My mentor, as I now look on her, moved to Swansea shortly before I sought help. She has helped me so much, building my confidence, including me in anything and everything related to SMART. She truly believes that I am capable of whatever I want to achieve. She has an uncanny knack of making you believe in yourself. Most unnerving. I was always going to do the facilitator training, even if it was just about giving myself a better grounding of the tools, but now, I know that I have to see how far this can go.

There are five steps to recovery. First is pre-contemplation. This is when you don't think that you have a problem, you are in denial. You have no thoughts of changing, and you use excuses to explain your behaviour. Second up is contemplation, when you are starting to realise that what you are doing may not be the best for you. Often this can entail a mixture of procrastination and apprehension, along with some ambivalence, weighing up the pros and cons of change. Third comes preparation. This is when you investigate various options available and the assistance and support that is available, researching groups, agencies, medical treatments and possible health concerns. Next up is action. This is the stage where you reach out and ask for help. You start attending meetings, maybe undergo detox and/or rehab, start taking medication and engaging with services. Finally comes maintenance. This is about continuing your life without your previous helping hand.

This is the most precarious, complacency can set in, you think that you are cured. Most of the time, you will be fine, but there will always be times that you will need to guard against. It is important to remember that you can still ask for support and keep mindful about where you can find it.

I feel that I am just entering the maintenance stage of my recovery. Through the denial of my substance use issues, I have gone straight from pre-contemplation to maintenance. I don't know how this will play out. My recovery in terms of mental health has followed the sequence detailed above, so hopefully, that will be enough. It is impossible to go back to the beginning and start again without putting everything that has happened over the last six months in jeopardy.

Barod is a fantastic agency. Previously called Drugaid, it is a progressive, forward-thinking organisation. Although I don't do too much with them directly, I have renewed my first aid certificates and actually played the drums for the first time in about 15 years when they had a musical drop-in. Still got it! There really wasn't that much to lose.

The Anxiety and Depression groups at Mind are great meetings. People with a range of mental health conditions, all trying to help each other. It is impossible not to grow to care about the people you meet in mutual aid settings such as this. We all try to help each other with issues from the trivial to extremely deep emotional problems. It is an incredible form of support, everybody has something to say that may be insightful and of value to someone else. This is a general rule of life, I believe. It's just what you choose to say. If the content of your words is encouraging, then you should never be afraid to speak up. If you want to sow discord and spit venom, then you can just fuck off as far as I am concerned.

A lot of the time, I feel like a complete and utter fucking fraud. I have just written 90,000 words on my attempts to commit suicide, and yet, I have never actually come that close to death, physically. This doesn't detract from the fact that on numerous occasions, I have made a very conscious decision to try and end my life. I'm just not very good at it. Time for a new hobby.

You cannot make a distinction between a suicide attempt and a cry for help. There most probably have been times where, subconsciously, I have left a safety net for myself. Maybe I have put some sort of contingency in place, something to give myself away, but this doesn't mean that I wasn't trying to kill myself at that time. Suicide is not an exact science. If you are trying to give the impression that you are attempting to kill yourself, then there is a very real danger that you could be successful. Pushing yourself right to the brink has an inherent risk. When you get to that point, you are no longer in control and you are putting yourself in genuine peril.

Cutting myself began as something borne out of curiosity. I never believed at the time that it would become something that I would use to such an extent. As with drugs and alcohol, it helped at the time. The sight of my blood running had some strange calming influence on me. Even when I was mutilating myself to the point that I did earlier this year.

I have always tried to keep my self-harm secret, cutting myself in places that were easily hidden. When I did start on my forearms, I would be in long sleeves for months after. I may just be in long sleeves for good this time. Just because somebody cuts themselves and leaves the wounds visible does not mean that they are an attention-seeker. If you are prepared to go to such lengths to make yourself noticed, then you are already unwell. This is not rational behaviour, and anybody who does so needs help. Urgent help. Believe me, as cannabis can be a gateway to harder drugs, scratching your flesh with something can all too easily lead to proper wounding and even an assault on your wrists.

For months, I felt like a fraud at SMART Recovery meetings. I didn't have a substance problem, I kept telling myself. My using had certainly never been at the level of some of the others that I met. I only ever drank lager, I only ever did Charlie when I drank, I never touched heroin, and crack only once. Blah, blah, blah. Bollocks!

There is no hierarchy in addiction. This belief that alcohol is better than controlled substances, purely because it is legal, is complete and utter nonsense. Heroin is perceived as the absolute worst, but I have met recreational heroin users who have never behaved in the manner that I have. For fuck's sake, heroin users tend to be much better versed on the health side of things than other recreational drug users.

Whatever your poison, when it becomes all-consuming, when it becomes your raison d'être, then you will do whatever it takes to feed it. All of this bullshit about 'When the fun stops, stop' is nothing more than a token gesture from people who know that there is money to be made. When the fun stops, it is too late. You will keep convincing yourself that you are having fun long after it has stopped. You will continually chase the good times that have left forever.

This isn't exclusive to substances. Gambling addiction is most probably the quickest way to leave yourself destitute. You can only do so much cocaine at one time, but you can lose all of your money in zero second flat gambling. Gaming addiction is becoming more prevalent now. This leads to isolation and

229

withdrawal from life. If you need to learn about the dangers of this, please see above.

Every addiction is harmful and self-destructive. You are trying to fill a void that is there. You are trying to replace something that is missing from your life. Most of the time, you probably don't even know what you are trying to replace. Anybody who feels the need to change their reality constantly cannot be happy in their life. One thing is for sure, you are trying to escape from something.

I have felt that I shouldn't be taking part in the majority of groups that I have attended at Mind. In the main, things have been going well for me since I started going there, and I have felt that I am taking up somebody else's time. Somebody who actually needs the support. My problems are not of the level of many who attend.

Most people have got a diagnosis of some kind, often multiple. I am 'normal'.

These groups do benefit from people with good news. I take encouragement from others in the group who have had some level of achievement, or just had their first good week after months of struggle. You can learn from people who are struggling just as much from people who are soaring, and they can learn from you. To be able to know that you have encouraged and helped someone is incredibly empowering, and everybody that I have come across in these groups has the capacity to do just that.

Many of the books that I have read recently are true stories of people who have overcome real adversity. Holocaust survivors, victims of abuse and abduction, people who have returned from war zones in one capacity or another. These are stories of true courage and strength.

Outside of the loss that death brings the only trauma that I have had in my life I have brought upon myself. Death is an inevitable part of life, and there is no single way to cope with it. When I look at the little things that it has taken for me to completely crumble, I feel like the weakest person to ever have walked the earth. I could never have survived the situations that I have read about. I don't know whether I am a fraud or just unbelievably weak.

I have picked up some potentially harmful pieces of information from my reading. I now know that the potential danger from a paracetamol overdose is there for the next seven days. If I wake up after an overdose in the future, I would just be able to carry on and try again, rather than coming up with some concoction of stronger painkillers. Knowledge is power, and a little power is a dangerous thing.

I feel strong in my abstinence. I have no cravings for drink or cocaine and have been in situations where I know that it would make things easier, but I never really considered it. Don't get me wrong, I do miss having a pint. I genuinely enjoyed the taste of a cold pint of lager.

For me to have a real urge to drink, I have to consciously put an excuse into my own head. This means that I am in control. I am currently very aware that my thoughts are just that, thoughts. If my conscious and sub-conscious are going to start ganging up on me, then I am going to need to find another level of self-awareness. If I do this, do I give myself more ammunition to attack myself with? It feels like a game of Jenga. I'm striving to get to a higher level than my thoughts, but every time I discover something new, am I actually disturbing the stability of what I have in place at the moment? I fucking hate Jenga! I've never had the steadiest of hands, and I certainly don't have the steadiest of minds.

Socialising has become a problem. That feeling of always being on the periphery is back with a vengeance. I feel relaxed in group sessions, but if I meet a group of two or more people from any group out and about, then that sense of isolation in a crowd returns.

I went out twice over Christmas. I spent the afternoon of Christmas Eve with my sister and her husband in the club. It's a big, open space, and it was sparsely populated with people that I knew, yet I found myself increasingly becoming uncomfortable and was only too pleased to leave. On Christmas Day, my brother and I popped to a different pub for a couple of hours. I used to go here occasionally, and it is a smaller place than the club. It was absolutely rammed and, besides my brother, I only knew one other person in there. I felt comfortable the whole time that I was there.

I am now more relaxed in a roomful of strangers than around the presence of friends and acquaintances. This is a real problem. If somebody does strike up a conversation with me or asks me to join them, I convince myself that it is all out of pity, and that I am impinging on their time. I have real trouble accepting friendships.

After the incident in June, I knew that I had to make more effort to keep in touch with people. I now regularly correspond with a few people, local and from further afield. A lot of the time, this is just the odd meme or "Hi, how are you?", but it does alleviate some of that feeling of isolation. However, I am incredibly aware that I don't make plans with anyone. I do everything alone, and the kicker is that I would struggle to accept an invitation due to the feelings that I have described. This is something that I have to change, but I have no idea how to go about that at the moment. This will take time.

No more 'What ifs'. This has to be my mantra from now on. The first half of my life has passed me by while I have been crippled by the fear of failure or rejection. If I don't change, then I will always lead a life of regret. The moment that I allow myself to be ruled by fear again is the moment that I give up and head for oblivion.

This doesn't mean that I have to accept every opportunity that presents itself to me. I have to take the time to contemplate it, though. This extends to every area of my life. Professionally, personally, romantically, I have to explore any avenue that is available.

I am aware that I am in an incredibly false situation at the moment. I have little or no responsibility, and I can't let this fact start to erode my faith in my recovery. I have to carry on down the path that I have chosen and make sure that I am totally prepared when the time comes to re-enter real life. I can't let my own irrational thoughts derail me.

My ultimate goal is to have a meaningful relationship with somebody. I keep telling myself that I must give myself time to meet someone, and this is the way that I would like things to happen, naturally. I am late-starting, however, and have to be prepared for things to be pushed a little. When I am further along my road, I will probably have to start looking at dating sites. I can't put this off indefinitely; one day, I will just have to put myself out there. This will be a massive step for someone who has such a poor image of himself that he hates every photo that exists of him.

Pictures of Labradors are OK on Facebook but probably won't cut it on Match.com.

I decided to try volunteering as a way to find some direction for a future career. Without looking too hard, I have found a promising path. I definitely want to work in mental health and, probably more specifically, recovery. I know that I am going to throw my lot in with UK SMART Recovery, and I have to see what comes of that. It may not lead to employment, but that is something to deal with when it comes to it. I want to start earning so that I can get on with the other things I want to achieve, but I know that this is the most crucial part of the puzzle.

If I can find work in an area where I have a true passion, then half the battle is won.

Everything that is to come, I will approach with a certain level of trepidation. The first thing that I want to do is get my driving licence. I have detailed the problems that driving has caused me previously. I know that to achieve my ultimate goals, this is imperative, and so, for the first time ever, I am going to learn to drive for myself because I want to. I know that I am going to need to have a good experience in my first lesson, so I will have to make sure that I am in a good state of mind. I can't procrastinate though.

Finding fulfilling work is important. I have real confidence in my abilities now. I am starting to prove more and more to myself. I have always rushed into work, my self-esteem almost entirely relying upon doing a day's work. This has led to me continually taking thoroughly inappropriate jobs for me, often low-paying and with little opportunity for progression or personal advancement. It doesn't take a genius to see that this has been detrimental to my sense of self-worth. I take pride in my willingness to fully commit to the most menial or mundane tasks, but this has also been counter-productive. I need something that I have a passion for. I need to occupy my mind. Unfortunately, I am aware that I have had so many false dawns in employment over the years. I know that I can go into a new position and thrive. I also know that I have real problems with responsibility and maintaining that success. I have no track record of settled, prosperous employment. This has to change, and that can only come from me.

I am having trouble when I don't make any tangible progress for a while. Standing still, treading water, if you will. Mentally, it feels like I am trying to ascend a descending escalator. I am perfectly in sync with the steps, and so, maintaining a status quo. I am comfortable with this, but I obviously feel the need to push other developments; failure to do so does leads to a noticeable drop in my mood. I wake up some mornings thinking what's the point. I still get up though. As long as I keep getting out of bed each morning, I will be OK. I have to learn to be patient. If I go too fast, I risk everything.

Branching out and living on my own will be a huge step. I know that I can survive on my own. I have no problem with domesticity; it is a large part of what I want from the future. I can do that on my own, but the danger comes in the time that I will spend alone. I enjoy my own company, but too much can lead to a real struggle for me. If I am going home from work every day to live alone, I could start to toil after a single bad day. After a couple of bits of bad news, I still get that feeling of impending doom, that an avalanche is coming to destroy everything. I can soon rationalise this, but will I be able to do this when I have endless hours to myself?

I also won't have my lifelong release of a couple of pints after work. If I can't socialise, then I could become isolated extremely quickly. Living alone would give me ample opportunity and time to bring about my own demise. I could conceivably plan for weeks, even months, and pick my moment when I know that I won't be disturbed, physically at least. I could lay the plans for several different attempts with contingencies in place. Frightening.

Should I even be thinking about starting a relationship when this is the way that I am thinking? I feel ready to be there emotionally for somebody, but can I be there emotionally for myself? Is it fair to bring somebody else into my twisted world? I am the only person who can drive me to suicide. That spectre of death at my own hands has never been very far away, and I wonder sometimes if it ever will be. I seem to be constantly walking a tightrope. The thought that there could be someone very close to me who would live the rest of their days wrongly blaming themselves for something that is entirely of my own doing is incredibly disturbing to me. How do you even bring up the subjects of self-harm, mutilated arms and suicide?

These are all irrational thoughts, but they are very real concerns to me. I like my irrationality to be logical, and when you can back this up with precedent and prior evidence, I find it difficult to counter this. It doesn't have to be that way again, but I know that I already have my excuses and my blueprint for despair tucked away, gathering dust, waiting for the day that I choose to unleash it. Even now, while trying to figure out a plan of self-preservation, I have to ask myself whether I am trying to talk myself back into it. It is oh-so clear to me now what I have been trying to escape all of this time, and I have no safety net in place. I can't stifle my problems anymore. I must fight them head-on.

As I type, I have no doubt that I can recover and prosper; what I can't do is get complacent or try and fight this alone. I know what I am up against, and I already have solid foundations on which to build. My support network has never been stronger, and I am acutely aware that those around me want to help. I'm fed up with always being the one who needs help, but by getting this period of my life right, I can start to provide the kind of support that I have received, for others. I can't do this for another 40 years, but I can choose to live a different way. And I do.

When I started this process, I expected to end up in a slightly more positive place. I am well aware of the enormity of what lies ahead. I just want to find my niche in life. I don't want much: a companion, a home and a purpose. Oh, and probably a dog. The trouble is that modern society is so avaricious that we are told that contentment shows a lack of ambition. Well, fuck you, society. I just want a bit of contentment, and there is nothing that you can do about it. It's up to me to make the best of the second half of my life, and I am the only person who can scupper that.

I know that I am going to fight myself all of the way. My awareness of how I am as a person is trying to tell me that it would be selfish to include anybody else in this. I must spend my life alone. I will only hurt anybody who allows me to get close. If I start to believe this, then I will end up alone, and I might as well go now. If I start to believe this, then I probably wouldn't be around very long anyway.

The thing is, I am as strong as I have ever been. I honestly feel that, and I'm only going to get stronger as long as I want to. I know that I have something to offer the right girl. I'm not interested in being with someone just for the sake of being with someone. People mistake sex for intimacy. Don't get me wrong, I enjoy sex, if my memory serves me correctly, but I want the intimacy of somebody trusting me with their greatest desires and their darkest fears. When I ask them how they are, I want them to feel that they can tell me even when they feel that they are at their absolute nadir. I want to enjoy rainy days cuddled up on the sofa, not feeling the need to talk, just enjoying each other's presence. I want to find a bench somewhere and just sit in each other's arms, enjoying the view. I want to see something in a shop and buy it for no better reason than it will put a smile on the face of somebody very special to me. I don't think that I am the boy for the big romantic gesture, but there would be little signs of my affection each and every day. I want to be there for someone, to help them grow, to help them be fulfilled. I may be an idealist, but I have to believe that that is out there for me.

This is year dot for me. Everything that has been has gone, and I can change nothing. I alone have influence over my future and my closing chapters. I intend to make it infinitely better than my past. I can no longer focus on how far along in life I am. I have beaten myself up about not getting on in life. Now, things will happen when they happen, when I am truly ready. I know that I have a fight with myself. That's why this is the critical period of my life. The longer I carry on, as

I have over the last six months, the existing muscle memory in my brain will start to atrophy. Worst case scenario, already, is no longer my default setting. Over time, the neural pathways in my brain will change. I have the ability to set myself on a happier path.

I am no longer living under any illusions. I have laid myself out bare in front of myself. I really haven't liked what I have found. The paradox here is that I am able to learn from all of the bad things that I have discovered about myself while documenting my past. I am learning about myself and can put things in place. Unfortunately, everything that I try and put in place can be used, by me, against me. Insight can only be a good thing, but it can also be counter-productive and set me up to fail. It's like poker. I see your self-awareness and raise you a new headfuck from a totally new direction! (Enough of the games metaphors!)

So there you have it. There is a fucked-up game's night (OK, last one) going on in my head, and I am just a spectator. Currently, I am just observing my thoughts, not trying to influence them, and this is fine. However, I am a partisan spectator, and I know, for definite, now which way I want this to go. I can intervene whenever I want, and I will when I need to. I feel that I am outside of my thoughts, looking in. If this wasn't my mind, I would find the whole thing quite entertaining. I think to sum it up. *My name is Steve and my head is fucked!*

Let's end on a positive note. I recently received my welcome pack from Mensa. I opened the folder that it came in, and there was a quote that struck an instant chord with me.

"It is never too late to be what you might have been."
George Eliot

Epilogue
Who Was That Bloke?

It is now Monday, 28 October 2019, and later today I will be sending off a signed copy of my first publishing contract. After sharing this story with a few close friends and family, I was encouraged to see about trying to get it published. Idly surfing on the internet, I came across Austin Macauley Publishers, a fairly new publishing firm who accepted submissions direct from first-time authors. As I type, I have absolutely no idea where this will lead, but I am extremely excited to see. I have been told that my words may help some people, and that is such an incredible thought.

A lot has changed. After having his right eye removed at the start of the year, Toby has continued to live life like only he knows how. He has become a wonderful, affectionate family member, retaining a penchant for moments of madness, stupidity and wilful disobedience. As for the rest of my family, everybody is in good health, including my grandmother who turned 100 in May. My parents continue to serve various churches and provide me with all of the love and support that I could ask for. My sister and her husband continue to live with Daisy and Tripod, their three-legged rescue cat. They too are still very involved with the church and are still an incredible source of encouragement. My brother is settled in Kent with his new partner and seems very happy, landscaping on a self-employed basis. A great reward for me is to know that I am no longer causing those closest to me pain and worry.

I qualified as a SMART Recovery Facilitator at the end of February. I started by running meetings as cover for other more established facilitators, but now, I take my own dedicated peer-led meeting on a Wednesday morning. This has come about through the support of the wonderful people at Barod in Swansea and, although my file was closed earlier this year, they continue to encourage and support me. As far as SMART is concerned, I am no longer working closely with the national co-ordinator but continue to promote SMART personally at every opportunity. I am currently training to become a volunteer for the Welsh Centre for Action on Dependency and Addiction (WCADA). This is another substance misuse agency in Swansea and the surrounding areas. I hope to start volunteering with them early in the new year.

I feel like a completely different person. I still haven't drunk alcohol or taken any recreational drugs, and there is a real possibility that I never will. For the first time in my life, I have genuine confidence, and I no longer sabotage myself. I see opportunity everywhere, and my life has opened up as a result. I am no longer crippled by self-doubt, and there is no bigger sign of this than the fact that I have got back behind the wheel. I have recently passed my theory test and have my practical test booked for early December. I genuinely feel that I have a decent chance of passing.

I have worked hard on re-engaging with who I truly am. I have managed to curb the feelings of self-loathing and feel now that I can trust my instincts. I never thought that I would say it, but I'm a decent bloke. Nothing arrogant in that, by being true to who I am, I have found a personal serenity, and I wake up each and every morning eager to see what the day has to offer. That undercurrent of anger and frustration has gone, and I find that I have time for everybody. The other side of this is that I also have the strength to recognise when someone isn't treating me fairly or respectfully, and I am more than willing to put boundaries in place to protect myself.

I can never allow myself to slip back to that place where I question my compassion and motives. It truly could be the difference between life and death. The person that you have just read about feels like somebody else, yet I still remember vividly every emotion that is described here. That life of torment can never be forgotten, but I have a chance to make the life that I convinced myself that I could never have. I intend to do just that.

Oh, one last thing. Since March, I have been lucky enough to spend a large proportion of my free time with the most wonderful girl. She is beautiful, witty, strong and compassionate. We have so much fun together, and our lives are filled with laughter, genuine laughter. She is, without a doubt, the greatest blessing of my recovery. It's early days, but I hope that my search for a companion may already be at an end

My life feels truly amazing, and to anyone reading this going through their own struggles, life can get better, please just hang in there.

If you, or someone that you know, have been affected by some of the issues covered in this book, below are contact details for three organisations that have been integral in my recovery. Some of these are regionalised, but there is definitely support out there, so please look, or ask.

UK SMART Recovery
Central Office
Third Floor Arthur House
Chorlton Street
Manchester
M1 3FH

0330 053 6022 (Monday–Friday, 9:30 a.m. – 4:00 p.m.)

www.smartrecovery.org.uk

Barod
73/74 Mansel Street
Swansea
SA1 5TR

01792 472002

www.barod.cymru

Swansea Mind
66 St. Helens Road
Swansea
SA1 4BE
01792 642999

www.smanseamind.org.uk